Climate Change Adaptation and Food Supply Chain Management

The success of the entire food supply chain depends on the prosperity of farms and local communities. The direct climate change risks faced by the agricultural sector are therefore also risks to businesses and food supply chains. Hence the importance of resilience at farm level, community level and business level when looking at food supply chain policy and management.

Climate Change Adaptation and Food Supply Chain Management highlights the issue of adaptation to climate change in food supply chains, the management and policy implications and the importance of supply chain resilience. Attention is given to each phase of the supply chain: input production, agriculture, food processing, retailing, consumption and post-consumption. European case studies demonstrate the vulnerabilities of contemporary food supply chains, the opportunities and competitive advantages related to climate change, and the transdisciplinary challenges related to successful climate adaptation. The authors argue for a redefinition of the way food supply chains are operated, located and coordinated and propose a novel approach enhancing climate-resilient food supply chain policy and management.

This book will be of interest to students, researchers, practitioners and policymakers in the field of climate adaptation and food supply chain management and policy.

Ari Paloviita is a Senior Researcher in the Department of Social Sciences and Philosophy at the University of Jyväskylä, Finland.

Marja Järvelä is a Professor (emerita) in the Department of Social Sciences and Philosophy at the University of Jyväskylä, Finland.

Routledge Advances in Climate Change Research

Local Climate Change and Society
Edited by M. A. Mohamed Salih

Water and Climate Change in Africa
Challenges and community initiatives in Durban, Maputo and Nairobi
Edited by Patricia E. Perkins

Post-2020 Climate Change Regime Formation
Edited by Suh-Yong Chung

How the World's Religions Are Responding to Climate Change
Social scientific investigations
Edited by Robin Globus Veldman, Andrew Szasz and Randolph Haluza-DeLay

Climate Action Upsurge
The ethnography of climate movement politics
Stuart Rosewarne, James Goodman and Rebecca Pearse

Toward a Binding Climate Change Adaptation Regime
A proposed framework
Mizan R. Khan

Transport, Climate Change and the City
Robin Hickman and David Banister

Toward a New Climate Agreement
Todd L. Cherry, Jon Hovi and David M. McEvoy

The Anthropology of Climate Change
An integrated critical perspective
Hans A. Baer and Merrill Singer

Planning Across Borders in a Climate of Change
Wendy Steele, Tooran Alizadeh, Leila Eslami-Andargoli and Silvia Serrao-Neumann

Climate Change Adaptation in Africa
An historical ecology
Gufu Oba

Carbon Governance, Climate Change and Business Transformation
Edited by Adam Bumpus, Blas Pérez Henríquez, Chukwumerije Okereke and James Tansey

Knowledge Systems and Change in Climate Governance
Comparing India and South Africa
Babette Never

Action Research for Climate Change Adaptation
Developing and applying knowledge for governance
Edited by Arwin van Buuren, Jasper Eshuis and Mathijs van Vliet

International Climate Change Law and State Compliance
Alexander Zahar

Climate Change Adaptation and Food Supply Chain Management
Edited by Ari Paloviita and Marja Järvelä

Community Governance and Citizen Driven Initiatives in Climate Change Mitigation
Jens Hoff and Quentin Gausset

Climate Change Adaptation and Food Supply Chain Management

Edited by Ari Paloviita and Marja Järvelä

LONDON AND NEW YORK

First published 2016 by Routledge

2 Park Square, Milton Park, Abingdon, Oxon OX14 4RN
711 Third Avenue, New York, NY 10017, USA

Routledge is an imprint of the Taylor & Francis Group, an informa business

First issued in paperback 2017

British Library Cataloguing-in-Publication Data
A catalogue record for this book is available from the British Library

Library of Congress Cataloging-in-Publication Data
Climate change adaptation and food supply chain management / [edited by] Ari Paloviita and Marja Järvelä
pages cm. – (Routledge advances in climate change research)
1. Food supply–Environmental aspects. 2. Food supply–Management.
3. Food supply–Government policy. 4. Climatic changes–Social aspects
5. Climatic changes–Economic aspects. 6. Sustainable agriculture.
7. Sustainability. I. Paloviita, Ari. II. Järvelä, Marja.
HD9000.5.C587 2015
338.1'9–dc23
2015006151

ISBN: 978-1-138-79666-9 (hbk)
ISBN: 978-1-138-10416-7 (pbk)

Typeset in Goudy
by Cenveo Publisher Services

Contents

Illustrations

Figures

Tables

Contributors

Marija Babović, PhD in Economic Sociology, is an Associate Professor at the Department of Sociology in the University of Belgrade, Serbia. She is the President of SeConS – Development Initiative Group, an NGO specialising in applied research and policy analyses. Her research focuses on sustainable development and gender equality.

Elena Battaglini, PhD in Spatial Sociology, is a Senior Researcher and manages the Research Area on Environment & Regional Development of ABT-ISF-IRES, Rome, Italy, where she has been working since 1992. Her main research focus is on regional endogenous development and its innovation processes.

Natalija Bogdanov, PhD in Agricultural Economy, is a Full Professor at the Department of Agricultural Economy in the University of Belgrade, Serbia, where she has been employed since 1986. Her research focus is on rural development, agricultural and rural development policy.

Gianluca Brunori is Full Professor of Food Policy at Pisa University, Italy, Department of Agriculture, Food and Environment. He is vice-president of the European Society for Rural Sociology. His research activities focus on sustainable rural development strategies and on marketing of local and sustainable food.

Hanna Hartikainen is a Researcher in the Natural Resources Institute Finland. She has expertise in carbon footprint methodology, environmental labelling initiatives and consumers' communication and desired information concerning food products. She has been involved in several food waste projects in close connection with the Finnish industry.

Lotta Heikkilä, MSc Food Economics, is a Research Scientist at the Natural Resources Institute Finland. At the moment she is working on measurement systems of food chain responsibility. In the future she would like to focus on new business opportunities and models based on food waste.

Mikael Hildén, PhD, is a Professor in the Finnish Environment Institute SYKE. He has analysed policies and practice related to the management of natural resources and climate change and studied national adaptation strategies across Europe. He leads the Climate Change Programme in SYKE.

Sari J. Himanen is a Senior Research Scientist at the Natural Resources Institute Finland, with a PhD from Environmental Sciences. Her current work focuses on sustainable intensification of agriculture and climate change adaptation at Finnish farms. She is particularly interested in how diversity might enhance multiple ecosystem services.

Suvi Huttunen, PhD Soc, has specialised in sustainability questions related to the utilisation of natural resources and related policy especially in rural areas. She works as a Researcher in the Climate Change Programme of the Finnish Environment Institute SYKE.

Pekka Jokinen, PhD Soc, is Professor of Environmental Policy at the University of Tampere, Finland. His recent work focuses on natural resource policy, sustainable food production and consumption, and local subsistence and sustainability.

Sirkku Juhola is an Assistant Professor in the Department of Environmental Sciences at the University of Helsinki, Finland, and a visiting scholar in the Department of Real Estate, Planning and Geoinformatics at Aalto University, Finland. She is the Deputy Chief Scientist of the Nordic Centre of Excellence NORD-STAR and the vice-chair of Finland's Climate Panel.

Marja Järvelä is Professor (emerita) of Social and Public Policy at the Department of Social Sciences and Philosophy, University of Jyväskylä, Finland. She has completed many research projects related to local sustainable development, ways of life and climate change. In addition to Europe, she has performed locality studies in Russia and West Africa. Presently, she is the second vice-chair of Finland's Climate Panel.

Helena Kahiluoto, DSc Agriculture and Forestry, is an Agroecologist leading research at the interface of food security, climate change and eutrophication. Her group applies resilience and sustainability transition approaches in interdisciplinary contexts.

Juha-Matti Katajajuuri is a Research Manager in the Natural Resources Institute Finland. He is the author of a number of scientific journals in the following fields: development and applying of life cycle assessment (LCA) and carbon footprinting in food case studies, sustainable production, sustainable consumption and food waste.

Teea Kortetmäki is a Researcher and PhD candidate at the University of Jyväskylä, Department of Social Sciences and Philosophy. She has specialised in environmental philosophy and environmental and ecological justice. She has published several journal articles on environmental ethics and co-edited the first Finnish book on climate ethics in 2013.

Miia Kuisma, MSc Env, is currently working as a Senior Research Scientist in the Natural Resources Institute Finland. Her research themes are related to sustainable nutrient economy in agrifood systems from local to global level. She is finalising her PhD dealing with the utilisation of agrifood residues.

Heikki Lehtonen is a Professor in the Natural Resources Institute Finland. His research has dealt with farm and sector level economic models of agriculture since 1995. He has analysed impacts of market and policy changes on economic, ecological and social dimensions of agriculture, including farm management.

Xing Liu, DSc Econ, works in the Natural Resources Institute Finland. She has focused on food market functionality, commodity market efficiency and risk management. She has also participated in dynamic economic modelling of farm management in response to current and future market as well as policy changes.

Johanna Mäkelä, DSc Soc, is Professor of Food Culture in the University of Helsinki, Finland. She is a sociologist specialised in food consumption. She has studied social and cultural aspects of eating since the 1990s and is particularly interested in meals and practices of eating. She uses both quantitative and qualitative research methods.

Hanna Mäkinen is a Research Scientist in the Natural Resources Institute Finland. Her PhD addresses response diversity which she applies in research of forage crops. Current projects are related to resilience, food security, climate change adaptation and adaptive capacity within agrifood systems, such as the agroforestry systems in Ethiopia.

Hanna Mela has an MSc in Geography. She has been involved in several research projects related to climate change adaptation and mitigation policies, as well as the impacts of climate change on various sectors of society. She works as a researcher in the Climate Change Programme of the Finnish Environment Institute SYKE.

Reijo Miettinen is Professor of Adult Education in the Institute of Behavioural Sciences of the University of Helsinki, Finland, and works in the Center for Research on Activity, Development and Learning. He has recently published a book, *Innovation, Human Capabilities and Democracy: Towards an Enabling Welfare State* (Oxford University Press, 2013).

Tuija Mononen, DSc Soc, is a Senior Researcher (Social Geography) at the University of Eastern Finland. She has focused on food research in social sciences (especially organic production), rural research, community experiences and local impacts of mining.

Tina-Simone Neset is an Assistant Professor at the Department of Thematic Studies – Environmental Change and the Centre for Climate Science and Policy Research (CSPR), Linköping University, Sweden. She is the head of the climate visualisation research cluster and one of the project leaders in the Nordic Centre of Excellence NORD-STAR.

Mari Niva, PhD Adjunct Professor, is a University Researcher at the Consumer Society Research Centre, University of Helsinki, Finland. Niva completed her doctoral thesis in 2008 and has specialised in the study of practices and ideals of food and eating. She has published articles in several journals.

Sami Paavola is a University Lecturer at the Center for Research on Activity, Development and Learning (CRADLE) at the Institute of Behavioural Sciences, University of Helsinki, Finland. His PhD dissertation was on abductive methodology (2006). He has worked on several research and developmental projects on tool mediated collaborative learning and work.

Ari Paloviita, DSc Econ, is a Senior Researcher in the Food System Studies Research Group in the Department of Social Sciences and Philosophy at the University of Jyväskylä, Finland. He is Adjunct Professor in Environmental Management (University of Eastern Finland) and specialises in food supply chain management and sustainable food systems.

Pirjo Peltonen-Sainio is a Professor in the Natural Resources Institute Finland. Her research focuses on adaptation of crops and production systems to conditions at northern latitudes and to climate change. Issues of sustainable intensification and food security underlie her work on the influence of environmental, climatic and genetic variation on crop production.

Hannele Pulkkinen is a Researcher in the Natural Resources Institute Finland working on climate impacts of agriculture and food production. She has expertise on international methodological developments of carbon footprints and labelling initiatives. She has worked with the food industry to develop a carbon footprint methodology and communication while conducting LCA studies.

Tuomo Purola, MSc Agriculture and Forestry, works in the Natural Resources Institute Finland and is a PhD candidate at the University of Helsinki, Finland, in the Department of Economics and Management. His PhD studies focus on integrated modelling of Nordic farming systems for sustainable intensification under climate change.

Antti Puupponen, PhD Soc. is a Post-Doctoral Researcher in the University of Jyväskylä, Finland, in the Department of Social Sciences and Philosophy, and he has specialised in food system studies. His doctoral dissertation dealt with sustainable development and localisation of food. Recently he has focused on climate change adaptation and food security.

Anu Reinikainen works as a Researcher in the Natural Resources Institute Finland. She has been working for more than 10 years on sustainability issues concerning food production systems. Recent research topics have focused on food waste and evaluation of regional sustainability

Karoliina Rimhanen, MSc Agroecology, is a Research Scientist in the Natural Resources Institute Finland and PhD candidate working on resilience of agri-food systems, synergies between climate change mitigation and adaptation, and food security. She applies qualitative and quantitative approaches in research addressing levels from soil to global in Ethiopia, Russia and Finland.

Rauno Sairinen, DSc Soc, is Professor of Environmental Policy at the University of Eastern Finland. He is also the scientific leader of the LYY Institute for Natural Resources, Environment and Society. His major research themes deal with environmental and natural resources governance, social impact assessment and environmental conflicts.

Tiina Silvasti is Professor of Social and Public Policy in the Department of Social Sciences and Philosophy at the University of Jyväskylä, Finland. She has studied structural change in agriculture, covering environmental issues. Her recent research interests lie in food system studies, particularly in food security and First World hunger.

Kirsi Silvennoinen, MSc Biosciences, is a Research Scientist working on several food waste projects, such as estimating volume and type of food waste, composition of waste in households and food services, impacts of food production and sustainable consumption of food.

Titta Tapiola has built her career in industry (PerkinElmer and Raisio Group) and currently in public research institute (Natural Resources Institute Finland). Tapiola has a Master's degree in biochemistry and in the near future will have a Master's degree in futures studies. Her main research interests are food system resilience and sustainability.

Foreword

There is growing evidence, confirmed by the Fifth Assessment of the Intergovernmental Panel on Climate Change (IPCC), that recent and ongoing climate change is already having impacts on the natural world and on human systems (Cramer *et al.* 2014). These impacts are gradually altering perceptions of the natural environment and its capacity to sustain livelihoods. In the agricultural sector, observed impacts of climate change include shifts in the length and intensity of the growing season and in the timing of crop development (Porter *et al.* 2014), as well as worldwide evidence of significant negative effects of warming on trends in yields of certain crops (Lobell and Field 2007). While coping strategies exist at the farm level for adjusting to the effects of short-term climatic variations, projections of accelerated climate change during the coming decades indicate an urgent need for more profound responses to manage changed risks and build resilience of the entire food supply chain – from farm gate to dinner plate.

Aside from direct weather effects on production, there are also many other risks to supply chains that need to be understood in determining their vulnerability under a changing climate. These include: changes in demand due to societal and cultural preferences (e.g. diet); economic exposure of regional firms to foreign and domestic competition and to world prices for energy and raw materials; susceptibilities in production and logistics at different upstream and downstream points along the chain; and fluctuations in product quantity and quality, often reflected in product prices (Beermann 2011). Other environmental trends such as nutrient depletion, soil erosion, air and water pollution and salinisation are also degrading the production environment over many areas. Moreover, food security in many regions is highly dependent on imported food whose availability is closely tied to commodity prices and international trade, which can themselves be affected by adverse climatic conditions that are geographically remote from the consumer region.

In European countries, elements of the food supply chain – inputs to production, agriculture, food processing, retailing, consumption and post-consumption – have developed over many centuries, but sensitivities to climate have changed little over that time. Continent wide, the decadal mean annual temperature over land areas during 2002–2011 was 1.3 °C (± 0.11) higher than the average during the second half of the nineteenth century (Kovats *et al.* 2014). This level of warming, which has accelerated in recent decades, has already prompted farmers across Europe to adapt their practices, in particular through changes in the timing of cultivation and selection of other crop species and cultivars (Olesen *et al.* 2011). However, awareness of climate change risks among other actors in the food supply chain is poorly understood and has been little examined.

This provides a backdrop for the research presented in this volume, which examines the challenges faced in adapting food supply chains to a changing climate in Europe. The primary regional emphasis is on northern Europe, reflecting research undertaken during the A-LA-CARTE project (A-LA-CARTE 2014), which has studied the implications of high-end climate change for agri-food systems and biodiversity in Finland. The project sought to examine the limits of adaptation to anticipated climate change, to investigate the extent to which present-day systems are resilient to changes in climate and to explore the options for enhancing this resilience.

Chapters in the book focus on developing strategies for reducing climate change and its impacts on food supply chains through climate-resilient pathways that integrate adaptation and mitigation within a risk management framework (Denton *et al.* 2014). Resilience is a recurring theme, targeting a future food system with enhanced buffering capacity to absorb disturbances such as climate change (Ericksen 2008). Some chapters go further, questioning the adequacy of conventional incremental approaches to adaptation (e.g. under scenarios of climate change towards the high end of projections) and arguing that there may then be a need for transformative adaptation that involves fundamental changes in institutions and in cultural values.

The authors have succeeded in presenting this new research in a most diverse and stimulating manner, and the editors are to be commended for collecting together these inter-disciplinary contributions and organising them in a way that is both novel and informative.

Timothy R. Carter
Finnish Environment Institute (SYKE)
A-LA-CARTE Consortium Leader

References

A-LA-CARTE (2014) *Assessing limits of adaptation to climate change and opportunities for resilience to be enhanced* was a consortium funded during 2011–2014 by the Academy of Finland as part of the Finnish Research Programme on Climate Change (FICCA).

Beermann, M. (2011) Linking corporate climate adaptation strategies with resilience thinking. *Journal of Cleaner Production*, 19: 836–842.

Cramer, W. *et al.* (2014) in *Climate Change 2014: Impacts, Adaptation, and Vulnerability. Part A: Global and Sectoral Aspects. Contribution of Working Group II to the Fifth Assessment Report of the Intergovernmental Panel on Climate Change*. eds C.B. Field *et al.* Cambridge: Cambridge University Press, pp. 979–1037.

Denton, F. *et al.* (2014) in *Climate Change 2014: Impacts, Adaptation, and Vulnerability. Part A: Global and Sectoral Aspects. Contribution of Working Group II to the Fifth*

Assessment Report of the Intergovernmental Panel on Climate Change. eds C.B. Field *et al*. Cambridge: Cambridge University Press, pp. 1101–1131.

Ericksen, P. J. (2008) What is the vulnerability of a food system to global environmental change? *Ecology and Society* 13. Available at: www.ecologyandsociety.org/vol13/iss12/art14/ (accessed 18 January 2015).

Kovats, R. S. *et al*. (2014) in *Climate Change 2014: Impacts, Adaptation, and Vulnerability. Part A: Global and Sectoral Aspects. Contribution of Working Group II to the Fifth Assessment Report of the Intergovernmental Panel on Climate Change*. eds C.B. Field *et al*. Cambridge: Cambridge University Press, pp. 1267–1326.

Lobell, D. B. and Field, C. B. (2007) Global scale climate–crop yield relationships and the impacts of recent warming. *Environmental Research Letters*, DOI:10.1088/1748-9326/2/1/014002.

Olesen, J. E. *et al*. (2011) Impacts and adaptation of European crop production systems to climate change. *European Journal of Agronomy*, 34: 96–112.

Porter, J. R. *et al*. (2014) in *Climate Change 2014: Impacts, Adaptation, and Vulnerability. Part A: Global and Sectoral Aspects. Contribution of Working Group II to the Fifth Assessment Report of the Intergovernmental Panel on Climate Change*. eds C.B. Field *et al*. Cambridge: Cambridge University Press, pp. 485–533.

1 Climate change adaptation and food supply chain management

An overview

Ari Paloviita and Marja Järvelä

Introduction

In the future, climate adaptation will become an inescapable task for the management of the food supply chain, both globally and locally. The gradual warming of the world's mean temperature and the increased frequency of extreme weather are expected to have a major impact on food supply chain performance and food security (IPCC 2014). Obviously, food supply chain performance and food security will be at risk and vulnerable, due to multiple other factors as well, thus it is an issue of high importance and high complexity – from a societal perspective – to find practical measures of adaptation for the world's food chains. Adaptation is also important for more conventional reasons because agriculture and the food sector form an important part of the world's economy, for instance, in the EU economy they provide 15 million jobs, 8.3 per cent of the EU's total employment and 4.4 per cent of the EU's GDP (Moussis 2013).

In trying to achieve a resilient food supply, global and local transformations are needed in both socio-economic and socio-ecological systems. When defining adaptation to climate change as a social action, we usually refer to processes and actions that help systems, such as households, organisations, communities, regions, countries, in order to better manage and adjust to changing conditions, stresses, hazards, risks or opportunities (Smit and Wandel 2006). In this book, we consider some of the main actors usually responsible for designing and operating a food system so that it takes on a more sustainable and/or resilient pattern of action. By considering food systems in a comprehensive yet operative manner, we focus on how food chain dynamics function as a whole, instead of studying parts in isolation from one another.

In more concrete terms, food is material we eat. But it is not just that; the discerning end-user may have strong cultural values related not only to the volume but also to the quality of the end product. Furthermore, the end-user may also have demands concerning how the food was produced and its origin. For example, at the upstream end of the food chain, a farmer looking for an alternative concept to his current, not-so-profitable pig farm may wish to start a more environmentally friendly alternative, such as raising wild boars. How can he know that the entire food chain will adjust accordingly?

To start a wild boar farm instead of continuing with a conventional pig farm, the farmer first needs to reform his feed provision and build suitable facilities for grazing. Second, he needs to know who would be his main customers for the boar meat. This involves the external food industry and the requirement to make contracts with retail, restaurants or other customers. Finally, the consumer, or a consumer group, needs to accept the replacement of at least some part of his/her conventional pork with boar meat. This plan may appear a quite simple and viable model. However, we live in a complex world with global driving forces where hardly any actor is free to act in an entirely autonomous manner. Instead, we make choices that are not just the influence of morals, taste and market dynamics but which are also affected by rules and regulations in every stage of the food chain. This makes the topic of food chain management adapting to climate change challenging but also stimulating.

Beyond mitigation, beyond vulnerable agriculture, beyond the business case

A *food supply chain* is an economic subsystem of a broader socio-ecological system. By adapting the definition of supply chain by Christopher (1998), the food supply chain can be defined as a network of organisations that are involved, through upstream linkages to farms and downstream linkages to consumers, in the different processes and activities that produce value in the form of food products and food services for consumers. The food supply chain concept is driven by business management scientists in the fields of logistics, physical distribution, operations management, marketing and supply chain management. Hence, *food supply chain management* has traditionally focused on developing *economic value* within the food supply chain network through value-adding activities and efficiency.

However, a food supply chain is not an island. It is a subsystem of a broader *food system*, which is a concept originally promoted by rural sociologists in the 1990s (Ingram 2011). Similar to the food supply chain, a food system includes activities from production to consumption, i.e. a chain of activities from the field to the table – from farm to fork. The key difference between a food supply chain and a food system is that the latter includes *the interactions between and within the biogeophysical and human environments* and also *the societal outcomes* of the activities (Ericksen 2008). Conceptually, environmental and social values are addressed on a par with economic values in a food system.

Sustainable food supply chain management has been introduced as a management concept in order to address environmental and social issues in food supply chain management. According to Seuring and Müller (2008), sustainable supply chain management "is the management of material, information and capital flows as well as cooperation among companies while integrating goals from all three dimensions of sustainable development, i.e. economic, environmental and social, which are derived from customer and stakeholder requirements". In a sustainable food supply chain, management issues such as food safety (not to be confused with food security), quality assurance, tracking and tracing practices, the origin of the food products, the inputs used during production, the labour standards, the treatment of animals and the environmental impact of production are important (Beske *et al.* 2014). However, the typical outcome of corporate sustainability activities in a food supply chain is to create economic value (see Figge and Hahn 2012). Social and environmental issues are addressed as far as there is a "business case". Moreover, sustainable supply chain management has been traditionally more concerned about the impacts of food supply chain activities on the environment and society rather than the impacts of global environmental and social changes on the business environment.

According to Dyllick and Hockerts (2002), there are three types of capital – economic, natural and social – relevant to economic, environmental and social sustainability. These types of capital are non-substitutable, for example, higher wages cannot substitute for the loss of clean water. In addition, the deterioration of natural and social capital is irreversible and the loss of biodiversity and the impacts of climate change are definite. Hence, the loss of cultural diversity is equally definite. Taking all that into account, it is clear that it is necessary to move beyond the business case in food supply chain management because environmental and social outcomes should not be subordinate to financial outcomes. Rather, corporate sustainability strategies should create environmental and social value alongside economic value (Figge and Hahn 2012). Identifying the *societal case* and the *natural case* for food supply chain management is a critical step towards creating a sustainable food system.

Climate change adaptation is an example of a societal case for food supply chain management. Specifically, it is a social learning process in which the intermediate goal should be to empower all actors in a food system so that they learn how to adapt to climate change (FAO 2014). Also in the management literature, the organisational learning model is the most highly developed attempt to understand how, why and when organisations will adapt to climate change (Nitkin *et al.* 2009: 26). As an issue demanding a societal perspective, climate change adaptation is firmly related to major global issues such as hunger, food security, food waste, water supply and energy supply. The world's food systems are extremely vulnerable to climate change – whether through extreme weather conditions, gradual changes in climate, or a combination of both. At the same time, climate change adaptation is a local approach associated with local livelihood, rural entrepreneurship and community development. Global food supply chains need to address both global changes in the world's food systems and the value of localisation. The majority of business discourse on climate change adaptation is concerned with *risk mitigation* and takes an indirect approach to climate change adaptation, tending to frame adaptation in terms of *vulnerability* and *adaptive capacity*, *risk* and *opportunity* (ibid.: 17). The indirect aspects of climate change adaptation in the business literature are regulatory, financial, physical, litigation, reputational and competitive risks (ibid.: 18). Accordingly, climate change will affect food supply chains in varying ways, depending on the complexity of the supply chain and on the degree of inter-connectedness and dependency of and on other industries (Beermann 2011).

There are barriers towards effective climate change adaptation in food supply chains. First, the institutionalisation of climate change mitigation is still an ongoing process. One goal of climate change mitigation is to reduce greenhouse gas emissions, especially carbon dioxide emissions. However, this aim has not achieved consensus at the inter-governmental level. In the light of recent IPCC reports, it must be admitted that climate change mitigation policy has, to a large extent, failed. Consequently, climate change impacts will affect economies and societies in fundamental ways but, because governments have not succeeded in climate change mitigation at the global level, climate change adaptation must take place at local, regional and national levels. However, adaptation is still being confused with mitigation (Nitkin *et al.* 2009: 19). Hence, a shift in focus from the inside-out impacts of a food system, i.e. emissions, from food system activities, to outside-in impacts, i.e. the physical and regulatory climate change impacts on food system activities, is required (Porter and Reinhardt 2007). Second, the majority of the literature dealing with climate change adaptation in food systems has focused on agricultural activities. This rather obvious, but limited, view of climate change adaptation in the food system has neglected other critical activities beyond the farm gate, such as the food industry; processing and manufacturing activities; the logistical system and the infrastructure supporting food supply chains; wholesale and retail; and consumption and post-consumption activities. As Eakin (2010: 78) puts it, a shift in focus is needed from concentrating on vulnerable agriculture to focusing on food system vulnerability. Third, food supply chain management is solely based on the business case and consequently biased towards financial performance. It has been generally suggested that companies should shift their focus beyond the business case and financial performance in order to deal with relevant societal issues (Vaara and Durand 2012). Hence, a shift in focus from the food supply chain to the overall food system is required. It must also be noted that climate change adaptation is embedded in the social and cultural worlds and is highly influenced by political processes, which means that depoliticising climate change adpatation and treating it as separate from societal processes runs the risk of exacerbating inequities and vulnerability (Mosberg and Eriksen 2014).

The link between climate change adaptation strategies and resilience thinking has been generally acknowledged in academia (e.g. Beermann 2011). Resilience is a useful concept in understanding the importance of adaptive capacity and coping strategies in order to decrease the vulnerability of the food system. Resilience can be examined at the farm level, the community level, the food company level, the food supply chain level and the household level. According to Ericksen *et al.* (2010: 73), managing food systems for resilience is an approach focusing on the dynamic processes of change that produce feedback in the food systems. A sustainable food system approach, in turn, can be ensured by integrating intra- and inter-generational justice and by deliberately taking the planetary boundaries into consideration (Gold and Heikkurinen 2013).

Vulnerable spaces and resourceful places: local responses

While sustainable development has been stated and confirmed as a universal policy target, globalisation has increased pressure on local economies and food systems. The pressure on agriculture and small and medium-sized enterprises (SME) processing and manufacturing in particular has been varied, including heavy price competiton from global markets, imported, novel food items and lower standards in farm employment in low-income countries. In view of the global competition, the mainstream policy answer has been further modernisation, ameliorated technological efficiency and increased competitiveness in agriculture, food processing and food manufacturing. Consequently, it is important to remember that all political attempts – whether local or global – that aim at climate change adaptation also need to fit in with the main trends of current policies.

From the point of view of the traditional local diversity of food production, modernisation has reduced diversity as a result of the increased standardisation of the food supply, economics of scale, longer delivery distances and related vulnerabilities in the food supply chain. However, another implication of this trend is that the producers and end-users in a food supply chain are socially and spatially increasingly distant from one another, even if they buy and sell at either end of the chain. Therefore, this mega-trend of modernisation is being realised in an ever more fierce struggle between local traditional farming and small-scale processing, at one end, and the "McDonaldisation" of food at the other end. Recently, however, a critical cultural factor has entered the scene; first, it manifested as critical views on overly standardised bulk production and, second, as an increasing demand for alternatives, such as quality food and organic production, and finally as active local food movements. Potentially, all these alternatives increase the diversity of the food chain, provided that alternative production is feasible for farmers and SMEs, and that all the players in a food chain can adapt their strategies to accommodate these alternatives. Hence, social structures, the role of locality, local micro-business networks and business network relationships that contain farmers and SMEs should be acknowledged by food chain researchers as critical aspects of sustainable performance (Bourlakis *et al.* 2014) and climate change adaptation.

Even if much of this experimenting on the local "re-rooting" and the "re-routing" of the food supply has followed dynamics other than deliberate adaptation to climate change, it may also serve either directly as mitigation or indirectly aid mitigation by contributing to local climate adaptation mechanisms. In general, it is important to recognise that these re-localisations generate new arenas for interaction for food chain actors who were isolated from each other by modernisation. According to many case studies (including some presented in this volume), re-rooted local communication and co-operative action for alternative food concepts can increase social capital and community resilience.

However, these emerging trends to adjust food chains so that they become sustainable and can adapt to climate change are remarkably embedded in particular localities and regions. Thus, the prerequisites for these to emerge and prosper are evidently strongly related to both socio-cultural and socio-economic assets that can be mobilised (Marsden and Smith 2005). Natural resources and spaces need to be translated into places enabling food chain initiatives that have real meaning to those who will take the initiative to build more resilient food chains (Battaglini *et al.* 2009).

Local assets for food chain management are obviously very different in terms of social and economic resources according to space and place. In the long-term European tradition, the spatial structures of food production were formed by seeking an effective balance between three different types of land use, namely ager, saltus and silva (Pinto-Corrreia and Vos 2004). Each of these types of land use needs their own adaptation dynamics, yet also a mutual balance based on both material and cultural basics is required. For example, some localities are more suitable for large-scale ager type cultivation while others would profit most from saltus-type grazing areas with more natural vegetation, or even from sustainable forestry relying on silva type of localities. Under the circumstances of major uncertainty, set up by the local impacts of future climate change, it is of great importance to consider how we understand the human-natural world metabolism in the long term through both agriculture and the world's food chains.

When considering our capacity to act and alleviate the threat of climate change, the above exploration of the food chain, the food system and the food chain management reveals major issues that must be tackled. These issues have their origin in the increasing complexity of our food chains and the broader food systems. Some constellations of these problems seem to lead to paradoxes that are difficult to unlock. Perhaps it is limiting to propose only one generalisable solution for any of these problems, and it is more desirable to look for at least a double solution that would benefit from functioning parallel dynamics. Having more than one option might better match the landscape of the increasing uncertainties that are prevailing, even though the volume of climate change research is increasing. Flexibility and rapidly applicable alternatives are clearly needed in circumstances where both natural and societal shocks are likely to emerge. An obvious limitation in the existing business case-dominated supply chain management literature on sustainability performance and climate change adaptation is the exclusion of farms and SMEs (Bourlakis *et al.* 2014).

Farm size and family farm

One of the intriguing issues that seems to come up constantly when trying to figure out the next steps to enhance resilience in food production is the social mode of farming. This issue is often linked to the recommendable scale of on-farm production, because building resilience is connected to the capacity for affordable investment in new equipment and facilities. In many countries, family farms still produce the majority of food. Simultaneously, however, farms are adjusting their activities more and more so that they fit into patterns of modern private entrepreneurship. Many studies, including some in this volume, highlight the transformations required on family farms in order to adapt to the shocks typical of global markets and ultimately of climate change (Wilson 2008; Darnhofer 2010). Again, it seems that there is no single solution for everyone in this adaptation. In the midst of a globally competitive economy, the traditional mode of the family farm seems to survive or even thrive, depending on its flexibility and capacity to modify production lines and farming practices, even if the true challenges brought to the fore by climate change remain distant and quite fuzzy to farmers and their close business partners.

The other major issue of social resilience connected to the social mode of production appears to be the problem of the size of the farms (e.g. Bindi and Olesen 2011). Currently, mainstream modernisation is trying to attain efficiency though economies of scale. At the same time there are many indications that social resilience on farms can more likely be achieved through measures that increase the "economy of scope", that is, the variety of product and production, rather than by means of economies of scale (Marsden and Smith 2005). Nevertheless, looking at the issue globally, the operative farm size seems to have risen with the level of economic development, especially in the twentieth century. However, Eastwood *et al.* (2010) argue that there are marked exceptions to this trend, such as the high prevalence of small farms in parts of North-West Europe and diminishing farm sizes in South Asia, despite economic growth. Therefore, it seems that increasing farm size is not necessarily the most effective measure with which to build food chains with a high adaptive capacity for the future. There is also the empirical evidence that small firms in the food supply chains are the top performers in terms of sustainability performance measures due to their flexibility and responsiveness (Bourlakis *et al.* 2014).

Besides, relatively small-scale and family farm management seem to fit together. The fact that the family remains the main source of farm labour seems to bring some advantages in building good and resilient farming practices. Family management, however, can also appear as an impediment to radical transformation or major investment. One interesting aspect of this complexity of the driving forces involved in the adaptation is the issue of the effect of generational shift on working practices. It seems that major transformations are often connected to successful generational turnover.

Actors in the food chains: complexities to be dealt with

One way to understand the present modernisation of the world's various food systems is to focus on the capacity building of the actors in these processes (Marsden and Smith 2005). Then it is possible to say that these actors are not only present in farm management, but also in the entire food chain. Consequently, the actors' capacities and their mutual cooperation can be the decisive assets to enhance resilience in all its main aspects. Furthermore, the issue of scale is very relevant to the resilience of the entire food chain and its operators. Many researchers have found that in local communities there might be a major discrepancy between the size of the actors which have to co-operate with one another, leading to inequalities in power and influence. For example, local food industries may be small-scale and numerous. However, a few well-organised, large companies might simultaneously have the decisive, controlling power in the organisation of the market. Hence, it is not at all insignificant who will be the main business partners for farmers in such a situation.

Since the second half of the twentieth century, technology has been a major driving force behind food production and all related services. On farms, the rapid mechanisation of farm practices has had a major impact on both investment and the demand for labour. In particular, productivity per labour unit has increased dramatically in high consumption societies, leading to a major outflow of the rural population. Now, the prevailing socio-technical systems, based on high financial investment, may have, at least in the short run, a decisive impact on the capacities available to be mobilised for the adaption of food chains to climate change. A modern food chain has high technological requirements, not only for production, but also for transport and storing. All these assets may be extremely vulnerable to escalating climate change, thus obliging responsible actors to build professional capacities accordingly.

Developing technological systems for resilient food chain requires multiple methods to measure the impacts and to survey both direct climate change impacts and the efficiency of the measures established to mitigate and adapt to climate change. Indeed, many sets of indicators have been built and experimented with recently. Yet the question remains, how accurate can these indicators be when we are trying to facilitate appropriate and politically feasible societal practices? In fact, much of the current measurement of food chain resilience still has the status of work in progress, even if some of it has been strongly institutionalised by, e.g., the Food and Agricultural Organisation (FAO), the European Union (EU) and many nation states. On the other hand, it is widely recognised that farms and SMEs seldom have the time, resources or information required for mitigation and adaptation measurement, which also means that farms and SMEs do not have a clear understanding of their own performance with regards to mitigation and adaptation (Bourlakis *et al.* 2014). Several chapters in this volume tackle the problem of accurate measurement in food chain management, while some of them explore relatively new targets of systematic measurement, such as food waste.

The modernisation of agriculture and food chains has resulted in a paradoxical situation for the traditional producer and SMEs: though the key position of farm and SME food production is recognised as an indispensable part of the food chain, the farmer/entrepreneur often struggles with the multiple pressures of value acquisition because their share of the total food chain income tends to be shrinking – even below that of a living wage in some places. Moreover, large firms in a chain may start dominating others in it by demanding the others conform to their needs regarding what can be delivered and how. For example, Arend and Wisner (2005: 427) state that supply chain management "is not a good fit for SMEs on several performance measures" and that "conflict exists over how supply chain management affects small and medium-sized companies". This tendency has led to complex circumstances that can be challenging with regard to providing alternative models for the (re)organising of food chains through new modes of entrepreneurship and interactive practices, where even consumers are allowed to have a bigger say in sending a strong message up-stream towards farms – either directly or through the intermediate actors in a food chain.

Capacity building can happen individually or collectively. When considering the many pressures of modernisation, not just climate change, many of the actors have already done their best to solve adaptation issues on their own. And even if it is clear that climate change adaptation still requires the further enhancing of individual capacities or the capacities of basic units, such as family farms, SMEs, etc., the most important challenge is to find ways for more community-based and socially interactive patterns of production and consumption. This volume includes several chapters that highlight several such options for building a more resilient food chain based on the various actors' civic initiatives and mutual efforts. However, a constant issue is: how autonomously can these actors successfully operate with their new ideas? This issue is connected to the debate on the need for institutional support, which may be organised in a number of ways. Yet, in building a resilient food chain, the core of the organising dynamics often lies more at the local than the national level. Moreover, sectorial measures that may depend on the long-term administrative tradition may not be the most effective ones for building new capacities into a food chain, so that it becomes resilient.

New challenges for food chain research

The nexus between climate change adaptation and food supply chain management has appeared as an emerging area of research and practice in which there is much work to be done. The impetus to assess climate change vulnerabilities and to increase resilience in agriculture is clear, but climate change adaptation in the food supply chain and in the overall food system is a very new field. This book aims to fill this gap and will thereby complement the existing literature. There are specific chapters dedicated to each major phase of the food supply chain: input production (e.g. plant breeders in Chapter 4), primary production (e.g. farms in Part III), food processing and manufacturing (e.g. food processing firms in Chapters 7 and 16), retail (e.g. wholesalers and retailers in Chapter 16), consumption (e.g. culinary cultures in Chapter 14) and post-consumption (e.g. food waste in Chapter 15). As the food supply chain is affected by the socio-economic, socio-political and socio-cultural environment, an interdisciplinary approach will be required.

This book aims to move the whole agenda of climate change adaptation forward. It acknowledges the importance of climate change adaptation in agriculture, but extends the system boundaries in climate change adaptation to the entire food supply chain. It also acknowledges the importance of the business case in the food supply chains, but extends the boundaries in climate change adaptation to the overall food system. Hence, the relevance of climate change adaptation is examined as a business case *and* a societal case, which are presented through various perspectives in this book. The impacts of climate change will vary according to farm, company, location in the supply chain and geographical location. Vulnerability to climate change in a particular region, company or supply chain will depend on their exposure and sensitivity to weather extremes, climate variability and gradual changes in climate as well as to their adaptive capacity. The extent and the form of climate change adaptation will also vary as the identified risks and vulnerabilities alter. It should be noted, however, that this book does not aim to make a clear distinction between climate change adaptation and climate change mitigation, as adaptation is generally "interpreted in a wide variety of ways by a wide variety of actors and is a highly contextual process dependent on variables such as sector, region and size of firm" (Nitkin *et al.* 2009: 19). For example, climate change influences societal and cultural processes, but it is also intensified by societal and cultural processes, which means that successful adaptation approaches must include mitigation efforts in the long run (Beermann 2011). According to Adger *et al.* (2009: 3), adaptation and mitigation efforts "are invariably intertwined and feed into each other" at the local level.

The structure of this book

This chapter has introduced the focus of the book: climate change adaptation and food supply chain management. The subsequent chapters of this book include four core parts, with 15 chapters that address various aspects of and approaches to food supply chain vulnerability and resilience. The parts are here presented in thematic order.

Part I, 'Food supply chains: actors, products and relationships', introduces the broader themes of food security, vulnerability and resilience. Chapter 2 by Jokinen, Mononen and Sairinen deals with the vulnerabilities of the global food system by clarifying the links between food security and climate change. Chapter 3 by Tapiola and Paloviita focuses on the resilience of the Finnish food system by employing general resilience indicators. Chapter 4 by Paavola, Himanen, Kahiluoto and Miettinen gives an insight into the discussions between plant breeders and researchers on the response diversity of crop cultivars, which is one of the food systems' attributes for resilience. Hence, Part I of the book starts with a global food system focus and then concentrates on national food systems and finally elaborates on actor-level interactions.

The first two chapters of Part II, 'Local vs. regional vulnerabilities and opportunities', highlight the wider European context, whereas two other chapters are rooted in the Finnish context. Chapters 5–8 of Part II present concrete approaches to methodologies and strategies for assessing and coping with vulnerabilities and exploiting entrepreneurial opportunities. Chapter 5 by Juhola and Neset deals with the assessment of vulnerability and the adaptive capacity of food systems. The development of assessment methodologies is discussed based on a broad overview of the literature on vulnerability to climate change. Chapter 6 by Brunori and Silvasti presents climate-related vulnerabilities and opportunities in the food systems of Italy and Finland from the perspective of food security. In Chapter 7, Puupponen examines the links between climate change, vulnerability and local adaptation strategies from the perspective of food enterprises in Finland. The authors of Chapter 8, Hartikainen, Pulkkinen, Katajajuuri and Peltonen-Sainio, have collaborated with the Finnish food industry in order to develop a methodology for assessing the carbon footprints of different foods. They focus on communication with consumers in the food supply chain.

Part III, 'Sustainable livelihood, community and farm resilience', is dedicated to farm-level adaptation and farm resilience, which is the cornerstone of the entire food supply chain. Concepts such as good farming, territorialisation and the family farm are discussed in the context of climate change adaptation. The experiences of Part III are derived from the rural areas of Finland and Serbia. The effects of the cultural understanding of good farming on farm resilience are explored in Chapter 9 by Huttunen, Mela and Hildén, who examine how the farmers' understanding of farming practices relates to their ability to adapt to climate change. A case study on farm resilience in the Zlatibor region of Serbia is presented in Chapter 10 by Battaglini, Babović and Bogdanov, who analyse how farm resilience could be conceptualised as an inner dimension of the process of territorialisation. In Chapter 11, Lehtonen, Liu and Purola evaluate the role of farm-level socio-economic characteristics in climate change adaptation with regard to mitigation targets in Northern Europe. Farm-level economic models consistent with utility maximisation and risk aversion are used in simulating the rational choices of different farm types. Another approach to farm-level vulnerabilities and farm resilience is outlined in Chapter 12 by Järvelä and Kortetmäki, who focus on farm livelihood and rural development, which can be seen as forming the core of farm resilience.

Part IV, 'Climate-resilient supply chain management: upstream and downstream', integrates the perspectives of the different phases of the food supply chain: primary production, food industry, retail, consumption and post-consumption. Moreover, the final section deals with the key determinants and relationships in climate-resilient food supply chains. In Chapter 13, Kahiluoto, Rimhanen, Kuisma and Mäkinen provide insights into management options for resilient North European dairy systems. Mäkelä and Niva, in Chapter 14, analyse what people can do in their everyday diet and eating habits in order to reduce the environmental impact of food consumption. They also examine what kind of changes people are ready for and how they understand the environmental aspects of food and eating. The authors suggest the concept of sustainable culinary cultures, which, as a joint effort, would require collective action. Chapter 15, by Silvennoinen, Katajajuuri, Hartikainen, Heikkilä and Reinikainen, focuses on food waste and related climate impacts in the Finnish food chain. Finally, Paloviita formulates

Chapter 16 by elaborating upstream and downstream relationships in the food supply chain from the perspective of food processing firms/manufacturers and food wholesalers/retailers. The importance of the value chain approach, partnerships with farmers and consumers as well as the need for organisational, cultural and behavioural changes are highlighted in order to redefine food supply chains for resilience.

A more sophisticated form of food supply chain management, one imbued with a social purpose, is required. Climate change adaptation requires the recognition of new and better ways to develop food products and services and serve food markets, but society's overall interests should also be served. Climate change adaptation is clearly a process of producing societal benefits far beyond simply producing economic benefits for a small part of the world's population. For business managers, this book aims to explain the social and environmental issues required in order to move beyond the mere business case in climate change adaptation. Business involvement in climate change adaptation is important as companies have "skills, resources and management capability to lead social progress in ways that even the best-intentioned governmental and social organizations can rarely match" (Porter and Kramer 2011). For policy-makers, this book aims to improve knowledge and understanding about the food supply chain approach. More specifically, it aims to present an approach in which the concept of the broader food system would be taken into consideration. This approach would be required since it includes activities that are being neglected in the current climate adaptation policies because they are conducted beyond the farm gate. The role of governments in assisting with climate change adaptation is equally important because they construct regulations, can set social and cultural goals and set legal standards for actors in food supply chains. For academia, this book examines the relevance of the broader societal issues related to food systems, and it also asks for the themes discussed in this book to be made part of other research agendas.

Acknowledgements

This research was funded by the Academy of Finland through the research project A-LA-CARTE (decision no. 140870).

References

Adger, N.W., Lorenzoni, I. and O'Brien, K.L. (2009) *Adapting to Climate Change: Thresholds, Values, Governance*. New York: Cambridge University Press.

Arend, R.J. and Wisner, J.D. (2005) Small business and supply chain management: is there a fit? *Journal of Business Venturing*, 20: 403–436.

Battaglini, A., Barbeau, G., Bindi, M. and Badeck, F. (2009) European winegrowers' perceptions of climate change impact and options for adaptation. *Regional Environmental Change*, 9(2): 61–73.

Beermann, M. (2011) Linking corporate climate adaptation strategies with resilience thinking. *Journal of Cleaner Production*, 19: 836–842.

Beske, P.L., Land, A. and Seuring, A.S. (2014) Sustainable supply chain management practices and dynamic capabilities in the food industry: a critical analysis of the literature. *International Journal of Production Economics*, 152: 131–143.

Bindi, M. and Olesen, J.E. (2011) The responses of agriculture in Europe to climate change. *Regional Environmental Change*, 11: 151–158.

Bourlakis, M., Maglaras, G., Aktas, E., Gallear, D. and Fotopoulos, C. (2014) Firm size and sustainable performance in food supply chains: insights from Greek SMEs. *International Journal of Production Economics*, 152: 112–130.

Christopher, M. (1998) *Logistics and Supply Chain Management*. London: Pitman Publishing.

Darnhofer, I. (2010) Strategies of family farms to strengthen their resilience. *Environmental Policy and Governance*, 20(4): 212–222.

Dyllick, T. and Hockerts, K. (2002) Beyond the business case for corporate sustainability. *Business Strategy and the Environment*, 11(2): 130–141.

Eakin, H. (2010) What is vulnerable? In J. Ingram, P. Ericksen and D. Liverman (eds) *Food Security and Global Environmental Change*. London: Earthscan, pp. 67–77.

Eastwood, R., Lipton, M. and Newell, A. (2010) Farm size. In *Handbook of Agricultural Economics*. Burlington, VA: Academic Press, pp. 3323–3375.

Ericksen, P. (2008) Conceptualizing food systems for global environmental change research. *Global Environmental Change*, 18: 234–245.

Ericksen, P., Bohle, H-G. and Stewart, B. (2010) Vulnerability and resilience of food systems. In J. Ingram, P. Ericksen and D. Liverman (eds) *Food Security and Global Environmental Change*. London: Earthscan, pp. 78–86.

FAO (2014) LACC Project. Available at: www.fao.org/climatechange/laccproject/47741/en/ (accessed 10 December 2014).

Figge, F. and Hahn, T. (2012) Is green and profitable sustainable? Assessing the trade-off between economic and environmental aspects. *International Journal of Production Economics*, 140: 92–102.

Gold, S. and Heikkurinen, P. (2013) Corporate responsibility, supply chain management and strategy: in search of new perspectives for sustainable food production. *Journal of Global Responsibility*, 4(2): 276–291.

Ingram, J. (2011) A food systems approach to researching food security and its interactions with global environmental change. *Food Security*, 3: 417–431.

IPCC (2014) Summary for policymakers. In C.B. Field Barros, V.R. Dokken, D.J. Mach *et al.* (eds) *Climate Change 2014: Impacts, Adaptation, and Vulnerability. Part A: Global and Sectoral Aspects. Contribution of Working Group II to the Fifth Assessment Report of the Intergovernmental Panel on Climate Change*. Cambridge: Cambridge University Press.

Marsden, T. and Smith, E. (2005) Ecological entrepreneurship: sustainable development in local communities through quality food production and local branding. *Geoforum*, 36: 440–451.

Mosberg, M. and Eriksen, S. (2014) The politics of climate change adaptation: taking stock of academic and practitioner experiences. Conference summary report. Available at: www.nmbu.no/sites/default/files/pdfattachments/conference_summary_report.pdf (accessed 16 December 2014).

Moussis, N. (2013) *Access to European Union: Law, Economics, Policies*. Rixensart: Intersentia.

Nitkin, D., Foster, R. and Medalye, J. (2009) Business adaptation to climate change: a systematic review of the literapture. *Network of Business Sustainability*. Available at: http://nbs.net/wp-content/uploads/NBS_Systematic-Review_Climate-Change.pdf (accessed 18 June 2014).

Pinto-Correia, T. and Vos, W. (2004) Multifunctionality in Mediterranean landscapes – past and future. In R. Jongman (ed.) *The New Dimensions of the European Landscape*. Wageningen: Springer.

Porter, M.E. and Kramer, M.R. (2011) Creating shared value. *Harvard Business Review*, 89(1–2): 62–77.

Porter, M.E. and Reinhardt, F.L. (2007) A strategic approach to climate. *Harvard Business Review*, October 22–26.

Seuring, S. and Müller, M. (2008) From a literature review to a conceptual framework for sustainable supply chain management. *Journal of Cleaner Production*, 16(15): 1699–1710.

Smit, B. and Wandel, J. (2006) Adaptation, adaptive capacity and vulnerability. *Global Environmental Change*, 16: 282–292.

Vaara, E. and Durand, R. (2012) How to connect strategy research with broader issues that matter? *Strategic Organization*, 10: 248–255.

Wilson, G.A. (2008) From 'weak' to 'strong' multifunctionality: conceptualising farm-level multifunctional transitional pathways. *Journal of Rural Studies*, 24: 367–383.

Part I

Food supply chains

Actors, products and relationships

2 Climate change and food security

Three case studies on uncertainty

Pekka Jokinen, Tuija Mononen and Rauno Sairinen

Introduction

Climate change is characterised by its immense complexity and, consequently, by uncertainty ranging from the lack of relevant data on environmental change, to the inadequate understanding of environmental system interactions, as well as the complex political system governing decision-making. Climate change also relates to several security concerns such as human security, food security and energy security (Report on Climate Security 2007; GECHS 2010). Therefore, communication and policies pose significant cognitive, psychological and political challenges and make the public anxious. As O'Brien (2009) has claimed, climate change adaptation should first and foremost satisfy security and survival values linked to physiological needs, safety needs and the social order.

On the international political agenda, food security is intimately linked to the discussions on the green economy that dominated the Rio+20 UN Conference on Sustainable Development in 2012. Food security is ultimately based on the enormous global challenge of how to feed the growing population in an environmentally, socially and economically sustainable way. This has been defined by Food and Agriculture Organisation (FAO) (2008) as the state when "all people, at all times, have physical and economic access to sufficient, safe and nutritious food to meet their dietary needs and food preferences for an active and healthy life". According to several estimates, food production will have to double by 2050 in order to sustain global food security (e.g. Tomlinson 2013).

Food security appears to be an issue of long-term environmental sustainability and of healthy and enriching food options (Newman and Ostry 2008; Sage 2012; Vermeulen *et al.* 2012). Various factors such as the volatile food prices and the increasing environmental impacts of meat consumption have revealed the unsustainability of the current food system (Lang *et al.* 2009). The development of biofuels and policy changes related to energy production are also factors affecting global food security (Murphy *et al.* 2011). Also climate change is projected to affect food security by decreasing crop productivity in lower latitudes (IPCC 2007). The food production and distribution system's interdependencies on these various factors thus result in a "wicked trilemma challenge": the growing demand for food is combined with increasing global demand for transport energy under conditions of declining petrochemical resources and the urgent need to reduce greenhouse gas emissions (Harvey and Pilgrim 2011).

This chapter focuses on the vulnerabilities of the global food system and aims to clarify the links between food security and climate change. By using three case studies based on a literature review, we will explore biofuel policies, the novel phenomena known as land grabbing and the issue of food production. In all cases, the role of climate change and the need for adaptation strategies appear to be uncertain and complex. The cases also highlight the competing interests related to land use. Biofuel policies are contested due to their land use requirements and are in direct conflict with lands available for food production. Land grabbing is another concern and refers to the large-scale land deals or transactions in developing countries carried out by transnational corporations or foreign governments. It is motivated both by the production of food and biofuels. The final case study discusses the methods of food production: conventional, genetically modified (GM) and organic food production.

Three case studies on uncertainty

Case study 1 – Biofuels: climate policy with complex and severe impacts on food security

The need to replace oil as the energy source in traffic and transportation is a global challenge for our modern culture (EIA 2010). In this respect, the development of biofuels has received increased attention in recent times as a means to mitigate climate change, alleviate global energy concerns for traffic and transportation and foster rural development and the bio-economy (Dufey 2006; Fischer *et al.* 2009). In the first-generation biofuels, the source of carbon for the biofuel is sugar, lipid or starch directly extracted from a plant. The crop is actually or potentially considered to be in competition with food. In the second-generation biofuels, the biofuel carbon is derived from cellulose, hemicellulose, lignin or pectin. This may include, for instance, agricultural and forestry wastes or residues, or purpose-grown non-food feedstocks (e.g. Short Rotation Coppice, Energy Grasses). In the third-generation biofuels, the carbon is derived from aquatic autotrophic organisms (e.g. algae).

Until now, biofuel production has mainly relied on first-generation conversion pathways (Fischer *et al.* 2009). Bioethanol can be produced from any feedstock that contains a high starch or sugar content, such as maize, wheat, sugar cane and sugar beet, by the fermentation of carbohydrates. The shift to biofuels in cars was relatively seamless in the beginning, because bioethanol could be blended with gasoline in any proportion of up to 10 per cent without the need for engine modification (Dufey 2006). Biodiesel, on the other hand, is produced through a chemical process called transesterification of vegetable oils from crop plants, such as oil palm, rapeseed, soya bean and jatropha. Similar to bioethanol, biodiesel can be used in pure form but requires specially adapted vehicles or blended with automotive diesel (ibid.). First-generation biofuel technologies were at first extensively employed in Brazil (sugar cane for bioethanol), the United States of America (maize for bioethanol) and the European Union (oilseeds, mainly rapeseed for biodiesel) (Fischer *et al.* 2009). First-generation pathways reduce greenhouse gas in the range of 20–70 per cent compared with fossil fuels (ibid.).

The rapid growth of first-generation biofuels production has raised many concerns with regard to sustainability issues and the threat posed to food security (Fischer *et al.* 2009; Raman and Mohr 2014). There are several reasons why the optimistic views on biofuels, as a straightforward solution to global problems, have dissipated.

The first argument is that biofuels can only provide a part of the solution. According to the OECD Round Table, biofuels could provide roughly 23 per cent of the demand for liquid fuels in 2050, as foreseen in the IEA's baseline scenario, without taking the economics of biofuels into account (Doornbosch and Steenblik 2007).

Second, greenhouse gas savings from the use of biofuels only replace fossil oil gradually over time. As a consequence, net greenhouse gas savings, resulting from the rapid expansion of first-generation biofuels, will only be reached after several decades. For shorter periods until 2030, the net greenhouse gas balance is dominated by carbon debts due to direct and indirect land use changes (Fischer *et al.* 2009).

Third, one of the most crucial problems in increasing biofuel production is that it competes for resources with food and food-related uses (Fischer *et al.* 2009; Koizumi 2013). There are two dimensions of competition between biofuel and food: the competition with food and food-related demand and competition with agricultural resources. In addition, it has been argued that the production of biofuels may pose a threat to biodiversity (Fischer *et al.* 2009; Palmer 2014). Many experts have stated that the biggest constraint on biofuels production is not the technology or the economy, but the adequacy of land. The production of biofuels requires large amounts of agricultural land for feedstock cultivation. According to UN estimates (UNEP 2008), biofuel crops covered about 1 per cent of the world's arable land and accounted for 1 per cent of road transport in 2007. The future projections also show increases to 4 per cent by 2030, with the biggest increases in the United States and Europe.

Fourth, there are already remarks that the agricultural commodity prices for the main feedstock crops are rising in international markets because of biofuel production (Palmer 2014). Naylor *et al.* (2007) worry about the trend:

> If energy markets begin to determine the value of agricultural commodities, the long-term trend of declining real prices for most agricultural commodities could be reversed … Over the short term, this reversal, while helping net food producers in poor areas, could have substantial consequences for the world's food-insecure, especially those who consume foods that are direct or indirect substitutes for biofuels feedstocks.

There is little doubt that current patterns of fossil fuel-based energy use are unsustainable and that a change in direction is needed. There is, however, no obvious technological fix available that will supply the world's traffic with a source of fuel that is cheap, clean, flexible and easily scalable. The current push to expand the use of first-generation biofuels is creating its own unsustainable tensions that will create new problems (Doornbosch and Steenblik 2007). In this context, it is important to clarify what exactly is at stake in the assessment of biofuels. It is clear that biofuel policies need very conscious and flexible governance in order to positively contribute to global sustainability problems.

Second-generation biofuel technologies are attracting great interest today. This is due to their low carbon dioxide emissions and the possibility of using non-food feedstock, such as residues and by-products from the agricultural and forestry industries, and from dedicated non-food-related feedstock (e.g. woody and herbaceous plants such as perennial energy grasses and fast-growing tree species; lignocellulosic biomass; non-edible vegetable oils; and algae) (Dufey 2006; Fischer *et al.* 2009; Gupta and Verma 2015). Second-generation biofuels are expected to reduce CO_2 emissions by a significant amount (from 70–100 per cent). For example, to produce agro-residues, there is no need for separate land, water and energy requirements and they do not have food value (Gupta and Verma 2015). Second-generation biofuels are, however, not without effect on the food systems. In his analysis in both China and Japan, Koizumi (2013) argues that non-food-based biofuel could have a negative impact on the most vulnerable populations, primarily on undernourished households due to the impacts on food availability. Anyhow, technological breakthroughs will be needed to reduce the overall cost of using second-generation biofuels. The required scale of operation will be large and substantial transport costs will be involved in getting the raw materials to the processing facilities. It is estimated that second-generation biofuels may only become commercially viable in the next 10–20 years.

Recently, some critical commentators have argued that the biofuel–food dilemma is an artefact of broader globalised industrial agricultural system issues and that the biofuels have been unfairly demonised before proper scrutiny (Wenner 2012; Raman and Mohr 2014). Nuffield Council on Bioethics (2011) has observed that the actual role of biofuels in the food price spikes of 2007/2008 is contested. Already in 2008, the UK Renewable Fuels Agency acknowledged that the effect of biofuels on food prices is complex and difficult to model, but observed that the poorest people are likely to be the most adversely affected. Raman and Mohr (2014) have suggested that the pertinent questions when analysing the "food-versus-fuel" dilemma are: which land, whose food and whose fuel sources are at stake? This means that the potential conflicts between biofuel and food security are contextual and have different spaces and scales.

Case study 2 – Land grabbing threatening food security

In the past few years, various countries such as Saudi Arabia, China, India and Japan have begun to buy and lease agricultural land for their own food maintenance from Africa, Asia, as well as the post-Soviet Eurasia (Visser and Spoor 2011). This process promoted by foreign governments and private investors is known as "land grabbing", "land-grab" or "global land acquisition", sometimes also "aggressive land acquisition", emphasising the fierceness of transactions (Borras *et al.* 2010). Such large-scale, cross-border land deals are often related to food security by finance-rich but resource-poor countries. The aim is to ensure a stable and steady supply of food for their populations in the aftermath of the food crisis of 2007–2008 (Kugelman 2009; Zoomers 2010; Hallam 2011). Even nations at the greatest risk of food insecurity appear as net-sellers of their farmland (Robertson and Pinstrup-Andersen 2010).

There are numerous interconnected factors and incentives for land acquisitions that may lead to radical changes in land ownership and land use (Cotula *et al.* 2009; Zoomers 2010). Accelerating urbanisation and changing diets are certainly pushing up food demand. Also the expectations of high food prices can tempt nations to land grab since the food crisis demonstrated that the world cannot continually enjoy low food prices. Energy security is the main impetus for land grabbing and, indeed, roughly a quarter of the land grab is for biodiesel production (Naylor *et al.* 2007; Kugelman 2009; Borras *et al.* 2010; Vermeulen and Cotula 2010). As well as for food and biofuel production, investments resulting in land use change are made for nature conservation, ecotourism, infrastructure projects and for tourist centres, for instance.

Land grabbing is a difficult phenomenon to study empirically since little is known about it as of yet. According to estimates, 15–20 million hectares of farmland have changed hands in developing countries since 2006, which corresponds to a quarter of the whole cultivation area in Europe (Von Braun and Meinzen-Dick 2009). Yet, much higher numbers have also been presented, estimating up to 51–63 million hectares under trade considerations (Friis and Reenberg 2010). A case study of five African countries – Ethiopia, Madagascar, Mali, Mozambique and Sudan – identified the key characteristics of land grabbing (Cotula *et al.* 2009; Cotula *et al* 2011; cf. Hall 2011). It was found that the scope of land grabbing is significant and land-based investments are increasing both in terms of projects and allocated agricultural land area. Also the size of single acquisitions is increasing even though there is substantial variation among the case countries. The private sector tends to dominate land deals but the governments often support trade processes both politically and financially. Foreign investors dominate land grabbing, though domestic investors also have a major role. Large-scale land claims may address a small proportion of the total land but the pressure is growing on higher value lands with irrigation potential or proximity to local markets.

Optimistic views consider external land acquisition as a positive option for host countries and for the local people's livelihood. For instance, the Food and Agriculture Organisation of the United Nations (FAO) has stated that international investments will outstandingly contribute to the countryside development if the objectives of the investors are suitable for the agricultural policy of the host country. The critics, on the contrary, highlight the unequal negotiation positions between the investors and local communities as the essential dimension of global land acquisition (Robertson and Pinstrup-Andersen 2010; Vermeulen and Cotula 2010). Therefore, the uneven power relations built into land grabbing are seen as a serious threat to food security and local livelihoods (Zoomers 2010).

Ecological concerns related to land grabbing are mainly because of the short-term orientation of the foreign investors; large-scale intensive agricultural production particularly threatens biodiversity and carbon stocks (Mackenzie 2008; Meinzen-Dick and Markelova 2009). Interestingly, as Friis and Reenberg (2010) write, climate change can have both negative and positive incentives for land grabbing. For instance, with changing weather patterns, agriculturally fertile land can be at risk due to the lack or abundance of rain. Climate awareness is also leading to a rapidly growing interest in green energy and biofuels and thus resulting in the increase in demand for global cropland. Land demand is also related to the implementation of the Kyoto Protocol's Clean Development Mechanisms, which gives countries credit in their carbon accounts if they invest in reforestation or pay countries to refrain from deforestation (Friis and Reenberg 2010).

The current land grab appears to be the result of a combination of globalisation, the liberalisation of land markets and the worldwide boom in foreign direct investment (Daniel and Mittal 2009; Zoomers 2010). Globalisation and new technologies facilitate long-distance trade whereas the liberalisation of land markets has resulted in a novel commoditisation of natural resources. Several authors, however, have remarked that foreign investment in and acquisition of land in other countries are not a totally new phenomenon (e.g. Daniel and Mittal 2009; Meinzen-Dick and Markelova 2009; White and Dasgupta 2010). Yet, the current land grab has a different dynamic, scale and set of players, especially since food and energy security are the major factors behind the land deals.

Case study 3 – Method of food production

The question concerning the best food production methods in the era of climate change has become an increasingly important topic among social scientists since the 1990s as agriculture is one of the major contributors to methane emissions and to nitrous oxide emissions, largely from fertiliser use. With the focus on climate change policy, discussions rage about which of the following – conventional, organic or genetically modified (GM) food – will deliver the most in terms of reducing greenhouse gas emissions, feeding the people and remaining economically viable (Lang *et al.* 2009; Stolze and Lampkin 2009).

The main arguments connected to conventional food production are based on the clear need for increasing food production. The report of the International Assessment of Agricultural Science and Technology for Development (IAASTD 2009) states that business as usual is no longer an option in food production. The report questions the ability of conventional and GM food production to feed the world. More cropland is used to grow animal feed and biofuels than is used to grow food for human consumption, therefore catering only to those who can afford it. In the era of climate change, organic farming has been seen as one of the possible way of food production because artificial fertilisers or pesticides are not allowed to be used. This is seen as an environmentally friendly way of food production. On the one hand, and at the same time, it is a well-known fact that yields in organic production are lower, but on the other, methane emissions and nitrous oxide emissions will be lower.

Organic farming methods originated in the 1920s, but the wider breakthrough happened globally in the 1990s along with the public financial support and common legislation. Requirements relating to organic production are specified under EU legislation (Council Regulation (EC) No. 834/2007). Organic production is an overall system of farm management and food production. It plays a dual societal role, where it provides for a specific market based on consumer demand, and delivers public goods contributing to the protection of the environment and animal welfare, as well as to rural development. GM methods are not allowed in organic food production (EUR-Lex 2014).

Genetic modification is the practice of transferring specific pieces of DNA from one organism to another. Plants are generated in a laboratory by altering their genetic make-up and are tested in the laboratory for the desired qualities. This is usually done by adding one or more genes to a plant's genome, using genetic engineering techniques. The motivation for developing GM food varies, and many supporters believe that it has the potential to feed the world because it can produce higher yields with less arable land and in a shorter growing period. The GM plants can be designed to be more resistant to diseases, pests and extreme weather. This also reduces or eliminates the need to use chemicals that may have a harmful effect on the ecosystem and human health (Randall 2009; Azadi and Ho 2010; Osterveer and Sonnenfeld 2012). At a global scale, food security has been employed as a means to justify and promote GM food (Woods 2012: 127).

The renewed focus on food security is perceived as a key challenge for organic farming due to its lower yields compared to conventional food production (Stolze and Lampkin 2009). Increased food production will be essential in the future and GM plants and other industrialised methods are seen as playing a significant role. Lawrence and McMichael (2012) argue that, "given that healthy ecosystems are essential to human life, the centrality of a sustainable form of agriculture to civilization is clear". Ericksen *et al.* (2009) state that increasing concerns about food security will require a wide range of sustainable agricultural practices combining organic and conventional practices to fulfil the food demand of the world's growing population.

Organic farming offers some clear environmental advantages in terms of not applying inorganic fertilisers or most synthetic pesticides (Lang *et al.* 2009). Yet, it is often criticised for deepening food insecurity for its lower yields. Lang *et al.* (ibid.) also found that with reduced production levels, organic farming is not necessarily efficient in terms of land-to-energy input ratios or in terms of greenhouse gases (GHG) emissions. Also Stolze and Lampkin (2009) write that lower yields and thus lower productivity of organic farming are weaknesses of the method. Organic farming also relies on livestock as an integral part of the system. It is seen as a significant way to reduce fossil energy inputs, the nitrous oxide emissions associated with the manufacture and use of nitrogen fertilisers and to provide opportunities for soil organic carbon sequestration. According to Badgley *et al.* (2007), organic farming has the potential to provide enough food to feed the world and it opens the door to the creation of a new kind of food system based on agro-ecological production principles. They also argue that this is possible on the current agricultural land base, while maintaining soil fertility. In fact, the models suggest the possibility that the agricultural land base could eventually be reduced if organic production methods were employed.

There is a growing scientific consensus that agro-ecological farming methods offer the most sustainable solution both in social and environmental terms (Rosin *et al.* 2012). Some experts have argued that food security will not be gained by increasing yields or by arable land expansion. The real alternative is to keep arable land as productive as possible. It has also been suggested that organic material as fertiliser (in farming land) should be increased (Scherr and Sthapit 2009). In other words, artificial fertilisers made from oil can be replaced by composting, and using green manure. Organic farming can affordably recapture carbon from the air and effectively re-store it in the soil (ibid.).

The issue of whether GM food or organic food – or both – can contribute sufficiently to the future food security is still being debated. To investigate the challenge between different food production methods, Azadi and Ho (2010) compared the advantages and disadvantages of GM food and organic food and concluded that it is difficult to "give a straight answer or simple solution on how food insecurity is being solved".

Discussion

The food system comprises numerous subsystems with their own rationalities. Even if the subsystems are internally rational as such, the whole system can be continuously unstable. As our case studies confirm, global food security and climate change create a web of complex interdependencies. On the one hand, climate change has serious consequences for food security, while, on the other, the increase in food production accelerates global environmental change. Further, national food systems are extremely vulnerable to global crises. An increase in the oil price raises the costs of food production (e.g. the fertilisers and transport). High oil prices also increase the demand for biofuels, which in turn, leads to the strengthening competition for the use of agricultural land (Gomiero *et al.* 2010). The rise of biofuel production is thus combining food production and energy production.

Food security has traditionally been considered a Third World problem of little relevance to Western countries, but this is likely to change in the future as the effects of climate change are increasing the probability of a global food market crisis. Major policy players, such as the USA, the EU and China, support their own biofuel production, irrespective of the oil price as a measure for domestic rural development (Lehrer 2009). Many cultivated plants, which are used as raw material for biofuels (e.g. sweetcorn, cassava, sugar cane and palm oil), constitute a main part of the diet of the world's poorest population. Therefore, their increasing prices cause serious problems for food security (Godfray *et al.* 2010).

Also the connections between land grabbing and food security are obvious since food security is the main driver of external land acquisition. As illustrated by case study 2, various countries are attempting to ensure the supply of food for their populations by acquiring global farmland. High food prices will likely maintain this dynamics in the future, but it is also clear that land grabbing is a serious threat to food security, particularly in Africa (Robertson and Pinstrup-Andersen 2010). Several Sub-Saharan African countries, which are strongly dependent on international food aid and have a large percentage of their population suffering from undernourishment, are net sellers of agricultural land.

According to Lang *et al.* (2009), the new food policy task should not just be feeding the people but feeding them appropriately, sustainably and equitably. Thus, the forthcoming food governance should be based on understanding the interconnection between the vulnerability of the food system and climate change (Thompson and Scoones 2009).

Given that a sufficient amount of food for the global population is already produced (UNEP 2009), the real challenges in the near future are related to the just distribution and effective use of food. If those challenges were fulfilled, a major policy change could appear, thereby leaving behind the goal of continuously increasing food production. This introduces a new food regime. The current food policy is steered by powerful countries and economic blocs though global civil society is becoming increasingly involved in the food policy discussion (e.g. Ericksen *et al.* 2009). Citizen-consumers' campaigns, which emphasise health and environmental questions as well as alternative food systems such as organic and local food, are calling for a stricter control of the food system (Thompson and Scoones 2009). The profound issues are what kind of governance processes will determine the dynamics of the global food system and how alternative food systems would promote sustainability (Horlings and Marsden 2011).

Conclusion

The global food system basically is failing when it comes to food security and environmental change. The attempt to strengthen food security by intensified food production is accelerating climate change whereas climate change is weakening food security particularly in vulnerable areas. Guaranteeing global food security thus appears a vicious circle that is extremely difficult to break. Yet, if the estimates by UNEP (2009; cf. also Badgley *et al.* 2007) are valid, even a decrease in farmland area can guarantee food security. The key challenge in the near future is how to produce a sufficient amount of food of good quality in climate-friendly ways and without deforestation. The regional variance of the conditions for food security is then of primary interest.

Most of the discussion about food security and farming methods has been concentrated on organic and GM food. More attention, however, needs to be given to sustainable and productive agriculture. Horlings and Marsden (2011) suggest that agro-ecological approaches could significantly contribute to feeding the world and thereby contribute to a real green revolution. This requires, however, a more radical move towards a new type of agri-food eco-economy. Under the current conditions of food crisis and food insecurity in many parts of the world, the challenge remains whether the heterogeneous variety of sustainable agri-ecological practices can offer a viable alternative compared with the conventional food production market.

Overall, because of the interdependency of food insecurity and climate change, the need for an improved land use policy is urgent. Besides co-operation at different governance levels, development of the capacity of local people to manage their farmland is required (Brown and Funk 2008). This applies also to the use of agricultural land for biofuel production (Borras *et al.* 2010). Farmers and local communities, which are responsible for land use, are significant actors in the mitigation of climate change even though the most central driver is the way developed countries steer food and biofuels production (Scherr and Sthapit 2009; Tilman *et al.* 2009). Large landowners and the global food industry have the main effect on land use policy.

References

Azadi, H. and Ho, P. (2010) Genetically modified and organic crops in developing countries: a review of options for food security. *Biotechnology Advances*, 28: 160–168.

Badgley, C., Moghtader, J., Quintero, E., Zakem, E., Chappell, M., Avilés Vázquez, K., Samulon, A. and Perfecto, I. (2007) Organic agriculture and the global food supply. *Renewable Agriculture and Food Systems*, 22: 86–108.

Borras Jr, P., Saturnino, M., McMichael, P. and Scoones, I. (2010) The politics of biofuels, land and agrarian change: editors' introduction. *Journal of Peasant Studies*, 37: 575–592.

Brown, M. and Funk, C. (2008) Food security under climate change. *Science*, 319: 580–581.

Cotula, L., Vermeulen, S., Leonard, R. and Keeley, J. (2009) *Land Grab or Development Opportunity? Agricultural Investment and International Land Deals in Africa*. Rome: FAO/London: IIED/IFAD.

Cotula, L., Vermeulen, S., Mathieu, P. and Toulmin, C. (2011) Agricultural investment and international land deals: evidence from a multi-country study in Africa. *Food Security*, 3: 99–113.

Daniel, S. and Mittal, A. (2009) *The Great Land Grab. Rush for World's Farmland Threatens Food Security for the Poor*. Oakland. CA: The Oakland Institute.

Doornbosch, R. and Steenblik, R. (2007) *Biofuels: Is the Cure Worse than the Disease?* OECD Round Table on Sustainable Development. Available at: http://media.ft.com/cms/fb8b5078-5fdb-11dc-b0fe-0000779fd2ac.pdf (accessed 1 August 2014).

Dufey, A. (2006) *Biofuels Production, Trade and Sustainable Development: Emerging Issues*. Sustainable Markets Discussion Paper No. 2. London: IIED.

EIA (2010) *International Energy Outlook*. Available at: www.eia.doe.gov/oiaf/ieo/pdf/highlights.pdf (accessed 1 August 2014).

Ericksen, P., Ingram, J. and Liverman, D. (2009) Food security and global environmental change: emerging challenges. *Environmental Science and Policy*, 12: 373–377.

EUR-Lex (2014) Eur-lex.europa.eu (accessed 1 August 2014).

FAO (2008) *Climate Change and Food Security: A Framework Document*. Rome: FAO.

Fischer, G., Hizsnyik, E., Prieler, S., Shah, M. and van Velthuizen, H. (2009) *Biofuels and Food Security*. Vienna: International Institute for Applied Systems Analysis.

Friis, C. and Reenberg, A. (2010) *Land Grab in Africa: Emerging Land System Drivers in a Teleconnected World*. Copenhagen: GLP-IPO.

GECHS (2010) *The Global Environmental Change and Human Security*. Available at: www.gechs.org/human-security/ (accessed 1 August 2014).

Godfray, H., Beddington, J., Crute, I., Haddad, L., Lawrence, D., Muir, J., Pretty, J., Robinson, S., Thomas, S. and Toulmin, C. (2010) Food security: the challenge of feeding 9 billion people. *Science*, 327: 812–818.

Gomiero, T., Paoletti, M. and Pimentel, D. (2010) Biofuels: efficiency, ethics, and limits to human appropriation of ecosystem services. *Journal of Agricultural and Environmental Ethics*, 23: 403–434.

Gupta, A. and Verma, J.P. (2015) Sustainable bio-ethanol production from agro-residues: a review. *Renewable and Sustainable Energy Reviews*, 41: 550–567.

Hall, R. (2011) Land grabbing in Southern Africa: the many faces of the investor rush. *Review of African Political Economy*, 38: 193–214.

Hallam, D. (2011) International investment in developing country agriculture: issues and challenges. *Food Security*, 3: 91–98.

Harvey, M. and Pilgrim, S. (2011) The new competition for land: food, energy, and climate change. *Food Policy*, 36: 40–51.

Horlings, L. and Marsden, T. (2011) Towards the real green revolution? Exploring the conceptual dimensions of a new ecological modernisation of agriculture that could 'feed the world'. *Global Environmental Change*, 21: 441–452.

IAASTD (2009) *Agriculture at a Crossroads. Synthesis Report*. Washington, DC: IAASDT.

IPCC (2007) *Climate Change 2007: Synthesis Report*. Geneva: IPCC.

Koizumi, T. (2013) Biofuel and food security in China and Japan. *Renewable and Sustainable Energy Reviews*, 21: 102–109.

Kugelman, M. (2009) Introduction. In M. Kugelman and L. Levenstein (eds) *Land Grab: The Race for the World's Farmland*. Washington, DC: Woodrow Wilson International Center for Scholars, pp. 1–23.

Lang, T., Barling, D. and Caraher, M. (2009) *Food Policy. Integrating Health, Environment and Society*. Oxford: Oxford University Press.

Lawrence, G. and McMichael, P. (2012) The question of food security. *International Journal of Sociology of Agriculture and Food*, 19: 135–142.

Lehrer, N. (2009) (Bio)fueling farm policy: the biofuels boom and the 2008 farm bill. *Agriculture and Human Values*, 27: 427–444.

Mackenzie, D. (2008) Rich countries carry out '21st century land grab'. *New Scientist*, 2685: 8–9.

Meinzen-Dick, R. and Markelova, H. (2009) Necessary nuance: toward a code of conduct in foreign land deals. In M. Kugelman and L. Levenstein (eds) *Land Grab: The Race for the World's Farmland*. Washington, DC: Woodrow Wilson International Center for Scholars, pp. 69–81.

Ministry of the Environment of Japan (2007) *Report on Climate Security*. Sub-Committee on International Climate Change Strategy, Global Environment Committee, Central Environment Council, Ministry of the Environment of Japan. Available at: www.env.go.jp/en/earth/cc/CS.pdf (accessed 1 August 2014).

Murphy, R., Woods, J., Black, M. and McManus, M. (2011) Global developments in the competition for land from biofuels. *Food Policy*, 36: S52–S61.

Naylor, R., Liska, A., Burke, M., Falcon, W., Gaskell, J., Rozelle, S. and Cassman, K. (2007) The ripple effect: biofuels, food security, and the environment. *Environment: Science and Policy for Sustainable Development*, 49: 30–43.

Newman, L. and Ostry, A. (2008) From seed to table: the challenge of creating sustainable food systems, *Environments Journal*, 36: 1–4.

Nuffield Council on Bioethics (2011) *Biofuels: Ethical Issues*. Available at: http://nuffieldbioethics.org/wp-content/uploads/2014/07/Biofuels_ethical_issues_FULL-REPORT_0.pdf (accessed 1 August 2014).

O'Brien, K. (2009) Do values subjectively define the limits to climate change adaptation? In N. Adger, I. Lorenzoni and K. O'Brien (eds) *Adapting to Climate Change*. Cambridge: Cambridge University Press, pp. 164–180.

Osterveer, P. and Sonnenfeld, D. (2012) *Food, Globalization and Sustainability*. London: Earthscan.

Palmer, J. (2014) Biofuels and the politics of land-use change: tracing the interactions of discourse and place in European policy making. *Environment and Planning* A, 46: 337–352.

Raman, S. and Mohr, A. (2014) Biofuels and the role of space in sustainable innovation journeys. *Journal of Cleaner Production*, 65: 224–233.

Randall, E. (2009) *Food, Risk and Politics: Scare, Scandal and Crisis – Insights into the Risk Politics of Food Safety*. Manchester: Manchester University Press.

Robertson, B. and Pinstrup-Andersen, P. (2010) Global land acquisition: neo-colonialism or development opportunity? *Food Security*, 2: 271–283.

Rosin, C., Stock, P. and Campbell, H. (eds) (2012) *Food Systems Failure: The Global Food Crisis and the Future of Agriculture*. London: Earthscan.

Sage, C. (2012) *Environment and Food*. London: Routledge.

Scherr, S. and Sthapit, S. (2009) Farming and land use to cool the planet. In Worldwatch Institute, *State of the World 2009*. Washington, DC: Worldwatch Institute, pp. 30–49.

Stolze, M. and Lampkin, N. (2009) Policy for organic farming: rationale and concepts. *Food Policy*, 34: 237–244.

Thompson, J. and Scoones, I. (2009) Addressing the dynamics of agri-food systems: an emerging agenda for social science research. *Environmental Science and Policy*, 12: 386–397.

Tilman, D., Socolow, R., Foley, J., Hill, J., Larson, E., Lynd, L., Pacala, S., Searchinger, T., Sommerville, C. and Williams, R. (2009) Beneficial biofuels – the food, energy, and environment trilemma. *Science*, 325: 270–271.

Tomlinson, I. (2013) Doubling food production to feed the 9 billion: a critical perspective on a key discourse of food security in the UK. *Journal of Rural Studies*, 29: 81–90.

UNEP (2008) *Global Environment Outlook GEO-4*. Available at: www.unep.org/geo/geo4.asp (accessed 1 August 2014).

UNEP (2009) *The Environmental Food Crisis*. Available at: www.unep.org/pdf/FoodCrisis_lores.pdf (accessed 1 August 2014).

Vermeulen, S., Aggarwal, P., Ainslie, A., Angelone, C., Campbell, B., Challinor, A., Hansen, J., Ingram, J., Jarvis, A., Kristjanson, P., Lau, C., Nelson, G., Thornton, P. and

Wollenberg, E. (2012) Options for support to agriculture and food security under climate change. *Environmental Science & Policy*, 15: 136–144.

Vermeulen, S. and Cotula, L. (2010) Over the heads of local people: consultation, consent, and recompense in large-scale land deals for biofuels projects in Africa. *Journal of Peasant Studies*, 37: 899–916.

Visser, O. and Spoor, M. (2011) Land grabbing in post-Soviet Eurasia: the world's largest agricultural land reserves at stake. *Journal of Peasant Studies*, 38: 299–323.

Von Braun, J. and Meinzen-Dick, R. (2009) *Land Grabbing by Foreign Investors in Developing Countries: Risks and Opportunities*. IFPRI Policy Brief 13. Available at: www.ifpri.org/sites/default/files/publications/bp013all.pdf (accessed 1 August 2014).

Wenner, C. (2012) Biofuels industry does not deserve to be demonized. *The Guardian*, 16 October.

White, B. and Dasgupta, A. (2010) Agrofuels capitalism: a view from political economy. *Journal of Peasant Studies*, 37: 593–607.

Woods, M. (2012) *Rural*. London: Routledge.

Zoomers, A. (2010) Globalisation and the foreignisation of space: seven processes driving the current global land grab. *Journal of Peasant Studies*, 37: 429–447.

3 Building resilient food supply chains for the future

Titta Tapiola and Ari Paloviita

Introduction

Modern food systems consist of the networks of activities and infrastructure needed to feed a certain population. The key activities of food supply chains involve input industries, primary production, food processing and manufacturing, distribution, retail, food services and consumption. Essential inputs into the food system, such as energy, fertilisers, pesticides and machinery, are vital and are often imported into Finland as they are mainly produced from or by using fossil fuels. Modern food systems are heavily dependent on these inputs to be able to function properly. It could be said that modern food systems run on oil (Bomford 2010: 121–122; Woods *et al.* 2010: 2991–2992).

All the activities above have social, cultural, economic, environmental and political aspects, including the governing and research institutions and organisations. According to Ericksen (2008b: 16) the main objective of food systems is food security. In Europe, food security is associated, for example, with improved understanding of the sources of food waste, which is significantly produced at all levels of the food supply chain (Kumar *et al.* 2013). Food security can also be viewed as part of the corporate social responsibility strategies of the food industry and the retailing companies (Manning 2013). Hence, there is a close interdependence between food security and the sustainable food system.

Global drivers influence the modern food systems, for example, climate change, a growing population, a growing elderly population, urbanisation, changes in diets, and economic crises that influence food prices, and so on (Misselhorn *et al.* 2012: 8). In addition, possible peak oil costs, structural changes in food systems, such as homogenisation and concentration, plus diminishing natural resources, will also entail risks and opportunities for future food systems and food security (Ericksen 2008a: 235, Ericksen 2008b: 20; Rockström *et al.* 2009: 473; Woods *et al.* 2010: 2991–2992, 2998). Food is also interlinked with water and energy (fossil fuels) (Stigson 2013: 2). Water scarcities, on the one hand, and flooding, on the other, are estimated to increase as the climate change proceeds and both have impacts on food security (Wheeler and von Braun 2013).

When considering unlikely phenomena and not knowing a lot about their measures, managing food systems for resilience and building resilience for food security provide a useful approach. It is possible to be prepared for or at least plan for phenomena that we know about, and have some well-informed scenarios on climate change adaptation and other issues. Nevertheless, there will doubtless be shocks and stresses that it is not possible to foresee or forecast. Casti *et al.* (2011: 4–5) list five reasons for the emergence of unexpected events: (1) increasing complexity and a limited human ability to understand and control the behaviour of complexities; (2) flat-world instability, i.e. the interdependencies of individual actions on a global level; (3) paradigm shifts representing major large-scale discontinuities, e.g. technological innovations; (4) unresolved global drivers reaching their tipping point and the subsequent consequences; and (5) some current characteristics of modern societies, such as the appreciation of individualism, specialisation and short-sightedness, which can work against long-term thinking.

Food systems are vulnerable to events caused by complexity, global interdependency, paradigm shifts and unresolved global drivers, such as climate change and even the fundamental characteristics of our society. Concern about the resilience of modern food systems and food supply chains raises many questions about their present and future resilience. Therefore this chapter is looking for answers to two questions: (1) How do food system experts perceive the current resilience of the Finnish food system, and (2) In what way do these same experts foresee the current resilience to have changed by 2050?

It is somewhat worrying how little time is spent thinking about our potential futures with regard to the long term, or in preparing ourselves for how food systems might be different in the future. The aim of the theories used in this work is not to explain what might be or will be. It is not possible to predict futures, but it might be possible to open new windows to consider the endless opportunities and threats, thus influencing decisions taken today and leading our future development in more preferable directions. This chapter aims to raise awareness of resilience thinking and to inspire key actors in the food supply chain to take action towards securing a preferable future for our common food system.

General resilience and resilience assessment

Resilience is a system-level concept and, unlike sustainability, it is not fundamentally normative, i.e. it does not include specific choices about performance measure. Usually there is a need to define the "resilience of what to what" (e.g. resilience of a certain system to a certain disturbance or event). When "resilience of what to what" has been defined, it is referred to as a specified resilience, e.g. resilience of a certain food supply chain to climate change.

On the other hand, general resilience refers to a broader set of system attributes, such as the amount of change a system can withstand, self-organising behaviour, connectedness, diversity, modularity and the capacity for learning (see Walker and Salt 2006: 121, 145–148; Carpenter *et al.* 2012). General resilience leaves external conditions more open to shocks, including unlikely events. Specified resilience, i.e. having more carefully defined system boundaries, is close to the concept of robustness (Resilience Alliance 2007, 2010; Anderies *et al.* 2013).

Food systems are complex examples of the socio-ecological system (SES). There have been many attempts to operationalise the measurement of the resilience of SESs, but only with some success, which is often connected to the systems having a well-defined spatial and temporal scale (Walker and Salt 2006). The measurement of resilience is difficult because it actually requires measuring the thresholds or boundaries between different regimes. That is why the resilience of a SES is not observable or directly measurable. However, Carpenter *et al.* (2005) list four approaches to develop indicators or surrogates: (1) aspects of the resilience of an SES are identified by using stakeholder assessment; (2) models – scenarios, computer simulations – are used to examine the potential thresholds; (3) historical profiling is used to compare similar SESs and regime shifts; and (4) case study comparisons are used to examine similar SESs. Each approach has its own strengths and weaknesses, therefore, a combination of them would secure more robust indicators. In connection with climate change, Engle *et al.* (2013) have constructed preliminary categories of a "hybrid" resilience framework with five groups of indicators: (1) governance and security; (2) natural resources; (3) social systems; (4) economic systems; and (5) infrastructure.

General resilience parameters are typically difficult to apply directly in practice, especially to complex systems such as food systems. However, one promising indicator framework is the behaviour-based indicator framework developed by Cabell and Oelofse (2012) to assess the resilience of agroecosystems. According to our literature review, these indicators can be applied and used in the general resilience framework. We will use 13 indicators of this framework to explore the resilience of the Finnish food system. Although these indicators were originally developed to measure the resilience of agroecosystems, their general resilience characteristics make most of them applicable to the overall food system. The indicators and their reference to general resilience parameters are described as follows:

1 "Socially self-organised" refers to the general parameters of self-organising behaviour, and the resulting innovation and experimentation (see Walker and Salt 2006: 121, 145–148). Meadows (2008: 79–80) defines self-organisation as a system's capability to make its own structure more complex.
2 "Ecologically self-regulated" refers to the general parameters of connectedness and feedbacks. The tightness of the feedbacks or responsiveness (connections) represents how quickly and strongly a change in one part of a system is felt in other parts of the system (Walker and Salt 2006: 121, 145–148). Carpenter *et al.* (2012) describe feedbacks as linkages in control and response variables. Davidson *et al.* (2013) list feedbacks as one of the critical resilience dimensions. Hence, an ecologically self-regulated indicator measures how ecological components self-regulate via stabilising feedback mechanisms that send information back to controlling elements.

3 "Appropriately connected" refers to the general parameters of connectedness and feedbacks, describing the quantity and quality of relationships between system elements.
4 "Functional and response diversity" refers to the general parameter of diversity, measuring the variety of ecosystem services and range of responses to the environmental change. Diversity highlights the number of different actors – people, species, business and food supplies – that form a system (Walker and Salt 2006: 121, 145–148).
5 "Optimally redundant" – a system that has optimally extra resources – refers to general parameters of modularity, independently functioning modules and back-ups. Modularity measures the separate components and links between the components of a system (ibid.: 121, 145–148). Carpenter *et al.* (2012) describe modularity as independent, and present similar systems or functions to secure functioning, even if one module fails. Hence, optimally redundant means critical components and relationships are duplicated to prevent failure. The amount of change a system can withstand while maintaining its main functions and structure is associated with its reserves (for the regeneration of key components) and redundancy (Carpenter *et al.* 2012). Sheffi (2005) identifies increased redundancy, i.e. keeping an extra food inventory, maintaining low capacity utilisation and the multi-sourcing of food, as a way to develop supply chain resilience, though it has limited utility.
6 "Spatial and temporal heterogeneity" refers to the general parameter of diversity, measuring patchiness (degrees of heterogeneity) across a landscape and changes over time. Diversity may also mean the diversity of land use – the opposite of monocultures (Walker and Salt 2006: 121, 145–148). On the other hand, self-organisation produces heterogeneity and unpredictability, but requires freedom and some disorder to occur (Meadows 2008: 80).
7 "Exposed to disturbances" refers to the general parameters of "practising" self-organising behaviour and the capacity for learning, meaning that the system can be exposed to low-level events that cause disruptions without pushing it beyond the critical threshold. According to Davidson *et al.* (2013), the likelihood of crossing critical thresholds is one of the critical resilience dimensions.
8 "Coupled with local natural capital" refers to the general parameters of modularity, self-organising and connectedness, meaning that the system functions mainly within a regionally available natural resource base and ecosystem services. According to Carpenter *et al.* (2012), nestedness is a concept that enables large-scale challenges to be turned into more natural scale, such as the village or community level.
9 "Reflected and shared learning" refers to the general parameter of the capacity for learning, which emphasises how individuals and institutions learn from past and present experimentation to anticipate change and create desirable futures. According to Davidson *et al.* (2013), openness to resilience thinking is one of the critical resilience dimensions.

10 "Globally autonomous and locally interdependent" refers to the general parameters of modularity, self-organising and connectedness, in which the systems have relative autonomy from global control and hence more local cooperation.
11 "Honours legacy" refers to the general parameters of the capacity for learning and trust, meaning that the current configuration and future trajectories of a system are influenced by past conditions and experiences. Trust enables effective collaboration and is developed in repeated interactions (Carpenter *et al.* 2012).
12 "Builds human capital" refers to the general parameters of the capacity for learning and trust, measuring the ability of a system to take advantage of and to build social relationships and memberships in social networks; leadership enables the building and maintenance of networks (Carpenter *et al.* 2012).
13 "Reasonably profitable" refers to the general parameter of the capacity for self-organising behaviour, measuring the ability of segments of society to gain a livelihood from the work they do without relying too heavily, for example, on subsidies or secondary employment.

In the next sections, the resilience of the current Finnish food system and its resilience in the year 2050 are assessed by using the abovementioned framework of 13 resilience indicators. We argue that this type of coarse information can be useful in profiling the degree of resilience of different food supply chain subsystems and will help to provide a starting point for resilience management.

Present resilience of the Finnish food system

The method used was an electronic survey of 63 experts (individual respondents). The invited experts were from research organisations, the food industry, the retail sector and the farmers' support organisation ProAgria. The behaviour-based indicator framework for assessing the resilience of agroecosystems was used when constructing the claims of the expert survey. It was also investigated whether, according to the experts' views, there are some types of farms (small, medium or large farms; organic, plant or livestock production farms), industries (small, medium or large businesses) or retail actors (local, national or international) that seem to be more resilient than others. The expert survey had four sections that respondents could choose from: primary production, food industry, retail and consumption. The respondent could also answer more than one section. There were 25–27 respondents (the variation is due to the fact that some respondents did not answer all the questions) in the section concerning primary production, 20–22 respondents in the food industry section, 13–14 respondents in the retail section and 36–37 respondents in the consumer attitudes and behaviour section. The scale used was the Likert scale (1–5). The Likert-scale data was complemented with written comments by the experts.

For each sub-system of the food supply chain system the most relevant set of indicators were selected, because primary production, the food industry, retailers and consumers operate in varying environments. Hence, only some of the indicators applied to all sub-systems. As the indicator framework used was primarily made to assess the general resilience of agroecosystems, the indicators were especially applicable to primary production, but many of them were also applicable to other sub-systems of the food system. The results (the means of the responses) are presented in Table 3.1.

The present resilience of primary production was measured by ten indicators. In general, organic farms are perceived as the most resilient farm type by the experts. Indicator 8, coupled with local natural capital, represents the lowest degree of resilience in primary production. Farms are typically dependent on imported natural capital, such as oil, fertilisers and pesticides. The highest degree of resilience is shown by indicator 9, reflected and shared learning, which means that farmers are able and willing to share their learning and know-how and have the capability to develop their livelihoods and possibly adopt new behaviours or structures if necessary. Some experts commented that farms have prepared for some rare but probable situations, such as power failure, but there were few opportunities to have or adopt redundancy (indicator 5) due to tight financial situations.

The present resilience of food industry was measured by seven indicators. In the food industry, it appears that larger businesses seem to have a higher resilience than smaller businesses. Indicator 5, optimally redundant, represents the lowest degree of resilience in the food industry. The experts believe the food industry operates very efficiently but that it does not have much redundancy if something unexpected occurs. The larger businesses were considered to have more redundancy or capacity available, which might be due to their wider range of resources and better access to resources.

The present resilience of the retail sector was measured by six indicators. International retailers seem to demonstrate a high degree of resilience regarding connectedness (indicator 3) as well as reflected and shared learning (indicator 9) compared to national and local actors. Presently the largest retail actors have appropriate connections to their stakeholders in order to minimise risks. In other words, they have plenty of connections to suppliers, several sales channels and customer groups. The experts did not see these connections as a trade-off to maintain flexibility, but as a necessity to minimise risks. However, international retailers demonstrate a low degree of resilience regarding coupling with local natural capital (indicator 8) as well as global autonomy and local interdependency (indicator 10). The retail sector as a whole is, according to experts, poorly associated with building local human capital (indicator 12).

The resilience of consumers was measured by four indicators – two of those indicators, (1) socially self-organised and (10) globally autonomous and locally interdependent, came from the general indicator framework. The indicators showed a medium degree of resilience, according to the experts. Two additional indicators measured the awareness of food waste and activities to reduce waste as well as consumer awareness of the environmental and social impacts of food.

Table 3.1 Present status of resilience of primary production, food industry and retail according to the expert survey

Indicator	*Primary production, i.e. farms*							*Food industry*				*Retail*			
	S	M	L	*Org.*	*PP*	*LF*	*All*	S	M	L	*All*	*Loc.*	*Nat.*	*Int.*	*All*
1. Socially self-organised	3.33	3.44	3.41	3.59	3.3	3.11	3.36	n/a	n/a	n/a	n/a	n/a	n/a	n/a	n/a
2. Ecologically self-regulated	2.79	2.57	2.43	3.61	2.5	2.79	2.78	n/a	n/a	n/a	n/a	n/a	n/a	n/a	n/a
3. Appropriately connected	2.38	2.67	3.13	3.04	3.04	2.71	2.83	2.55	3.36	3.82	3.24	3.07	3.64	3.86	3.52
4. Functional and response diversity	3.08	2.85	2.5	3.65	2.5	2.46	2.84	2.45	3.09	3.59	3.05	n/a	n/a	n/a	n/a
5. Optimally redundant	2.88	2.80	2.76	2.96	2.88	2.72	2.83	2.19	2.62	2.90	2.57	2.57	2.5	2.93	2.67
6. Spatial and temporal heterogeneity	2.96	2.88	3.00	4.08	2.69	3.31	3.15	n/a	n/a	n/a	n/a	n/a	n/a	n/a	n/a
7. Exposed to disturbances	3.30	3.41	3.22	3.93	3.37	3.22	3.41	n/a	n/a	n/a	n/a	n/a	n/a	n/a	n/a
8. Coupled with local natural capital	2.2	2.27	2.23	2.76	2.23	2.15	2.31	3.05	3.36	3.36	3.26	2.92	2.54	2.23	2.56
9. Reflected and shared learning	3.23	3.48	4.12	4.00	3.80	3.96	3.77	2.86	3.19	3.95	3.33	2.77	3.38	3.83	3.33
10. Globally autonomous and locally interdependent	n/a	n/a	n/a	n/a	n/a	n/a	n/a	3.43	3.10	2.38	2.97	3.31	2.92	1.69	2.64
11. Honours legacy	3.52	3.37	3.00	3.85	3.26	3.30	3.38	n/a	n/a	n/a	n/a	n/a	n/a	n/a	n/a
12. Builds human capital	n/a	n/a	n/a	n/a	n/a	n/a	n/a	3.43	3.29	2.90	3.21	2.46	2.62	2.31	2.46
13. Reasonably profitable	n/a	n/a	n/a	n/a	n/a	n/a	n/a	n/a	n/a	n/a	n/a	n/a	n/a	n/a	n/a
In total	2.97	2.97	2.98	3.55	2.96	2.97		2.85	3.14	3.27		2.85	2.93	2.81	

Notes: Primary production is divided into small (S), medium (M), large (L), organic (Org.), plant production (PP) and livestock (LF) farms. Food industry is divided into small (S), medium (M) and large (L) businesses. Retail sector is divided into local (Loc.), national (Nat.) and international (Int.) actors. Degree of resilience is illustrated as follows: low (white, mean of responses 0–2.6), medium (light grey, mean of responses 2.7–3.3) and high (dark grey, mean of responses 3.4–5).

According to the experts, the low level of awareness of food waste among consumers represents a serious resilience problem in Finland.

The resilience of the Finnish food system in 2050

The second part of the expert survey used the same indicators to ask questions about the future resilience of the Finnish food system. The results (the mean of the responses) are presented in Table 3.2. Overall, the experts believe the Finnish food system will be clearly more resilient by 2050 compared to today. There were only two indicators that were given a low degree of resilience in the future for certain types of actors, namely indicator 3, appropriately connected, which was a problem for small food industry businesses and indicator 10, globally autonomous and locally interdependent, which was a problem for large food industry businesses and international retailers. In addition, both indicators show a clear negative change for food industry businesses of all sizes from today to 2050.

In primary production, the indicators generally demonstrate a high degree of resilience in the future. Potential future resilience problems in primary production are associated with indicator 5, optimally redundant, and indicator 13, reasonably profitable. It appears that the experts believe that large farms will have the best opportunities to build a profitable business. On the other hand, farms may lack reserves and back-ups to cope with system failure.

The written replies to indicator 2, ecologically self-regulated, emphasised a well-known problem in Finland: the separation between livestock farms and plant production farms, which refers to the fact that manure produced by livestock is not exploited efficiently – often because of logistics. The respondents also stated that there is much to do before farmers really understand and exploit ecosystem services and local natural resources. However, organic farms were seen as positive exceptions. The relative change from the current situation to 2050 for organic farms appeared to be smaller than for other farm types because they already seem to behave resiliently. The comments also emphasised that it is critical and necessary for future sustainability and resilience to learn and exploit eco-system services and local natural resources sustainably. Some respondents commented that only when the prices of inputs – oil, fertilisers and pesticides – rise high enough will alternatives be sought and evaluated seriously.

The food industry and the retail sector are expected to build local human capital (indicator 12) in the future, with the exception being international retailers. On the other hand, only local retailers seem to be globally autonomous and locally interdependent (indicator 10). Experts do not foresee international actors in the retail business being globally autonomous because they would still acquire products from global markets. Regarding local actors, the experts foresee more autonomy from the global markets and less concentration.

Indicator 8, coupled with local natural capital, and indicator 9, reflected and shared learning, reflect a high degree of resilience in the future for all actors in

Table 3.2 Future resilience of primary production, food industry and retail according to the expert survey

Indicator	*Primary production, i.e. farms*							*Food industry*				*Retail*			
	S	M	L	Org.	PP	LF	All	S	M	L	All	Loc.	Nat.	Int.	All
1. Socially self-organised	3.74	3.63	3.52	3.89	3.59	3.44	3.64	n/a	n/a	n/a	n/a	n/a	n/a	n/a	n/a
2. Ecologically self-regulated	3.59	3.67	3.7	4.00	3.63	3.96	3.76	n/a	n/a	n/a	n/a	n/a	n/a	n/a	n/a
3. Appropriately connected	3.56	3.79	3.88	3.96	3.92	3.72	3.81	2.45	3.09	3.59	3.05	3.85	4.15	3.85	3.95
4. Functional and response diversity	3.73	3.73	3.54	3.92	3.65	3.35	3.65	3.33	3.71	4.05	3.70	n/a	n/a	n/a	n/a
5. Optimally redundant	2.96	3.08	3.00	3.20	3.16	3.00	3.07	2.81	2.90	3.00	2.90	2.75	2.85	3.15	2.92
6. Spatial and temporal heterogeneity	3.50	3.69	3.96	4.24	3.68	3.88	3.83	n/a	n/a	n/a	n/a	n/a	n/a	n/a	n/a
7. Exposed to disturbances	3.38	3.35	3.31	3.58	3.38	3.38	3.40	n/a	n/a	n/a	n/a	n/a	n/a	n/a	n/a
8. Coupled with local natural capital	3.96	4.23	4.24	4.38	4.19	4.23	4.21	4.00	4.14	4.05	4.06	4.38	4.08	3.69	4.05
9. Reflected and shared learning	4.16	4.24	4.40	4.36	4.32	4.36	4.31	3.81	3.95	4.10	3.95	4.00	4.08	4.25	4.11
10. Globally autonomous and locally interdependent	3.42	3.35	3.31	3.54	3.31	3.58	3.42	3.10	2.76	2.14	2.67	3.85	3.33	2.15	3.11
11. Honours legacy	3.7	3.56	3.37	3.78	3.59	3.59	3.60	n/a	n/a	n/a	n/a	n/a	n/a	n/a	n/a
12. Builds human capital	n/a	n/a	n/a	n/a	n/a	n/a	n/a	3.9	3.85	3.67	3.81	4.00	3.62	3.31	3.64
13. Reasonably profitable	2.62	2.85	3.42	3.15	3.12	3.31	3.08	n/a	n/a	n/a	n/a	n/a	n/a	n/a	n/a
In total	3.53	3.6	3.64	3.83	3.63	3.65		3.34	3.49	3.51		3.81	3.69	3.4	

Notes: Primary production is divided into small (S), medium (M), large (L), organic (Org.), plant production (PP) and livestock (LF) farms. Food industry is divided into small (S), medium (M) and large (L) businesses. Retail sector is divided into local (Loc.), national (Nat.) and international (Int.) actors. Degree of resilience is illustrated as follows: low (white, mean of responses 0–2.6), medium (light grey, mean of responses 2.7–3.3) and high (dark grey, mean of responses 3.4–5).

the food industry and retail. While the retail sector as a whole as well as large food industry businesses seem to be appropriately connected in the future (indicator 3), this is not true for smaller food industry businesses. In addition, large food industry businesses seem to be more resilient in terms of functional and response diversity (indicator 4).

The experts on consumer behaviour foresee only positive developments and no negative relative changes from the present to the future. The most significant changes they foresee are the diminishing of food waste and greater consumption awareness.

Implications for climate change adaptation

The indicator framework of this study measures the general resilience of the Finnish food system, whereas resilience to climate change would require additional specific measures. These specific measures would be very different in agriculture, the food industry, retail and consumption and require sector-specific indicators. Moreover, further disaggregated farm level, factory-level, store-level and even household-level measures would be required because climate change adaptation is notably a local activity in nature and calls for adaptive behaviour and practices at the local level. However, general resilience forms the foundation for all kinds of resilience, including climate change adaptation. The tightness of feedbacks, modularity, diversity and self-organising behaviour are all fundamental components of resilience in any kind of system. The critical factors and supply chain phases from the perspective of climate change adaptation are discussed in the following. It should be mentioned that the experts foresee the mean temperature change being about +2.3 degrees Celsius by 2050 and the impact of climate change on Finnish primary production to be slightly positive. This information can be useful when interpreting their responses concerning the future resilience of the food system.

There are various strengths in the Finnish food system for building resilience to climate change. Organic farms and larger farms are perceived as socially self-organised, which can promote innovations and experimentation to cope with climate change adaptation. Innovation, in terms of taking advantage of new circumstances due to discontinuities, is a crucial component of resilience (Beermann 2011). Climate change can involve risks as well as opportunities. In addition, organic farms are currently seen as the most ecologically self-regulated farms. A high degree of ecological self-regulation is seen as promoting short-term adaptation at the farm level in terms of returning to a defined starting point. Moreover, the experts perceive organic farms to be resilient in terms of spatial and temporal heterogeneity. Obviously crop rotation, which is effectively done in organic farms, increases their adaptive capacity to climate change as well. Moreover, experts believe organic farms are exposed to low-level disturbances more than other farms, helping them to practise self-organising behaviour and increasing their capacity for learning in "safe" circumstances without pushing beyond a critical threshold.

Organic farms and large food industry businesses are linked to functional and response diversity, according to the expert views. Responding to the disruptions caused by climate change and recovering from that by maintaining a continuity of food supply chain operations and objectives is expected to be enabled by accurate diversity. According to the experts, the food industry, especially large and medium-sized businesses, is currently coupled with local natural capital. The experts see the food industry as taking responsibility for its environment and respecting natural resources, including water resources and efficient waste management. Moreover, the Finnish food industry has been actively developing carbon labels for food products in cooperation with research organisations, as will be illustrated in Chapter 8.

There are also weaknesses in the Finnish food system that can restrict resilience building. Optimal redundancy is a measure which is not currently associated with the Finnish food system in our expert survey. That is why it is important to reach optimal redundancy, in which efficiency and resilience are in balance. In addition, the retail sector and the food industry, except for small businesses, are not particularly associated with building local human capital. In the future, however, the experts believe that both sectors will improve their performance in those areas. Within the whole food supply chain, the retail sector will probably face the most dramatic changes. Hence, retailers must reconsider their values, purpose and mission in the food supply chain.

Naturally small businesses and local retailers demonstrate a higher degree of resilience in terms of global autonomy and local interdependency compared to large businesses and international actors. According to the experts, this will be the case also in the future – they even see negative developments in terms of appropriate supply chain relationships, global autonomy and local interdependency. Due to the concentration and consolidation in the food industry and food retail, large businesses and international retailers will always face the risk of climate change disruptions in their global supplier networks. On the other hand, farmers, large food industry businesses and international retailers are associated with reflected and shared learning. As West (2014) suggests, adaptive management is a continual and iterative learning-by-doing process, which enables collective empowerment and accelerates organisational transformation. In food systems, these transformations are already taking place.

The profitability of farms is and will be a critical cornerstone of the overall resilience of primary production. To ensure food security and adequate supplies of food, the economic, social and environmental dimensions of the vulnerability of the food supply chain must be carefully assessed. Climate change introduces potential extra costs for farms that are already struggling with their finance. On the other hand, innovative farms and rural entrepreneurs can explore opportunities related to the changing climate. According to the experts, farmers are associated with honouring the legacy, which in turn demonstrates a high degree of trust in the communities of the primary producers. Trust enables horizontal cooperation between farms (supplier cooperation), which is a necessary condition in climate change adaptation.

Conclusion

The food system experts have very positive views concerning the resilience development of the Finnish food system in the future. The size of the company or farm does not necessarily indicate their degree of overall resilience as there are different kinds of vulnerabilities in small (local) and large (international) businesses. Depending on the resilience indicator, the critical phases of the food supply chain can be found in primary production, in the food industry, in the retail sector or in consumption. Along the whole supply chain, however, food system experts consider organic farms to be the most resilient actor. Maybe other actors in the food supply chain could learn something from the principles of organic farming in their process of resilience building. However, a comparison between the resilient behaviour of different subsystems should be made with caution, as the corresponding measures are partly different. Resilience is a multi-dimensional, multi-faceted and multi-disciplinary phenomenon that is the result of various building blocks. There is no single indicator measuring resilience, but a comprehensive set of resilience indicators is needed.

Resilience indicators can be considered a critical element of the internal side of risk, which includes the conditions of the community or the food system exposed to climate change, and resilience, which works closely with the capacities for coping and adaptation. This study used an indicator framework made to assess the resilience of agroecosystems, but similar frameworks and sets of indicators could be developed for the food industry, the food retail sector and consumption. It is equally important to develop indicator frameworks to measure resilience specifically for climate change. Measuring the adaptive behaviour and practices of different food supply chain actors, such as supply chain resilience and organisational resilience, with suitable measures could enhance adaptive management within the food supply chain.

References

Anderies, J.M., Folke, C., Walker, B. and Ostrom, E. (2013) Aligning key concepts for global change policy: robustness, resilience, and sustainability. *Ecology and Society*, 18(2): 8.

Beermann, M. (2011) Linking corporate climate adaptation strategies with resilience thinking. *Journal of Cleaner Production*, 19: 836–842.

Bomford, M. (2010) Getting fossil fuels off the plate. In R. Heinberg and D. Lerch (eds) *Post Carbon Reader: Managing the 21st Century's Sustainability Crisis*. Healdsburg, CA: Watershed Media in collaboration with Post Carbon Institute USA, pp. 119–127.

Cabell, J.F. and Oelofse, M. (2012) An indicator framework for assessing agroecosystem resilience. *Ecology and Society*, 17(1): 18.

Carpenter, S.R. Arrow, K.J., Barrett, S. *et al.* (2012) General resilience to cope with extreme events. *Sustainability*, 4(12): 3248–3259.

Carpenter, S.R., Westley, F. and Turner, M.G. (2005) Surrogates for resilience of social–ecological systems. *Ecosystems*, 8(8): 941–944.

Casti, J., Ilmola, L., Rouvinen, P. and Wilenius, M. (2011) *Extreme Events*. Helsinki: Taloustieto Oy.

Davidson, J.L., van Putten, I.E., Leith, P., Nursey-Bray, M., Madin, E.M. and Holbrook, N.J. (2013) Toward operationalizing resilience concepts in Australian marine sectors coping with climate change. *Ecology and Society*, 18(3): 4.

Engle, N.L., de Bremond, A., Malone, E.L. and Moss, R.H. (2013) Towards a resilience indicator framework for making climate-change adaptation decisions. *Mitigation and Adaptation Strategies for Global Change*, 19(8): 1295–1312.

Ericksen, P.J. (2008a) Conceptualizing food systems for global environmental change research. *Global Environmental Change*, 18(1): 234–245.

Ericksen, P.J. (2008b) What is the vulnerability of a food system to global environmental change? *Ecology and Society*, 13(2): 13.

Kumar, M., Srai, J., Pattinson, L. and Gregory, M. (2013) Mapping of the UK food supply chains: capturing trends and structural changes. *Journal of Advances in Management Research*, 10(2): 299–326.

Manning, L. (2013) Corporate and consumer social responsibility in the food supply chain. *British Food Journal*, 115(1): 9–29.

Meadows, D. (2008) *Thinking in Systems: A Primer*. New York: Chelsea Green Publishing.

Misselhorn, A., Aggarwal, P., Ericksen, P.J., Gregory, P., Horn-Phathanothai, L., Ingram, J. and Wiebe, K. (2012) A vision for attaining food security. *Current Opinion in Environmental Sustainability*, 4(1): 7–17.

Resilience Alliance (2007) *Assessing Resilience in Social-Ecological Systems: A Workbook for Scientists*. Available at: www.resalliance.org/index.php/resilience_assessment (accessed 27 September 2014).

Resilience Alliance (2010) *Assessing Resilience in Social-Ecological Systems: A Workbook for Practitioners* (Revised version 2.0). Available at: www.resalliance.org/index.php/resilience_assessment (accessed 27 September 2014).

Rockström, J., Steffen, W., Noone, K. *et al.* (2009) A safe operating space for humanity. *Nature*, 461(7263): 472–475.

Sheffi, J. (2005) Building a resilient supply chain. *Harvard Business Review*, 1(8): 1–4.

Stigson, P. (2013) The resource nexus: linkages between resource systems. In *Reference Module in Earth Systems*. Oxford: Elsevier, pp. 1–3.

Walker, B. and Salt, D. (2006) *Resilience Thinking: Sustaining Ecosystems and People in a Changing World*. Washington, DC: Island Press.

West, A. (2014) *The Long Hedge: Preserving Organizational Value Through Climate Change Adaptation*. Sheffield: Greenleaf Publishing.

Wheeler, T. and von Braun, J. (2013) Climate change impacts on global food security, *Science*, 341(6145): 508–513.

Woods, J., Williams, A., Hughes, J.K., Black, M. and Murphy, R. (2010) Energy and the food system. *Philosophical Transactions of the Royal Society B: Biological Sciences*, 365(1554): 2991–3006.

4 Making sense of resilience in barley breeding

Converting the concept of response diversity into a tool of reflection and decision-making

Sami Paavola, Sari J Himanen, Helena Kahiluoto and Reijo Miettinen

Introduction

Resilience is a widely used concept concerning the status and dynamics of social-ecological systems. The concept originates from the discourse of ecological systems, and there is a variety of interpretations (e.g. Holling 1973; Folke 2006; Folke *et al.* 2010; Davoudi 2012). Resilience emphasizes the unpredictable and non-linear nature of change in both natural and social-ecological systems. The inclusion of social aspects and human agency requires a reinterpretation of the concept of resilience. The inclusion of human agency seems to have effects on the uses of the concept of resilience by introducing issues such as the capacity for renewal and learning.

In this chapter we follow a targeted and specific attempt to develop a tool to enhance resilience in barley cultivation in Finland. The ecological concept of response diversity (Elmqvist *et al.* 2003) has been developed further by a group of agrifood researchers as a potential tool to assess and manage resilience in agri-food systems (Kahiluoto *et al.* 2014). The ecological concept refers to the diversity of responses to disturbance within a functional group, for example, among species contributing to the same function (Nyström 2006). However, resilience has been difficult to operationalize in more concrete measures (Cumming *et al.* 2005; Walker *et al.* 2006). It is important to characterize resilience also in smaller, more manageable social-ecological systems (Folke *et al.* 2010). In our study, the diversity of responses of barley cultivars used in Finland towards varying weather factors and agroclimatic conditions was discussed with plant breeders on the basis of the research results by Kahiluoto *et al.* (2014).

The aim of our study is to follow the development of the concept of response diversity and related methods in a dialogue between agrifood researchers and barley breeders. Potentially the tool could be used to conceptualize and take practical measures to enhance response diversity in barley cultivation. In this chapter, first, we briefly present the concept of resilience, and how social resilience challenges the traditional ecological concept. Second, we analyze how the clustering of barley cultivars towards critical weather conditions was developed.

Finally, we analyze the attempts of (agrifood) researchers and plant breeders to develop response diversity and clustering of barley cultivars as a practically oriented tool to enhance the resilience of barley breeding.

Enhancing resilience with response diversity

A basic way of understanding resilience has been to see it as a way of enduring surprising crises and retaining the same functions as before. Resilience has been defined as "the capacity of a system to absorb disturbance and reorganize while undergoing change so as to still retain essentially the same function, structure, identity, and feedbacks" (Walker *et al.* 2004; cf. Holling 1973: 14).

Resilience can be understood as the predictability of the systems in question and the return time after disturbances ("engineering resilience") (Holling 1996). However, the main emphasis has been on the fact that these systems are non-linear, containing uncertainties and surprises. Resilience means then the ability to cope with these unpredictabilities and changes and to persist even if the system does not return to its previous state but has multiple states of equilibria ("ecological resilience") (ibid.).

There has been a lot of discussion on how much "social resilience" changes the core meaning of resilience (Adger 2000; Folke 2006; Davoudi 2012). Even if ecological systems can deal with transformations and change, social systems are even more prone to transformations. For social systems, the capacity for renewal, development and coping with changes is important, and not necessarily only the retention of the existing structure and functions of the system. Davoudi (2012) has listed critical issues that are important when translating resilience from the natural to the social world: (1) intentionality of human actions, which means that human interventions can change existing cycles of change; (2) the importance of what the defining desirable outcomes of the resilience are, that is, the different normative judgements on the outcomes; (3) the definitions of the system's boundaries, that is, who are involved; and (4) issues of power and politics as well as justice and fairness. Davoudi concludes that even with these differences between natural and social worlds, resilience is a promising concept to be a bridge between natural and social sciences. But an important question is how to enhance the resilience of social-ecological systems.

One central characteristics of social resilience is learning. Resilience is seen as "the capacity to buffer change, learn, and develop" (Folke *et al.* 2002: 437). Similarly it has been defined as: "[t]he capacity to adapt and to manage resilience requires learning and the ability to make sense of things, especially in arenas of collaborative learning, using a combination of various sources of information and knowledge" (Walker *et al.* 2006). Learning is a central element of managing changes and transformations. This means that humans and institutions are active agents in social-ecological systems. The question then arises how to enhance learning and what kind of learning would provide resilience.

In this study, we use cultural-historical activity theory and its concept of activity and artifact mediation (Engeström 1987; Miettinen 2009) to make sense of the attempts to enhance resilience. It highlights that human agency is historically evolving and mediated by cultural means, signs and tools (Vygotsky 1978). Especially important in this study is the idea of *retooling*, the idea that change in practices requires the development of novel kinds of tools and artefacts which are used as practical means of activity (Miettinen and Virkkunen 2005). Tools and artefacts need to be made instruments for the actors, that is, actors must make and adapt them for specific uses within the activities in question (Béguin and Rabardel 2000). In this chapter, we are then not primarily aiming at finding characteristics or indications of resilience but rather will discuss how researchers and plant breeders worked in dialogue to develop a tool to enhance resilience, based on the idea of response diversity.

Our main research questions concerning the meetings between researchers and plant breeders in this chapter are: (1) What kind of uses and reservations were presented on response diversity by plant breeders? And (2) How did the approach of response diversity take shape into a practical tool during the meetings?

Tool development process to enhance resilience in barley breeding

We analyze a project to enhance resilience in barley breeding. Agrifood researchers have been developing an approach to empirically reveal response diversity in barley crop cultivars (Kahiluoto *et al.* 2014). The rationale of this project was that response diversity can provide a better means of enhancing resilience than traditional scenario-based approaches. The agrifood researchers maintained that it is really difficult to predict how climate and weather conditions will change in the future. Different kinds of scenarios about the future are made but they offer various kinds of predictions of the future weather. It is likely that extreme weather conditions will become more frequent because of climate change, which increases variation and uncertainty. How, in varying localities, and over which actual time-scale the climate will change is unsure. Both the effectiveness of climate change mitigation actions and long-term changes occurring can significantly influence the actual impacts. That is why it would be important to prepare for a multitude of potential changes and different kinds of extreme weather conditions rather than prepare oneself for one projection only.

> All in all, we are in an operational environment which is very complex and includes more and more uncertainties, and it is ever more difficult to approach this in the customary way, so that we are doing scenarios and evaluating how probable the change will be, and then we are going to adapt to this supposed change, for example, in plant breeding. So that … this is not on very firm ground.
>
> (Agrifood researcher, meeting 1)

Diversity is considered one key factor for making sense and enhancing resilience. Response diversity refers, not just to diversity in general, but to the diversity of responses within certain functional groups, such as the most important fodder cereal, barley, in Finland, to critical factors of change and variability (Elmqvist *et al.* 2003; Kahiluoto *et al.* 2014). A central idea is that larger diversity in itself does not necessarily mean larger diversity in those issues which are central from the point of view of retaining the specific functions. As an example, it was shown that even if there is greater diversity of barley cultivars grown in Finland than before, the diversity in responses to certain climate factors critical to the barley yield is decreasing in regions where most barley is cultivated in Finland (Kahiluoto *et al.* 2014). According to breeders, the situation may be, at least partly, due to the increased competition on the cultivar market, which forces them to continuously introduce new cultivars while keeping the costs down. According to agrifood researchers, the scenario-led adaptation debate may also have contributed to this development. The weather response cluster, which is almost the only one to affect the new cultivars, is one which benefits from an earlier spring – the projected change which is supposed to increase yield potential. This cluster is, however, drought-prone, and therefore vulnerable when the intensity and frequency of extremes regarding amount of rain increase.

The product: Barley cultivar

The agrifood researchers have been formulating a generic procedure to specify response diversity for different domains. Barley was selected as the first case to study, because it has an important function in the Finnish agrifood system: it is the most common fodder grain and therefore the cereal species that is most grown in the Finnish livestock-dominated agriculture. If the yields started to fail dramatically, barley imports would be needed to some extent. Consequently, the competitiveness of the domestic food and feed industry would decline. Barley has also the broadest range of cultivars of cereals cropped in Finland, and the Official Variety Trials provide a valuable data set. The availability of long-term cultivar trial data allowed an empirical assessment to be conducted on the responsiveness and sensitivity of the barley cultivars to several weather factors, which potentially are becoming more common in their occurrence due to increasing climate change.

The generic procedure developed using barley comprised collecting the long-term empirical data from various locations with different climatic conditions, identifying the most critical weather factors for barley yield using that data and clustering the barley cultivars according to yield responses to those critical weather conditions. The data consisted of barley cultivars (103 in total) used in Finland during 1980–2009. Critical agro-climatic conditions for the yield were identified on the basis of 12 critical weather variables. The results were validated with data from farms (Kahiluoto *et al.* 2014).

The factor analysis grouped the barley cultivars into four clusters according to their specific sensitivity to the following agro-climatic conditions: (1) heat stress; (2) precipitation; (3) temperature sum and effective global radiation; and 4) sowing time. Barley cultivars were then grouped into two main groups with nine sub-groups as follows:

1 Cultivars reacting strongly to temperature ("Temperature the most important")

   a Cultivars benefitting from heat and dryness (3 cultivars)
   b Cultivars benefitting from heat (4 cultivars)
   c Cultivars benefitting from coolness (9 cultivars)
   d Good heat tolerance (stable to weather conditions) (14 cultivars)
   e Good heat tolerance and benefitting from dryness and early sowing (rather stable) (11 cultivars)
   f Good heat tolerance (rather stable) (33 cultivars)

2 Cultivars reacting strongly to precipitation ("Dryness the most important")

   a Cultivars benefitting from dryness and heat (3 cultivars)
   b Cultivars benefitting from rain (stable to heat) (6 cultivars)
   c Cultivars benefitting from rain and heat (also dryness and early sowing) (20 cultivars)

Individual cultivars were then grouped on the basis of their strength in relation to critical agro-climatic conditions presented above (see an example in Table 4.1).

The findings of Kahiluoto *et al.* (2014) indicate that though diversity in cultivar use measured as number of cultivars (type diversity) has increased in major barley cultivation areas, the response diversity to key weather factors has decreased in the main cultivation area.

The key actors: agrifood researchers and breeders

As farmers are dependent on breeding efforts to be able to adapt their cropping to changing climatic conditions by selecting which cultivars and crops to grow, the agrifood researchers believed that the breeders have a significant role to

Table 4.1 An example of a grouping tool of barley cultivars in relation to critical agro-climatic conditions

Main groups of critical agro-climatic conditions				
Name of the cultivar	*Low heat stress*	*Low precipitation*	*High temperature sum and radiation*	*Dry and early sowing*
1) a. Cultivars benefitting from heat and dryness				
Hohto	4	5	5	5
Tolar	5	5	5	4
Prisma	5	4	1	5

Note: Numbers in the table are the strength of the factor in relation to the cultivar – "5" means that the cultivar reacts strongly to this factor.

play and might be interested in the results and the novel approach. The weather factors on the background of the clustering, and the cultivar composition of the clusters, were made explicit to the breeders so they could assess and comment on the work and to build trust. Finally, major 'baskets' of cultivars were formed. Selecting one or more cultivars from each basket ensures that part of the cultivars always produces a good yield, irrespective of the weather conditions. Such a robust set of cultivars for a farm, a region or a buyer of barley such as the fodder or brewery industry will secure the overall yield in conditions of uncertainty and variability of climate and weather. In the long term, barley breeding material comprising a high response diversity is an important public good to ensure Finnish food security.

On the basis of the findings from the cluster analysis, a more user-friendly decision-making tool was thought to have potential for the different actors involved in Finnish crop production and agrifood supply. The potential for decision-making became even more evident once the foundations of the grouping were validated by farm-based yield data (Kahiluoto *et al.* 2014). The end-users of a tool could be, for example, a plant breeder who reflects whether cultivars for different extreme conditions are or should be made available, or a farmer who tries to optimize the selection of cultivars in use for enhanced yield security. For the National Emergency Supply Agency, the grouping might provide a means of analyzing holistically the resilience of barley production in Finland. The food industry may look at the resilience of the cultivars that they use, and the tool could provide a means for strategic planning concerning the raw materials. The researchers thought that after the first-round discussions with the breeders, the tool should be introduced to a larger group of actors and national stakeholders.

Data: meetings in a commercial plant breeding company

Our main data consisted of three meetings held during November 2012 and February and May 2013 when the agrifood researchers presented the approach on response diversity and the classification of barley cultivars in a commercial plant breeding company in Finland. These meetings, called "meeting 1, 2, 3" in this chapter, lasted 3 hours, 2 hours 15 minutes and 1 hour 15 minutes, respectively. The participants of these meetings varied somewhat during the process but in total there were four agrifood researchers, two social scientists and 12 people from the plant breeding company participating in these meetings (all the authors of this chapter were participants). People from the plant breeding company represented different kinds of occupations, ranging from the management to the different positions in plant breeding. All of them are called "plant breeders" below for the sake of anonymity. The agrifood researchers and some of the plant breeders had previously collaborated.

In the meetings, the results of the research on the response diversity were presented to the plant breeders. The aim of these meetings was to discuss whether the idea of response diversity could be used or developed as a practical tool to enhance resilience in plant breeding or more generally with other stakeholders in the food production chain (farmers, industry, trade, etc.). In the first two meetings, the agrifood researchers presented the idea of response diversity and the more detailed results on barley cultivar responses to varying weather. The last meeting pursued a more general kind of discussion concerning the grouping tool designed by the researchers. The main topic of discussion in the meetings was barley breeding since the analysis was done with barley. It was, however, kept in mind that the same approach could be used for other crop species.

All the meetings were recorded and transcribed. We coded: (1) all utterances where the response diversity was discussed, as well as utterances on (2) uses and (3) hesitations and tensions of response diversity and clustering. The main occurrences of the uses and hesitations are summarized in the next section. We focus on how the plant breeders discussed the foundations and validity of the clustering and the possibility of using it as a tool in plant breeding activity.

Discussions on response diversity in the researchers–plant breeders meetings

Main interests of researchers and plant breeders

The main interest of the researchers was to discuss whether practitioners find this kind of an approach promising and should it be developed further for more practical purposes in the plant breeders' own work. The researchers presented different application areas for the approach and asked for whom this kind of a tool could be useful. The analyses behind the clustering were complex, which emphasized the need for participants to think collaboratively on how to interpret these clusters and further develop the tool. The researchers asked if the specific analyses and clusters made sense and made the plant breeders interested. The researchers wanted to know if any results seemed strange or anomalous to the plant breeders, and they discussed potential reasons for surprises in the data.

The plant breeders were clearly interested in the new method. One motivation for this was the worry about climate change itself and about new things that are not taken into account in their existing practices. It was quite obvious that climate change was thought about and discussed frequently in the work of plant breeders: "Concerning the weather factors, what came to my mind is of course the climate change which we are pondering very much with breeding; how we should react" (Plant breeder, meeting 3).

The response diversity approach was considered interesting as the plant breeders' perspective regarding the breeding goals of the future is somewhat different, and consequently they had not analysed the cultivars' weather responsiveness from the point of view of response diversity. The breeders were interested in this method though they were hesitant about its practical usability. It seemed to give a complementary perspective to their own analyses, also targeting the development of well-adapted barley genotypes to provide farmers with environmental stability and yield security under varying production conditions. Targeting for phenotypic plasticity has a somewhat similar goal, but the means to assess it were different.

A special interest for plant breeders was the long-term perspective provided with the response diversity. A realistic time perspective was also an issue that created discussion and hesitation among breeders, but one main strength and motivation of the response diversity was seen in the longer-term perspective. The relevance of the response diversity and the time perspective was emphasized:

> But, on the other hand, with a longer time perspective, we surely need to think also that we have that diversity there ... So then this is, at least in my opinion, such an idea that we could surely apply it here ... Because we are creating all the time materials for the future cross-breeding.
>
> (Plant breeder, meeting 2)

For the long-term perspective, further collaboration concerning pre-breeding with other stakeholders such as universities and national administrative authorities was discussed.

Main tensions and problems of implementation

The breeders presented different kinds of reservations and questions concerning the use of response diversity to enhance resilience. In plant breeding, goal-setting is a long-term action. However, plant breeding needs to meet the short-term cultivar requirements of the customers. The public good can be taken into consideration in the long-term breeding goal-setting and planning. The discussion agreed that the responsibility for a long-term perspective cannot be just down to one actor but other stakeholders should be involved: "What a commercial firm can do is quite restricted, so that you might get a wrong impression that we can do quite a lot" (Plant breeder, meeting 1).

The plant breeders agreed with the results on response diversity that even if the number of cultivars is higher in the market, the cultivars are often genetically quite similar to each other and more like to each other than before. It is reasonable that the high-yielding cultivars that are well adapted to particular locations serve at least partly as parental material for future improved cultivars. Breeding is long-term work and a limited number of properties are targeted for improvement most acutely at a time. The discussion agreed that there should probably be other means of ensuring a longer-term perspective. A commercial firm can be part of this kind of collaboration but cannot probably be solely responsible for it. The plant breeders also stated that finance to undertake research on pre-breeding is difficult to obtain in the Nordic countries. They speculated that the situation is better in Germany and the USA where universities can do more longer-term work with pre-breeding.

Another discussed challenge was related to methodological design, as there was a need to use a sufficient number of cultivars to achieve reliable clustering and to validate the results using farm-based data. However, many of the cultivars included in the analyses were no longer used in breeding or in the market. For the plant breeders, this seemed to provide a backward-looking method. They would prefer the same analyses to be done with only those cultivars that are currently used. The time perspective was also otherwise an area of hesitation in these discussions. Some of the plant breeders emphasized that they need to work with quite a short-term perspective. On the other hand, other breeders pointed out that they need to think also about including a longer time perspective in their own work, especially in the pre-breeding stage.

One clear area of potential joint development was the classification of the response diversity itself. Different kinds of issues were brought up during the meetings which helped the researchers to develop the tool further. A new kind of clustering was presented in the final meeting. However, the results of clustering were not easy to interpret for the plant breeders. On the one hand, the approach on response diversity and the results seemed clear but, on the other, the plant breeders realized that they were unsure if they understood how to interpret the results, especially certain weather factors.

Some results contradicted the plant breeders' previous experience, and the use of old data introduced hesitation about the usefulness for their own work. At some point in the discussions some of the plant breeders got quite sceptical about the use of the approach in their own work:

> So that some kind of a meta-analysis can be made on this [using response diversity] ... But in the practical work on breeding, this knowledge comes too late or it cannot be produced. So that this societal message can be recognized from this, but maybe the applicability here ...
>
> (Plant breeder, meeting 3)

Some of the plant breeders pointed out that they are already taking these kinds of issues into account in their work, at least to some extent. These comments partially defended their own work but were also aimed at pointing out what is potentially relevant for their own work in the response diversity: "We are also in practice making different kinds of cultivars and in that way we are taking into account that [i.e. a different potential future]. But how different are they worth making?" (Plant breeder, meeting 3).

When discussing the potential usefulness of the response diversity for different stakeholders, plant breeders also presented other specifications that were useful for the researchers. They pointed out that farmers do not necessarily always have much freedom to make choices on cultivars and especially in cases where the industry prefers and contracts certain cultivars.

Collaboration between researchers and the breeding company is an ongoing process so we do not know how it will take shape. We identified, however, the concrete suggestions and results presented during these meetings. During the process the researchers clarified the clustering by making the clusters clearer and naming them anew. This was not a simple task, as the clustering required the technical skill to perform quite complex analyses (two biometricians carried out the analyses). The plant breeding company has discussed with farmers the meaning of the selection of cultivars with regard to controlling risks but without using the concept of response diversity explicitly. The company is interested in developing this approach further to involve other relevant stakeholders in the discussion.

It was suggested that the use of response diversity could be discussed with a larger group of stakeholders in a workshop or a seminar. Special interest was shown in the researchers and the plant breeding organization having discussions with the National Emergency Supply Agency if the longer-term perspective on resilience seemed to be within their area of interest.

Conclusion

This chapter has followed an attempt to develop a practical tool based on an empirical assessment of response diversity in barley cultivars. Resilience of barley cropping requires ways of preparing for uncertainty and surprises. Instead of trying to predict what the weather conditions in the future will be, the idea of this project has been to prepare for different kinds of extreme weather conditions.

In order to make the approach and the clustering of cultivars (developed in research) useful for barley breeding, the trade and farmers, simplified versions concentrating only on relevant cultivars need to be developed. The interests of various stakeholders need to be taken into account as well. The interests of a commercial company seem to be different from the long-term perspective analyzed with the response diversity. The plant breeders also suggested that probably public actors (such as the National Emergency Supply Agency, or universities) should take more responsibility for ensuring resilience with barley breeding in the longer-term perspective. On the other hand, the plant breeders are the ones doing the pre-breeding with the barley, largely determining the future availability of the cultivars, so the tool with response diversity might be useful for them in some form also.

The meetings between the researchers and the plant breeders helped to clarify the development of the tool of response diversity, and also the potential main partners involved in the future collaboration. The agrifood researchers gained feedback on the clustering and the tool, which enabled them to clarify the way of presenting the data. Researchers learnt that in order to serve current needs, the data has to represent the currently available cultivars. The concept and the terms that emerged from the research, such as the titles of cultivar groups, need to be made explicit and clear to make them usable in practical decision-making.

The tool development process on response diversity in barley cultivation is still ongoing. The next step is an extension of the discussion with other relevant partners involved; industry and seed retailers to serve immediate needs as well as the national emergency supply agency and the authorities to serve long-term needs. The tool development process to enhance resilience and make cropping more adapted to face future climate change requires perseverance, collaboration and initiatives from all the actors involved.

Acknowledgements

This study was supported by the Academy of Finland, the projects A-LA-CARTE 2011-2014 (decision no. 140870) and ADIOSO (decision no. 255954). We thank the representatives of the plant breeding company for a detailed reading of and commenting on the manuscript.

References

Adger, W.N. (2000) Social and ecological resilience: are they related? *Progress in Human Geography*, 24(3): 347–364.

Béguin, P. and Rabardel, P. (2000) Designing for instrument-mediated activity. *Scandinavian Journal of Information Systems*, 12: 173–190.

Cumming, G.S., Barnes, G., Perz, S., Schmink, M., Sieving, K.E., Southworth, J., Binford, M., Holt, R.D., Stickler, C. and Van Holt, T. (2005) An exploratory framework for the empirical measurement of resilience. *Ecosystems*, 8: 975–987.

Davoudi, S. (2012) Resilience: a bridging concept or a dead end? *Planning Theory & Practice*, 13(2): 299–307.

Elmqvist, T., Folke, C., Nyström, M., Peterson, G., Bengtsson, J., Walker, B. and Norberg, J. (2003) Response diversity, ecosystem change, and resilience. *Frontiers in Ecology and the Environment*, 1: 488–494.

Engeström, Y. (1987) *Learning by Expanding*. Helsinki: Orienta-Konsultit.

Folke, C. (2006) Resilience: the emergence of a perspective for social-ecological systems analyses. *Global Environmental Change*, 16: 253–267.

Folke, C., Carpenter, S., Elmqvist, T., Gunderson, L., Holling, C.S. and Walker, B. (2002) Resilience and sustainable development: building adaptive capacity in a world of transformations. *Ambio*, 31: 437–440.

Folke, C., Carpenter, S.R., Walker, B., Scheffer, M., Chapin, T. and Rockström, J. (2010) Resilience thinking: integrating resilience, adaptability and transformability. *Ecology and Society*, 15(4): 20. Available at: www.ecologyandsociety.org/vol15/iss4/art20 (accessed 17 December 2014).

Holling, C.S. (1973) Resilience and stability of ecological systems. *Annual Review of Ecology and Systematics*, 4: 1–23.

Holling, C.S. (1996) Engineering resilience versus ecological resilience. In P.C. Schulze (ed.) *Engineering within Ecological Constraints*. Washington, DC: National Academy Press.

Kahiluoto, H., Kaseva, J., Hakala, K., Himanen, S.J., Jauhiainen, L., Rötter, R.P., Salo, T. and Trnka, M. (2014) Cultivating resilience by empirically revealing response diversity. *Global Environmental Change*, 25: 186–193.

Miettinen, R. (2009) *Dialogue and Creativity. Activity Theory in the Study of Science, Technology and Innovations*. Berlin: Lehmanns Media.

Miettinen, R. and Virkkunen, J. (2005) Epistemic objects, artefacts and organizational change. *Organization*, 12(3): 437–456.

Nyström, M. (2006) Redundancy and response diversity of functional groups: implications for the resilience of coral reefs. *Ambio*, 35(1): 30–35.

Vygotsky, L.S. (1978) *Mind in Society: The Development of Higher Psychological Processes*. Cambridge, MA: Harvard University Press.

Walker, B.H., Gunderson, L.H., Kinzig, A.P., Folke, C., Carpenter, S.R. and Schultz, L. (2006) A handful of heuristics and some propositions for understanding resilience in social-ecological systems. *Ecology and Society*, 11(1): 13. Available at: www.ecologyandsociety.org/vol11/iss1/art13/ (accessed 17 December 2014).

Walker, B., Holling, C.S., Carpenter, S.R. and Kinzig, A. (2004) Resilience, adaptability and transformability in social-ecological systems. *Ecology and Society*, 9(2): 5.

Part II

Local vs. regional vulnerabilities and opportunities

5 Vulnerability to climate change in food systems

Challenges in assessment methodologies

Sirkku Juhola and Tina-Simone Neset

Introduction

While the ability of societies to produce adequate amounts of food has varied significantly over centuries, the amount produced has steadily increased. Over the last two centuries we have seen an exponential growth in the production of food globally, leading to a situation where the overall global quantity of food has never been higher. Increasing trends of urbanisation, particularly in the developing world, and population growth continue to place a demand for growth in food production globally. It is estimated that the global population is set to increase to over 9 billion by 2050 (UNFPA 2014).

However, this has evidently not resulted in the disappearance of hunger and famine. The Food and Agricultural Organisation of the United Nations (FAO) estimates that there continue to be over 800 million people who are deprived of adequate nutrition (FAO *et al.* 2014). While incidences of hunger occur globally, it is estimated that two-thirds of those facing hunger live in seven countries, India, China, the DR Congo, Bangladesh, Indonesia, Pakistan and Ethiopia (Lal 2013).

In addition to these trends, the threat of climate change and its impacts on food systems itself has been of interest to many. The most recent assessment of the Intergovernmental Panel on Climate Change (IPCC) states that climate change will have considerable impacts on agricultural production (IPCC 2014). It is also acknowledged that impacts will vary greatly across regions globally and that there can be both negative and positive impacts.

In Europe, it is estimated that positive effects can include earlier sowing, a decrease in the risk of freezing and increased plant productivity due to a rising mean temperature, as well as potential increases in yield due to the fertilising effect of amplified carbon dioxide in the atmosphere (EEA 2004). The most common negative impacts are related to weather extremes, droughts, flooding and potential increases in pests and diseases.

Much of the impact of climate change on the food system depends on complex interactions between vulnerability, risk and exposure (IPCC 2014). The concept of the food system is relatively new and the complexities of the food system itself have been of interest to many researchers in the field, covering a wide spectrum of approaches and methodologies. At one end of the spectrum, research related to food and agriculture covers crop science and agricultural production while the other end addresses issues of food access, distribution and safety.

It has been argued that there is a need for a more systematic application of existing science to cover the entire food chain to unpack some of this complexity and contribute to the goal of meeting future food needs (Fresco 2009). The aim of this chapter is to review the ways in which the climate change vulnerability of food systems can be assessed. By adopting a conceptually holistic perspective of food production, distribution and consumption, it is possible to see how the current literature has approached and assessed food system vulnerability.

In order to do this, this chapter uses the concept of a food system to review the literature to see how vulnerability has been assessed in different parts of the food system. The chapter also discusses the main challenges associated with the use of these types of assessments in policy-making.

The complexity of food systems

The concept of food security is intimately linked to that of a food system, which has emerged as the key concept in this decade, also as a response to the concern over global environmental change (Ericksen 2008). Key issues in understanding food systems are, first, the definition of boundaries as to what constitutes a food system and, second, understanding the dynamics of that system and its scale dependencies.

This systemic understanding has also followed calls for sustainability within these systems. According to Fresco (2009), a sustainable food system would exhibit a number of features, including the capacity to respond to changing demands in quantity and quality. Furthermore, a sustainable system is characterised as being resource-efficient in relation to land, labour and the use of energy. Efficiency of energy use within the system is also considered important in the context of mechanisation of agricultural production.

There is a need to conceptually broaden the definition in order to understand how food security cannot be reached by an increase in production only, as there are significant issues related to access and safety that also need to be considered (Ericksen 2008). Thus, a broader definition of a food system includes not only the activities related to agricultural production but also those of processing, distribution and consumption. Furthermore, it is argued that a systems-based approach can aid an understanding of the critical factors that lead to particular outcomes or interactions that govern a specific behaviour.

According to this definition, a food system first of all consists of the interactions between and within biogeophysical and human environments. This includes understanding the environments within which crops are cultivated and how they interact with the natural systems. Second, these systems determine and underlie the activities within a food system themselves. These activities cover production through to consumption, i.e. how crops are grown, harvested, processed and finally consumed. Third, a food system encompasses the outcomes of the activities, i.e. contributions to food security, environmental security and social welfare. In addition, it also includes other determinants of food security that are related to the interactions between the food system and biogeophysical systems.

The food system (see Figure 5.1) is considered to consist of activities that determine the outcome of food security, which itself consists of three dimensions: food utilisation, access and availability (Ericksen 2008). Thus, the drawing of boundaries within a food system here would include the identification of what kinds of activities are included and what dependencies are included between these activities. First, food utilisation consists of both nutritional values present in food as well as those associated with it through social norms, and issues of food safety. Second, access to food is determined by the affordability of food, allocation of it as well as preference for foods that are culturally and socially acceptable. Third, availability is considered to include the production, distribution and exchange of food.

Here the focus is on identifying how climate change-related vulnerabilities have been assessed in food systems, with a focus on food system activities, i.e. from production to consumption in order to identify how assessments have covered these activities.

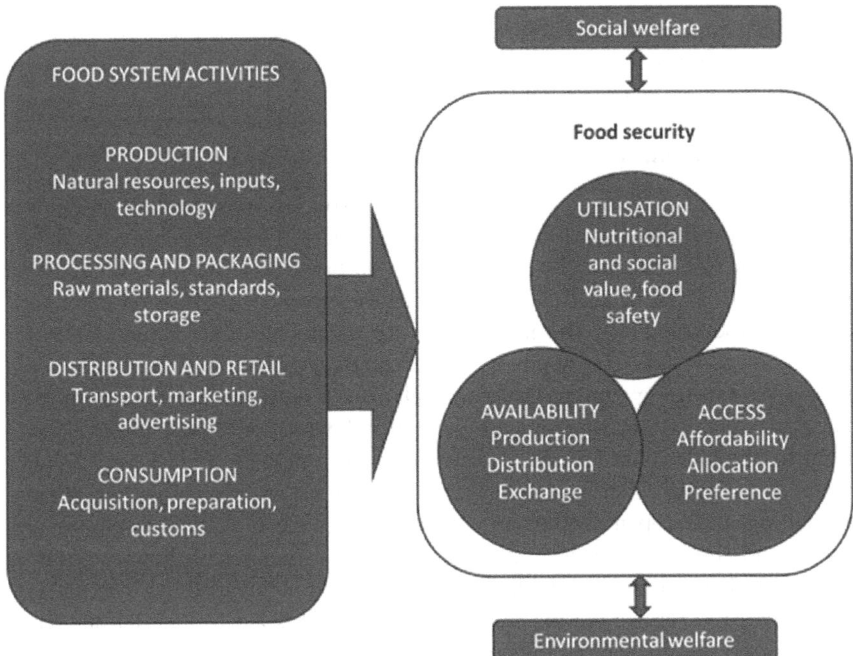

Figure 5.1 The food system

Source: Adapted from Ericksen *et al.* (2009).

Assessment methodologies for food system vulnerability

The vulnerability of regions to climate change depends on the exposure of the system, on the sensitivity of the system and finally on its adaptive capacity (IPCC 2007). Assessing the vulnerability of a specific sector, such as agriculture, or the food system, brings a number of inherent methodological challenges. These challenges already occur when defining the spatial and temporal system boundaries as well as the indicators for exposure, sensitivity and adaptive capacity. For any given food system, the selection of relevant indicators that are included in the assessment can have a significant influence on the final results (Jones and Andrey 2007). Furthermore, weighing and summarising methods that are frequently used in quantitative vulnerability assessments have been shown to lead to different measurements of vulnerability (Wiréhn *et al.* 2015), but are often not visible in the assessment process. Assessment methodologies for vulnerability range from participatory methods that include stakeholders to more desk-based approaches that include model-based simulations and the use of indicators based on statistical sources (Hinkel 2011).

As any changes in the food system are intrinsically linked to resource flows and sustainability challenges, the assessment of a food system's vulnerability to climate change does not provide a complete picture if other related dynamics, such as land use change, fertiliser requirements or logistical challenges, are not taken into account. Often such linkages imply trade-offs between sustainability challenges and impact on the sustainable management of the food chain in relation to e.g. water security, nutrition safety, phosphorus vulnerability or soil quality (Neset and Cordell 2012).

Vulnerable agriculture

Unsurprisingly, in terms of the food system activities, most studies on climate change vulnerability have focused on food production. Assessments have developed in the last decade from early attempts to bring together climate and crop modelling to assessments that also bring in the human factors in terms of agricultural production, i.e. the farmers' ability to change their behaviour in an anticipatory or reactive manner. A persistent problem has been the scale mismatches in using climate models in relation to crop models (Challinor *et al.* 2007). Climate change models are generally downscaled to the regional level from the global climate models, while many crop models operate on a smaller scale. It is argued that particularly early attempts to bring together climate modelling and crop modelling encompassed a range of different regions and crops, and the uncertainty ranges derived from a number of different sources (e.g. spatial variability in yield, uncertainty in climate/emissions information, differences in crop simulation methods) (ibid.). This led to a situation where yield impact studies sampled uncertainty randomly and the estimates of uncertainty were not very precise.

One way of approaching this has been to examine a single climate stimulus and its impacts on productivity. Simelton *et al.* (2009) assessed how small droughts can sometimes trigger serious losses, while in some instances even larger droughts have no serious impact on the food security of a particular area. The authors developed a crop-drought vulnerability index by identifying socio-economic indicators and using harvest and rainfall data and examined sensitivity and resilience to drought for each of China's main grain crops. The index results show that there were significant differences in the sensitivity or the resilience of the crops, depending on their geographical location. This enabled the researchers to develop a drought-vulnerability typology based on factors such as land, labour, capital, agricultural technology and infrastructure that either buffer or exacerbate the drought's impacts.

The issue of scale has been subject to a persistent scientific discussion, with assessment ranging from a landscape-level approach to cover continents. Early on, Fraser (2006) argued that there are existing assessments that fall along a continuum that starts from large-scale generalisations, i.e. macro-level assessments, to site-specific assessments, i.e. micro-level. It has been argued that the selection of a system border and scale has to be in line with the aim of the vulnerability assessment as well as relevant to the exposure parameter (Cordell and Neset 2014). For some studies, the national scale is relevant to include agricultural policies and food import, while a regional scale might be more relevant for studying specific climatic exposure indices.

An early example of a landscape approach was developed by Fraser *et al.* (2005), who argue that it is a good level to estimate the vulnerability of a food system to future shocks. According to this approach, the system is conceptualised as consisting of three generic characteristics: (1) the wealth available in the system; (2) how connected the system is; and (3) how much diversity exists in the system. There are a number of methods to assess these characteristics, drawing on development economics, such as assessing financial risk, as well as tools from chemistry to assess the connectivity within the system. The authors conclude that wealthy but non-diverse and tightly connected systems are most vulnerable to shocks.

Beyond the landscape approach, a Europe-wide assessment looked into the ways in which climate change might affect the continent's agriculture (Olesen *et al.* 2011). It is estimated that climate change will bring increased temperatures and a change in precipitation that will vary strongly between seasons and across the region in the context of ongoing cereal grain yield stagnation and increased yield variability. Interestingly, in this case, the assessment of vulnerability drew on a qualitative and a quantitative questionnaire directed to experts. The questionnaires were distributed to a number of agro-climatic and agronomy experts in 26 countries in Europe that was divided into 50 environmental zones for the purpose of the exercise. The main questions were related to the vulnerabilities of crops and cropping systems and the estimates of climate impacts on them. The experts were also asked about the possible adaptation options, including those observed so far. The results show that farmers are currently adapting to changes already by changing cultivation timing and changing species and cultivars. While the respondents identified positive impacts, the majority are considered to be negative.

In the Mediterranean region, vulnerability in agriculture has been assessed with respect to water scarcity and crop production (Iglesias *et al.* 2007). This study related exposure parameters such as water availability, soil salinity and erosion to an adaptive capacity index for the agricultural sector in a number of Mediterranean countries. As water resources are anticipated to be even further strained and significant adaptation measures are required, it is expected that agriculture in many of the Mediterranean countries will become vulnerable to climate variability (ibid.).

There are also examples of assessments that have focused on individual crops but that have combined a number of different modelling approaches. Elsgaard *et al.* (2012) modelled the impact of climate change on specific crop yields for Europe. Based on two different regional climate models, this study indicates a general increase in the share of maize per agricultural area, while there was no strong increase for oats in any specific area. Wheat is projected to gain a higher share of agricultural area in the northern parts of Europe while decreasing in the southern parts.

Fraser *et al.* (2013) combined a hydrological model with agricultural, meteorological and socio-economic data to develop models of adaptive capacity. By combining the hydrological and adaptive capacity models, the authors were able to identify vulnerability hotspots for maize and wheat. The results indicate that adaptive capacity as well as vulnerability can vary significantly across the globe. In Europe, the north-eastern Mediterranean was identified as a vulnerability hotspot for both wheat and maize.

Increasingly, modelling approaches have been developed for cropping systems that go beyond the single crops but also take into account issues of adaptive capacity, for example. To consider things more broadly, the adaptive capacity of farmers and institutional development are important dimensions to include (Challinor *et al.* 2007). It is also argued that current research is dominated by hazard and impact modelling which draws on the tradition of risks associated with current climate variability (Nelson *et al.* 2010). A study of Australian agriculture shows how hazard/impact modelling can be complemented with more holistic measures of adaptive capacity to provide quantitative insights into the vulnerability of Australian rural communities to climate variability and change.

Similarly, in northern Norway, Kvalvik *et al.* (2011) have studied the vulnerability of the agricultural sector and argue that its vulnerability is dependent on the interaction between the changing biophysical conditions and socio-economic and policy-related factors. This study applied both quantitative and qualitative methods to study farmers' vulnerability and concluded that policy appears to be a greater challenge than climate change, but also that farmers are highly adaptive to the different exposure factors, such as rainfall and drought.

Matthews *et al.* (2013) recognise the potential of crop modelling to identify vulnerabilities and also as a useful tool in evaluating the possible trade-offs between potential adaptations. Furthermore, the authors suggest that there are four areas in crop modelling that are beneficial in relation to identifying vulnerabilities. First, modelling can help determine where and how well crops of the future will grow and, second, it can also contribute to crop improvement programmes. Third, they can identify which future crop management practices will be appropriate and, fourth, they can assess the risk to crop production in the face of greater climate variability. A similar approach was also applied in a case study of Wuchuan County (Dong *et al.* 2015). Applying a framework inspired by the IPCC, the authors introduced a six-step method to assess vulnerability by including sensitivity, exposure and adaptive capacity. The assessment uses predominantly meteorological and crop data and these are processed in a synthetical index method.

Targeting multi-scales and multiple indicators for farming

Assessments have also included multi-scales and multiple indicators. Applying the IPCC definition of vulnerability, a study by Antwi-Agyei *et al.* (2012) forms the basis of an integrated and multi-scale approach to explore the drivers of farming system vulnerability to drought at the national, regional, district and community levels. The aim of that study was to develop and apply a crop drought vulnerability index and socio-economic indicator approach to map vulnerability at national and regional scales. An experimental Hunger and Climate Vulnerability Index was designed by Krishnamurthy *et al.* (2014) to show the relative vulnerability of the food-insecure population at country level. The index uses a number of socio-economic and environmental indicators selected to reflect the different aspects of vulnerability that are further aggregated to a composite index. This index shows that there appears to be a high correlation between hunger and climate risks, particularly in areas where there is already a high level of food insecurity. This index is an example of a multi-dimensional assessment that goes beyond crop yields and also assesses the capacities that are available for adaptation.

A recent example of combining complex models is provided by Bär *et al.* (2015). It brings together the DPSIR-model with the IPCC understanding of vulnerability. This is done to gain a better understanding of the causal relationships and the dynamics within the agricultural system to identify vulnerabilities. The authors argue that logical links between different indicators need to be combined into a model to reduce the discrepancy between the theoretical framework and the analysis process. The authors apply the framework to assess the vulnerability of agricultural water resources in the Black Sea catchment area and to identify particularly vulnerable regions. Although the authors recognise that modelling a complex system is possible, the more comprehensive the system is, the more difficult it becomes. In particular, the authors point out that interrelationships between many of the elements of the system are not adequately defined, either theoretically or empirically. This means that, for example, the role of policy and economic developments in the availability of water resources is unknown.

Vulnerable food system beyond agricultural activities

As mentioned before, it is hardly surprising that most of the vulnerability assessments developed to assess food systems have focused on the production part of the food system. However, it is also worth noting that there are further food system activities that contribute to food security. Nevertheless, these activities, which include processing and packaging, distribution and retail and food consumption, have received far less attention in terms of their vulnerability to climate or environmental change.

Processing and packaging of food have received some attention in national assessments. One example of this is a systemic study that was recently conducted in Ireland with an emphasis on national food safety (Lennon 2015). Lennon suggests that climate change influences the occurrence of pests and diseases, toxin generation in crops and has consequences for trade networks in the food system. Distribution and retail of food have not been explicitly addressed, despite the fact that climate change is likely to affect transport both globally and locally.

The issue of food consumption has not been explicitly addressed either. The closely related issue of food supply chain losses, caused by inefficiencies in processing, distribution, retail and consumption, is, however, an issue of adaptive capacity on a global scale. Kummu *et al.* (2012) estimate that 23–24 per cent of total resource use for food production (i.e. water, cropland and fertilisers) is used to produce losses and wastage globally. Reducing these losses demands changes in all parts of the food system, though losses are greater in the production and storage in developing countries, while industrialised countries contribute more significantly to the losses in distribution, retail and consumption (Gustavsson *et al.* 2011).

Mirgalia *et al.* (2009) argue that perhaps the production-side issues are widely investigated but that safety of food and feed is an issue that has received less attention so far. In a review of these issues in Europe, the authors state that most vulnerabilities arise, among others, from mycotoxins formed on plant products during storage, from pesticide residues and from the presence of pathogenic bacteria in foods following more frequent extreme weather conditions, such as flooding and heatwaves. The authors highlight the need for further research in this field, as do Tirado *et al.* (2010), who also examine the issue of food contamination and acknowledge that there are many challenges to food safety at various stages in the food chain.

While in the general food security literature, the access to food is recognised as increasingly important, the impacts of climate change have not been explored, with the exception of a few case studies from Sub-Saharan Africa. A recent study suggests that the indirect impact of climate change on wages and food prices is likely to lead to further vulnerability of poor households in Sub-Saharan Africa (Skjeflo 2013). Skjelflo argues that the vulnerable household groups cannot be identified by examining production only but one needs to consider their position in and access to markets also, as exemplified through a case study from Malawi.

According to Skjelflo (ibid.), households with large rural land holdings may benefit from climate change but the urban poor are more likely to be adversely affected because they spend more of their income on food.

Studies have also shown that access to food and the reduction of food security are similarly conditioned by access to other things. This is also related to the third food security outcome, availability. Availability in this context means distribution and exchange of food. A study of 12 countries in Sub-Saharan Africa shows that the ability of households to reduce their vulnerability is due to access to weather information, household and agricultural production-related assets and participation in local social networks and institutions (Wood *et al.* 2014). The authors further call for methods to accommodate cultural differences in understanding household-level decision-making.

Use of assessments in policy

In the literature there have been calls for the use of vulnerability assessments and scenarios to support decision-making in food systems. Vervoort *et al.* (2014) argue that the development of decision-making tools needs to consider three issues to increase their relevance. First, it is necessary to ensure the appropriate scope for action within a food system. Second, it is important to move beyond simplistic intervention-based decision guidance to support local activities that can build adaptive capacity. Third, this capacity should then be harnessed for longer-term strategic planning in order to ensure sustainability in the future.

Webber *et al.* (2014) note that crop models are currently the primary tool to assess the impacts of climate change on crop productivity and they assess their role and suitability for informing decision-making in the African context specifically. The authors argue that climate change alone is rarely the driving force behind decisions to change farming practices but other factors, such as access to credit and labour availability, play a larger part in this. According to the authors, crop models are useful for a number of purposes, for example, for testing which changes are most robust to future climate scenarios, either linked to economic, farm system or livestock models to scope potential impacts, or to probe interactions of cropping systems. Furthermore, Webber *et al.* argue that the greatest benefit of linking crop modelling with other disciplines is to provide a platform for debate and discussion for stakeholders from different disciplinary backgrounds in order to better assess the impact of climate change on food security.

Also, Krishnamurthy *et al.* (2014) argue that the index they developed can be used to monitor vulnerability, evaluate potential effectiveness of programmes and/or examine plausible impacts of climate change by introducing scenarios into the vulnerability model. Similarly, Bär *et al.* (2015) argue that sticking to a single but meaningful vulnerability index can be used to transfer knowledge to policy-makers. It not only allows the policy-makers to understand the underlying causes of vulnerability but also to identify possible policy actions.

However, it is worth keeping in mind that assessment methodologies can lead to different results (Wiréhn *et al.* 2015), complicating their use. A fully transparent vulnerability assessment method would thus require an individual selection of indicators by experts, stakeholders or other end-users of the information. It could also include a system that enables users to both select indicators, determine their weight and their classification (e.g. if an indicator such as soil fertility or employment rate in the agricultural sector should be included as a sensitivity factor or rather as an indicator of increased or decreased adaptive capacity). As Cordell and Neset (2014) argue, we also acknowledge that there is no right or wrong in assessing vulnerability. Choices between methodologies are dependent on selecting the most appropriate tools that suit the context and objectives of the assessment.

Conclusion

This chapter has discussed the role of vulnerability assessments in the context of food systems. While most studies hitherto have focused on the vulnerability of the production stage of the food system, assessments of processing, distribution, retail and consumption are important to identify key challenges for current and future food security. As Ericksen *et al.* (2009) point out, food system vulnerabilities are linked across multiple scales, and adaptive actions to decrease the vulnerability of the food system might involve unintended negative consequences on another scale. This phenomenon, also identified as maladaptation in the recent climate adaptation literature (Adger *et al.* 2010; Barnett and O'Neill 2010; Dow *et al.* 2013), includes adaptation actions that have high opportunity costs, reduce the incentives to adapt, or lead to unsustainable path dependencies, for instance (Barnett and O'Neill 2010). While research in climate change adaptation has contributed to the development of several methodological strings in recent years, issues related to maladaptation have not yet been sufficiently addressed (Adger *et al.* 2010; Dow *et al.* 2013). Methods that enable the study of these issues need to address the changing understanding of vulnerability, identify the specific food supply system and its parts, and enable the assessment of adaptation measures and their potential unintended negative consequences that might result from them. Direct trade-offs between actions that decrease a system's vulnerability to climate change but increase the vulnerability or imply negative consequences for other resources or systems also come under the category of maladaptation, and might be easier to identify. Like Fresco, we argue for a sustainable approach to food system policy, one that recognises the need to adapt plant, animal and food systems to changing temperature, nutrient and water conditions (Fresco 2009) and one that recognises the context of multi-functionality, globalisation and global markets.

References

Adger, W.N., Brown, K. and Conway, D. (2010) Progress in global environmental change. *Global Environmental Change*, 20(4): 547–549.

Antwi-Agyei, P., Fraser, E.D., Dougill, A.J., Stringer, L.C. and Simelton, E. (2012) Mapping the vulnerability of crop production to drought in Ghana using rainfall, yield and socioeconomic data. *Applied Geography*, 32(2): 324–334.

Bär, R., Rouholahnedjad, E., Rahman, K., Abbaspour, K.C. and Lehmann, A. (2015) Climate change and agricultural water resources: a vulnerability assessment of the Black Sea catchment. *Environmental Science & Policy*, 46: 57–69.

Barnett, J. and O'Neill, S. (2010) Editorial: maladaptation. *Global Environmental Change*, 20: 211–213.

Challinor, A., Wheeler, T., Garforth, C., Craufurd, P. and Kassam, A. (2007) Assessing the vulnerability of food crop systems in Africa to climate change. *Climatic Change*, 83(3): 381–399.

Cordell, D. and Neset, T. (2014) Phosphorus vulnerability: a qualitative framework for assessing the vulnerability of national and regional food systems to the multi-dimensional stressors of phosphorus scarcity. *Global Environmental Change*, 24: 108–122.

Dong, Z., Pan, Z., An, P., Wang, L., Zhang, J., He, D., Han, H. and Pan, X. (2015) A novel method for quantitatively evaluating agricultural vulnerability to climate change. *Ecological Indicators*, 48: 49–54.

Dow, K., Berkhout, F. and Preston, B.L. (2013) Limits to adaptation to climate change: a risk approach. *Current Opinion in Environmental Sustainability*, 5(3): 384–391.

EEA (2004) *Impacts of Europe's Changing Climate: An Indicator-Based Assessment*. EEA Report No. 2/2004. Copenhagen: European Environment Agency.

Elsgaard, L., Børgesen, C.D., Olesen, J.E., Siebert, S., Ewert, F., Peltonen-Sainio, P. and Skjelvåg, A.O. (2012) Shifts in comparative advantages for maize, oat and wheat cropping under climate change in Europe. *Food Additives & Contaminants: Part A*, 29(10): 1514–1526.

Ericksen, P.J. (2008) Conceptualizing food systems for global environmental change research. *Global Environmental Change*, 18(1): 234–245.

Ericksen, P.J., Ingram, J.S.I. and Liverman, D.M. (2009) Food security and global environmental change: emerging challenges. *Environmental Science & Policy*, 12(4): 373–377.

FAO, IFAD and WFP (2014) *The State of Food Insecurity in the World 2014. Strengthening the Enabling Environment for Food Security and Nutrition*. Rome: FAO.

Fraser, E.D. (2006) Food system vulnerability: using past famines to help understand how food systems may adapt to climate change. *Ecological Complexity*, 3(4): 328–335.

Fraser, E.D., Mabee, W. and Figge, F. (2005) A framework for assessing the vulnerability of food systems to future shocks. *Futures*, 37(6): 465–479.

Fraser, E.D., Simelton, E., Termansen, M., Gosling, S.N. and South, A. (2013) "Vulnerability hotspots": integrating socio-economic and hydrological models to identify where cereal production may decline in the future due to climate change induced drought. *Agricultural and Forest Meteorology*, 170: 195–205.

Fresco, I.O. (2009) Challenges for food system adaptation today and tomorrow. *Environmental Science & Policy*, 12(4): 378–385.

Gustavsson, J., Cederberg, C., Sonesson, U., van Otterdijk, R. and Meybeck, A. (2011) *Global Food Losses and Food Waste: Extent, Causes and Prevention*. Rome: Food and Agriculture Organization (FAO) of the United Nations.

Hinkel, J. (2011) Indicators of vulnerability and adaptive capacity: towards a clarification of the science–policy interface. *Global Environmental Change*, 211: 198–208.

Iglesias, A., Garrote, L., Flores, F. and Moneo, M. (2007) Challenges to manage the risk of water scarcity and climate change in the Mediterranean. *Water Resources Management*, 215: 775–788.

IPCC (2007) *Climate Change 2007: Impacts, Adaptation and Vulnerability, Working Group II to the Fourth Assessment Report, et al.* Cambridge: Cambridge University Press.

IPCC (2014) *Climate Change 2014: Impacts, Adaptation, and Vulnerability. Part A: Global and Sectoral Aspects. Contribution of Working Group II to the Fifth Assessment Report of the Intergovernmental Panel on Climate Change.* Ed. C.B. Field, V.R. Barros, D.J. Dokken *et al.* Cambridge: Cambridge University Press.

Jones, B. and Andrey, J. (2007) Vulnerability index construction: methodological choices and their influence on identifying vulnerable neighbourhoods. *International Journal of Emergency Management*, 4(2): 269–295.

Krishnamurthy, P., Lewis, K. and Choularton, R. (2014) A methodological framework for rapidly assessing the impacts of climate risk on national-level food security through a vulnerability index. *Global Environmental Change*, 25: 121–132.

Kummu, M., de Moel, H., Porkka, M., Siebert, S., Varis, O. and Ward, P.J. (2012) Lost food, wasted resources: global food supply chain losses and their impacts on freshwater, cropland, and fertiliser use. *Science of the Total Environment*, 438: 477–489.

Kvalvik, I., Dalmannsdottir, S., Dannevig, H., Hovelsrud, G., Rønning, L. and Uleberg, E. (2011) Climate change vulnerability and adaptive capacity in the agricultural sector in northern Norway. *Acta Agriculturae Scandinavica, Section B, Soil & Plant Science*, 61(suppl. 1): 27–37.

Lal, R. (2013) Food security in a changing climate. *Ecohydrology & Hydrobiology*, 13(1): 8–21.

Lennon, J.J. (2015) Potential impacts of climate change on agriculture and food safety within the island of Ireland. *Trends in Food Science & Technology*.

Matthews, R.B., Rivington, M., Muhammed, S.S., Newton, A.C. and Hallett, P.D. (2013) Adapting crops and cropping systems to future climates to ensure food security: the role of crop modelling. *Global Food Security*, 2(1): 24–28.

Miraglia, M., Marvin, H., Kleter, G., Battilani, P., Brera, C., Coni, E., Cubadda, F., Croci, L., de Santis, B. and Dekkers, S. (2009) Climate change and food safety: an emerging issue with special focus on Europe. *Food and Chemical Toxicology*, 47(5): 1009–1021.

Nelson, R., Kokic, P., Crimp, S., Martin, P., Meinke, H., Howden, S.M., de Voil, P. and Nidumolu, U. (2010) The vulnerability of Australian rural communities to climate variability and change: Part II—integrating impacts with adaptive capacity. *Environmental Science & Policy*, 13(1): 18–27.

Neset, T.S. and Cordell, D. (2012) Global phosphorus scarcity: identifying synergies for a sustainable future. *Journal of the Science of Food and Agriculture*, 92: 12–16.

Olesen, J.E., Trnka, M., Kersebaum, K.C., Skjelvåg, A.O., Seguin, B., Peltonen-Sainio, P., Rossi, F., Kozyra, J. and Micale, F. (2011) Impacts and adaptation of European crop production systems to climate change. *European Journal of Agronomy*, 34(2): 96–112.

Simelton, E., Fraser, E.D., Termansen, M., Forster, P.M. and Dougill, A.J. (2009) Typologies of crop-drought vulnerability: an empirical analysis of the socio-economic factors that influence the sensitivity and resilience to drought of three major food crops in China (1961–2001). *Environmental Science & Policy*, 12(4): 438–452.

Skjeflo, S. (2013) Measuring household vulnerability to climate change: why markets matter. *Global Environmental Change*, 23(6): 1694–1701.

Tirado, M., Clarke, R., Jaykus, L., McQuatters-Gollop, A. and Frank, J. (2010) Climate change and food safety: a review. *Food Research International*, 43(7): 1745–1765.

UNFPA (2014) *The State of the World Population*. New York: UN Population Fund.

Vervoort, J.M., Thornton, P.K., Kristjanson, P. *et al.* (2014) Challenges to scenario-guided adaptive action on food security under climate change. *Global Environmental Change*, 28: 383–394.

Webber, H., Gaiser, T. and Ewert, F. (2014) What role can crop models play in supporting climate change adaptation decisions to enhance food security in Sub-Saharan Africa? *Agricultural Systems*, 127: 161–177.

Wiréhn, L., Danielsson, Å. and Neset, T-S. (2015) Assessment of composite index methods for agricultural vulnerability to climate change. *Journal of Environmental Management*, 156: 70–80.

Wood, S.A., Jina, A.S., Jain, M., Kristjanson, P. and Defries, R.S. (2014) Smallholder farmer cropping decisions related to climate variability across multiple regions. *Global Environmental Change*, 25: 163–172.

6 Food security during climate change

The challenge of European diversity

Gianluca Brunori and Tiina Silvasti

Introduction

Food security is the main outcome and the principal policy objective of food systems. According to the Food and Agriculture Organization of the United Nations (FAO 1996): "Food security exists when all people, at all times, have physical, social and economic access to sufficient, safe and nutritious food that meets their dietary needs and food preferences for an active and healthy life." Food security involves four dimensions: (1) adequacy of food supply or availability; (2) accessibility to food or affordability; (3) utilisation or quality and safety of food; and (4) stability of supply without seasonal fluctuations or shortages (UNEP 2009: 78). Food systems consist of food supply chains and include four types of activities: producing, processing and packaging, distributing and retailing, and consuming food. All these activities involve social, economic, political and environmental processes and dimensions.

Until recently, the dominant industrial food systems have been a great success. Increases in efficiency and the productivity of agriculture have reduced the prevalence of hunger and improved nutrition. However, in the current context of environmental, social, political and economic changes, food system activities also generate substantial threats (Ericksen 2008) because their environmental impacts – including climate impacts – are huge and unpredictable (UNEP 2009), thus food security is not fully guaranteed for all people, even in the richest countries of the world (Riches and Silvasti 2014).

The capacity of food systems to produce food security – previously considered self-evident in the industrialised world – is now endangered by challenges such as global population growth and urbanisation, environmental degradation, resource scarcity, climate change, economic and financial concentration, inequality and poverty. Consequently, the concept of food security has been reassessed. The 'old' analysis focused primarily on the problems of hunger and undernourishment in the developing world. The anticipated solution to the problem of hunger was to increase food production by investing in science, technology and the agribusiness. With intensified distribution and reduced wastage, this was thought to bring food prices down and improve the availability of and access to food. Such a productionist policy paradigm was strongly promoted internationally and state policies focused on farming and agricultural sectors rather than broader food system activities (Lang and Barling 2012). According to Lang and Barling (ibid.), the world food crisis in 2007–2008 showed that food systems are under serious stress and its indicators show that certain parts of it are in decline. The emerging 'from farm to food' approach to food security acknowledges a myriad of economic, social and ecological problems connected to food system activities. Besides the need to guarantee production, there is a desire for more complex analysis and policy design. It has become necessary to redesign sustainable food systems by applying social and environmental criteria in addition to economic arguments. To promote sustainable food systems in the long term, ecological impacts must be taken into consideration when determining the prerequisites for overall sustainability (Norton 1992).

There are no undisputed definitions for the concepts of vulnerability or sustainable food system. According to Ericksen (2008):

> [Vulnerability is] a function of exposure, sensitivity, and coping or adaptive capacity. Exposure means that a unit must be exposed to a shock, threat, or stress to be vulnerable to it. Identifying exposure as a separate component implies that the potential for harm is only one part of vulnerability ... environmental shock or stress may be the trigger that sends people into a vulnerable state, but other shocks, such as a change in agricultural policy, can coincide with or contribute to this underlying vulnerability.

The Sustainable Development Commission in the UK considers food systems sustainable when their core goal is to feed everyone equitably, healthily and sustainably in a way that addresses needs for availability, affordability and accessibility, and which is diverse, ecologically sound and resilient, while building the capabilities and skills necessary for future generations (SDC 2009: 10). Resilience is understood as the capacity of the system to absorb shocks and still maintain its functions as well as the capacity for renewal, re-organisation and development in a changing world where the future is unpredictable (Folke 2006).

This chapter focuses on climate-related vulnerabilities and opportunities as well as climate change adaptation in the food supply chains of two largely food-secure European countries located in different climate zones: Italy and Finland. The aim is to compare key elements of the climate change adaptation of the national food systems. This leads to the questions: What kind of nationally embedded policy measures have been applied? And is there any ground for a common European adaptation policy from the perspective of food security? The chapter begins with a presentation of the country cases of Finland and Italy, including the climate change adaptation measures that have been adopted. In the following two sections, a summary of the national adaptation measures is presented and the possibilities for common European adaptation policies – in the context of European diversity – are discussed.

Diversity of Europe's climate and adaptation measures

Europe has a hugely diverse climate. This diversity is not only clear between northern and southern Europe, but also even within many states. Thus, the climatic impacts set direct limits on what is feasible in terms of maintaining food security in a region. Furthermore, a variety of food system activities have an influence on food security outcomes. Yet, these outcomes vary according to historical, political and social contexts (Ericksen 2008). In addition, there can be genuine conflicts of interest between different dimensions of sustainability. It may be hard to find win-win-win solutions for ecological, social and economic problems, especially when different interpretations of sustainability or, for example, different regional interpretations of the risks and opportunities connected to climate change are taken into account. In the following, the cases from Italy and Finland are introduced.

Italy

Due to its shape and geographical location, Italy has a variety of climate systems, that range from regions with an average temperature below 10° Celsius (mainly in the Alps) to regions with averages between 28–30° Celsius in the summer (mainly in southern Italy). Also precipitations vary from 2500–3000 mm in the highest altitudes to below 500 mm in Sardinia and Sicily.

According to Cecchi *et al.* (2007), Italy has undergone an increase in maximum temperature by 0.6° Celsius in the north, and by 0.8° Celsius in the centre–south over the last 50 years; a decrease in precipitation together with an increase in precipitation intensity; an increase in the number of tropical nights between 1981 and 2004; an average reduction in the number of frost days. Furthermore, in the near future, Italy can expect a reduction in precipitation by up to 25 per cent in winter and an increase in average temperature.

Italy ratified the Kyoto Protocol in 2002. The Italian target under the Kyoto Protocol was to reduce total greenhouse gas (GHG) emissions by 6.5 per cent over the period 2008–2012 with respect to 1990. This target was not met, as the reduction in the given period was only 4.6 per cent (ISPRA 2014), thus Italy will have to activate some compensation mechanisms.

According to the Ministry of the Environment, in 2007, the agricultural sector contributed 6.7 per cent of Italy's national GHG emissions (Ministero dell'Ambiente 2009). According to the estimates of the project AGRICARBON (Rete Rurale Nazionale 2012), the share is higher: 19 per cent because transportation, packaging and industrial processing are included in their calculation. The reductions in greenhouse gases from agriculture amount to about 16 per cent (ISPRA 2014) and are due to the reduction in the number of animals, variations in cultivated surface/crop production and the use of nitrogen fertilisers, which are mainly linked to the Common Agricultural Policy (CAP) measures. It is expected that the 'greening' measures in the new CAP will contribute to a further reduction in GHG emissions.

The food industry, like other industrial sectors, has developed reduction strategies for GHG emissions in order to comply with Kyoto targets. According to Federalimentare (2010), a syndicate of food processing firms, since the beginning of the 1990s, food companies have reduced water consumption by 30–40 per cent. In the last decade, energy savings have reached about 15–20 per cent and packaging volume as well as package material weight have been reduced by about 40 per cent, also resulting in savings on transportation costs. Some companies have dealt with the targets of sustainable development by initiating a proactive approach. Among these, Barilla, an international leader in pasta and bakery, has developed a sophisticated environmental reporting system that documents progress in the reduction of the consumption of water, energy and materials used per unit of product. Granarolo, a dairy system of cooperatives, has issued an environmental product declaration (EPD) for a dozen of its products. Also, CoopItalia, the biggest retail chain in Italy, has launched a project 'CoopItalia for Kyoto' that involves 199 suppliers. Since the beginning of the project, CoopItalia reports an efficiency increase of 63 per cent and a decrease in the GHG emission rate from 0.194 to 0.182 CO_2/kg (CoopItalia 2014).

In addition, food companies increasingly communicate with consumers about their efforts to become more ecologically efficient. Barilla is one of the most active in this regard as, in addition to communicating its achievements in the field of ecological efficiency, it promotes campaigns for sustainable consumption and food security. The recent Milan Protocol, for example, offers a charter of principles that aims at encouraging political leaders: "To promote healthy lifestyles and fight obesity, to promote sustainable agriculture and to reduce food waste by 50% by 2020." The protocol has been launched by Barilla in collaboration with civil society organisations like WWF, Slow Food and many others. Despite these initiatives, however, the Italian food industry as a whole is not among the most active in making sustainability efforts, and the enduring economic crisis has made firms reluctant to invest in sustainable development.

Even if it is sometimes difficult to make a difference between mitigation measures and adaptation measures, it is fair to say that attention on climate change has focused mainly on mitigation during this first period. However, recent events have signalled to the public that the impacts of climate change are actually a present certainty and not merely a future possibility. As a consequence of reduced precipitation, a safe water supply has become a social and economic emergency in several regions. On the other hand, heavy precipitation events have increased the frequency of floods and landslides. Crop failures, as in the case of olives, in central Italy in 2014 have created panic and anxiety among farmers.

Extreme events make food systems more vulnerable. In an already fragile territory like Italy, floods and landslides put crops and herds at risk, plus they damage the transport infrastructure, undermining food distribution systems. Climate change also affects future food availability, for instance, the development cycle of many crops, such as grape, olive and wheat, has already been reduced, anticipating changing harvesting times and creating problems in the organisation of the operations of food chains. In addition, it is forecasted that the yield of the main summer crops might decrease, mainly as a result of the increase in the frequency of extreme climate events, such as increased rain during the Spring sowing time or climate stress during flowering or the course of the crop development stage. Also, as a consequence of change in the geographic range of pests – due to their ability to survive in regions where previously harsh winters would have killed them – new or more intense use of pesticides is foreseen. In Italy, regions that produce high quality food products are among the most vulnerable to the impacts of climate change. It is estimated that an increase of 2° Celsius in temperature would cause a loss of 0.7 per cent in the Italian GDP (Wolf and Menne 2007).

A consequence of this increased risk level has been that the debate on adaptation has intensified. Roundtables, research projects and other initiatives have been promoted or participated in by the Ministry of Agricultural, Food and Forestry Policies and by the Ministry of the Environment. The increased sensibility to the impact of climate change has raised the attention of the public regarding initiatives such as community gardens, zero km food chains and zero packaging shops. Also, the issue of waste has become central in the media, addressing company strategies as well as consumer behaviour.

Italy has a high external dependency on commodities like soybeans, wheat and maize, and concerns have been raised about the likelihood that climate change can influence their availability and affordability on international markets. Under these circumstances re-localisation initiatives have been taken by the food industry. For example, Barilla reports that it has developed a high quality variety of wheat suitable for growing in Italy, thus contributing to the re-localisation of sourcing (Barilla 2013). Another example of localisation in the Italian food systems is AsdoMar, a canned tuna producer, creating a 100 per cent Italian supply chain. At the same time, Italy relies upon regionally produced products for its export-oriented strategy, and there is evidence that many of the areas where Denomination of Origin products are produced are among the most sensitive to climate change conditions.

As a planned adaptation action the Ministry of the Environment released the "Strategy for Adaptation to Climate Change" in 2013 (Ministero dell'Ambiente 2013) for public consultation. In the section dedicated to agriculture, the report distinguishes between short-term and long-term adaptation actions. In the former, actions such as a change in the sowing date, changes in the cultivar and practices to retain soil moisture are considered. In the latter, the report lists land use change as well as investing in the improvement of the efficiency of irrigation systems and the modification of agricultural systems.

Moreover, the "Strategy for Adaptation to Climate Change" recognises the role of knowledge systems as a key factor in planned adaptation. Climate change alters the cognitive environment of the farmers, requiring the reconstruction of new cognitive environments that reflect higher instability, changes in the seasonality of biological cycles and the occurrence of new pests. Such reconstruction would be necessary in order to avoid inadequate responses to perturbations.

Monitoring and early warning systems would also have to become components of this environment as would investing in research, which is necessary if innovation is to be fostered.

Finland

Finland is one of the northernmost countries in the world, with a quarter of its territory within the Arctic Circle, which makes agriculture demanding. It is believed that global warming will improve farming conditions due to the rising average temperature and the lengthening of the growing season. It is also anticipated that arable land could be expanded further north and new crops like corn and alfalfa could be included in the agricultural variety (Peltonen-Sainio *et al.* 2009; Schulz 2009). Even after the risks have been identified, for example, new pests, plant and animal diseases as well as challenges in plant breeding, it is estimated that the short-term economic benefits of climate change may outweigh the farming disadvantages (MMM 2014: 13–14).

Finland also ratified the Kyoto Protocol in 2002. The target under the Protocol was to maintain emissions at the level of year 1990 over the period 2008–2012 and this target was met. According to Statistics Finland (2012), in 2011, the agricultural sector contributed about 9 per cent of Finland's national GHG emissions. However, the contribution of the Finnish food chain as a whole to climate change has been estimated to be somewhat larger, 14 per cent in all (Virtanen *et al.* 2010).

There are many ways to measure climate change adaptation in agriculture, though the methods are not particularly vigorous. In addition, it is difficult to separate the expressed measures of mitigation and some forms of adaptation from each other. For instance, in anticipatory adaptation, some resources in research and development are focused on charting, profiling and following the new risks resulting from disease, pests and extreme weather conditions. Furthermore, breeding and sustainable cultivation measurement techniques are being developed. At the same time, however, it is emphasised that agricultural environment and climate conditions are and have always been in a continuous state of change (MMM 2011).

However, the CAP, together with national agricultural and environmental policies, has established the most influential adaptation measures in Finland. Regular policy interventions, such as regulations for fertiliser use and manure processing, have been conducted to mitigate the climate impacts of farming (ibid.). Nevertheless, the most remarkable decrease in greenhouse gas emissions in Finnish agriculture occurred during the early 1990s when the agricultural industry adjusted to fit in with CAP – Finland joined the European Union and CAP in 1995 – by decreasing the number of farms, resulting in a decrease in the amount of livestock (Statistics Finland 2012). Given the continuous long-term economic pressures following the rapid structural change in agriculture and the temptation to increase productivity and economic profitability due to the anticipated improvements in farming conditions, it is likely that these changes will lead to contradictions and thus conflict between future economic and environmental goals. An example of this can already be seen in the Farmers Union opposing the legislation – later accepted by parliamentary majority – of a specific climate change law in Finland (MTK 2014).

In processing, packing, distribution and retail, it is emphasised that climate impacts should be explored in the context of the whole food supply chain, and that adaptation measures should be prepared in cooperation. According to the anticipatory adaptation strategy, multidisciplinary research that is focused on improving energy and resource efficiency, cutting down waste, rationalising logistics and developing packing materials and technologies is expected to improve cooperation. In addition, the importance of consumer behaviour is heavily underlined: it is crucial to find ways to guide consumers to make responsible, climate-friendly choices and decrease wastage.

In the processing sector, the adaptation measures seem to be mainly reactive. The need for energy efficiency as well as ensuring the quality of water under conditions of a rising average temperature have been recognised. It is also anticipated that the variety of raw materials will change as the crops farmed in Finland change. Additionally, fossil fuel dependency is mentioned as a potential risk and the need to develop renewable energy sources has already been identified (Molarius *et al.* 2010).

In distribution, the challenges of climate change are understood to be problems of guaranteeing food safety rather than guaranteeing food security. Food safety entails controlling temperatures in storage and transportation, developing early warning systems for microbes and harmful metabolites, and improving risk assessment systems and in-house control. Along with global warming, the relevance of hygiene and maintaining high-quality cold chains is expected to be increased.

The role of consumers is emphasised not only in connection with eco-friendly consumer choices but also in connection with health education. According to the new Nordic nutrition recommendations healthy and sustainable diets can easily be adopted, while food choices can also be made from the perspective of sustainable development. In addition to the effect of agriculture on the eutrophication of waters, the environmental impacts of food systems are being used as a means to illustrate climate change, for instance, through carbon footprinting. Local and organic food produce have been identified as eco-friendly products, while diets rich in vegetables and seasonal products are recommended for both health and environmental reasons. Additionally, the need to reduce food waste has been underlined (Terveyttä ruoasta 2014), leading to some catering services already offering 'climate lunches' in their daily menus. For example, AgriFood Finland, the National Institute of Health and Welfare, a few ministries, and some NGOs and enterprises have been involved in the development of the concept of the climate lunch. The basic idea is to give consumers the opportunity to easily make food choices that are climate-friendly and healthy.

In Finland, the grocery market is controlled by a strong oligopoly. There are two main retail chains – the S-Group and the Kesko Group – who dominate

80 per cent of the grocery trade. Some anticipatory as well as planned adaptation measures, like energy and resource efficiency in building, logistics and in-store recycling and waste recovery as well as decreasing packaging, will be and are used by them to mitigate climate change. The Kesko Group also has an experimental farm to promote Finnish agriculture. It invests in developing plant varieties and research to achieve sustainable cultivation methods and to improve domestic food production. The Kesko Group also aims to start an organic cultivation programme (Kesko 2013). The S-Group is investing in wind power and aiming to produce 50 per cent of all the power it needs via its own wind farms by 2016 (Sitoumus 2050 2014). Both these chains will increasingly reduce food waste by donating edible but unsellable food to charities, who will deliver it to people in need. While these chains have rebuilt their logistics to minimise climate impacts and maximise profits, one of the consequences of their success has been the closure of small shops, particularly in remote areas. Consequently, access to food has been endangered in remote rural areas due to the distance between the consumer and retailer.

Scanning adaptation strategies in Italy and Finland

Although it is sometimes difficult to separate the methods used to mitigate climate change impacts from various forms of adaptation, the food systems in Italy and Finland, which are responsible for producing food security, will be first explored here according to the four types of climate change adaptation presented by Fankhauser *et al.* (1999): (1) reactive adaptation, i.e. measures that are taken in response to climate change after the fact; (2) anticipatory adaptation, i.e. deliberate decisions to prepare for potential effects; (3) autonomous adaptation, i.e. natural or spontaneous adaptation when facing climate change; and (4) planned adaptation, which requires conscious intervention. Second, we will address some further policy issues of interest with regard to adaptation strategies in Italy and Finland.

In Italy, at least some of the short-term actions concerning the adaptation of agriculture, such as changes in the sowing date and the cultivar as well as practices to keep soil moist, will probably take the form of natural or spontaneous adaptation by farmers to climate change. In Fankhauser's terms, they could, thus, be classified as autonomous adaptation. However, in the "Strategy for Adaptation to Climate Change," Italian public authorities also address the long-term actions of adaptation and recognise the need for more deliberate public action in encouraging land use change, investments to improve the efficiency of irrigation and the modification of agricultural systems. Thus, both planned and anticipatory measures in agriculture are also on the agenda.

Along with the agricultural sector, other food system actors have foreseen the need for climate change adaptation in Italy. A major fluctuation in prices as well as reductions in the availability of some basic products, like soybeans, maize and wheat, on global markets is anticipated. Under these circumstances important re-localisation initiatives, which may be interpreted as anticipatory adaptation measures, have been taken by the food industry. However, it seems obvious that in the near future there will remain a serious need for further deliberately taken decisions to prepare for the potential effects of climate change. This need most emphatically concerns the development of anticipatory adaptation measures established to endorse the resilience of the many vulnerable regions producing high quality food, including the Denomination of Origin food products for export from Italy.

In Finland, the context of constructing adaptation measures is very different from Italy as global warming is expected to improve farming conditions in the country. A rising average temperature and lengthening growing period are foreseen as resulting in a situation where arable land could be expanded further north and new crops could be included in agricultural variety (Peltonen-Sainio *et al.* 2009; Schulz 2009). Although it identifies many risks, it is estimated that the short-term economic benefits of climate change will exceed the disadvantages for farms and farming.

However, in the name of anticipatory adaptation, some resources have been focused on the research and development of agriculture, for example, breeding and developing sustainable cultivation techniques. At the same time, it is also emphasised that both the agricultural environment and climate conditions are continually changing. Therefore, it is presumed that successful farmers will be able to spontaneously react to climate change by changing sowing and harvest times and the selection of crops accordingly, indicating trust in autonomous adaptation (MMM 2011).

Simultaneously, in packing, distribution and retail adaptation, mitigation and adaptation methods should be prepared in cooperation with the whole food supply chain. Notably, consumer behaviour is emphasised. The food industry and retail stores claim that they will, according to market logic, supply whatever consumers demand, suggesting an orientation towards reactive adaptation measures, even in the future. On the other hand, there is occasional debate on planned price policies or price controls based on climate protection, though no serious policy measures have been taken (Molarius *et al.* 2010).

According to these land case studies of food system activities in Italy and Finland, an array of nationally embedded climate change adaptation measures can be found in both countries. However, it seems to be quite problematic to separate the methods used to mitigate climate change impacts from those of climate change adaptation, both analytically and in practice. The most remarkable difference appears when interpreting the policy measures taken in practice. For example, after the ratification of the Kyoto Protocol and during the first period of attention on climate change impacts on food systems, the focus in Italy was mainly on mitigation measures. The primary goal was to reduce emissions in order to avoid negative climate impacts. Nevertheless, recent extreme weather events, like droughts, flooding and landslides, have convinced public opinion and food system actors and politicians that climate change with multiple environmental, economic and social impacts is not only a future possibility – it is a present-day certainty. Consequently, the mitigation of climate change impacts is seen as being inadequate and the development of adaptation measures is gaining more serious attention. At the same time, while concrete policy actions are fairly stable, the interpretation of the goals and practices has changed. Under these circumstances, earlier mitigation measures may be re-interpreted as measures of adaptation.

In the national context of Finland, the target set for the Kyoto Protocol was to maintain emissions at the level of the year 1990 over the period 2008–2012. The target was met, and though the contribution of the Finnish food supply chain to climate change is estimated to be about 14 per cent (Virtanen *et al.* 2010), there has not been any particular national pressure to cut emissions resulting from food system activities. In the Finnish food system, climate change adaptation has, so far, been more about monitoring and charting threats and possibilities rather than emphasising possibilities. However, the concrete adaptation measures initiated by food processing companies, distributors and retailers – improving energy and resource efficiency, reducing waste, rationalising logistics and developing packing materials and technologies – can be interpreted as mitigation measures. Thus, the actors are certainly informed about the need to prepare themselves for future climate change impacts. Nevertheless, the very same measures can also be interpreted as economically profitable business acts with potentially positive effects on climate change adaptation.

This examination of two geographically different European countries – located in different climate zones and which have differing anticipations and expectations concerning the impacts of climate change – shows how difficult it is to claim that adaptation policies could be arranged in a multi-level fashion within Europe's diverse climate regions. It seems to be clear that adaptation measures have to be tailored not just to national needs but also to regional needs – according to the specific natural and climate conditions. For example, Sicily differs greatly from the Italian Alps and Lapland, in the susceptible Arctic, differs greatly from southern Finland. When making these observations, it is important to consider the fact that there is no common policy for securing food supply in the EU. Nor is a national self-sufficiency in production emphasised in the CAP. Instead, self-sufficiency is now believed to be guaranteed through the common agricultural market, which means that sufficiency is market-based. In summary, this means that climate change adaptation policy should be included not only in CAP and national agricultural as well as environmental policies, but also in the corporate social responsibility policies of food processing companies as well as distributors and retailers. Educating consumers to make climate-friendly consumer choices will not be sufficient action, even if it is inevitable.

Conclusion

Finally, are there any grounds for common European policies for climate change adaptation from the perspective of food security? It is clear that the Common Agricultural Policy, together with national agricultural and environmental policies, has the power to establish influential adaptation measures, including environmental and climate subsidies, tax deductions and other "greening measures". Consequently, agriculture appears to be the main target for effective policy measures. CAP and national policies are relatively influential due to their power to sanction action through political means and the imposition of law. On the other hand, the production, distribution and retail sectors operate under market conditions, which will always involve market forces. This means that economic profitability will be a prerequisite for doing business, in which competition of some sort is generally understood to guarantee greater efficiency. In the name of consumer sovereignty, consumers cannot be forced by law to make certain choices, though they can be and should be educated to make responsible choices that indicate soft coordination between business concerns and the state with respect to long-term environmental food and environmental security. Therefore, it is essential that CAP policies and national policies maintain sensitivity to the regional particularities of the food chain when formulating new measures for climate change adaptation.

References

Barilla (2013) *Good For You, Good For the Planet: Sustainable Business Report 2013*. Available at: www.goodforyougoodfortheplanet.org (accessed 15 December 2014).

Cecchi, L., Orlandini, S., Morabito, M., Bindi, M. and Morindo, M. (2007) Ecosystems, forests and agriculture. In T. Wolf and B. Menne (eds) *Environment and Health Risks from Climate Change and Variability in Italy*. Copenhagen: World Health Organisation.

CoopItalia (2014) Press release: Coop for Kyoto. Available at: www.e-coop.it (accessed 15 December 2014).

Ericksen, P.J. (2008) What is the vulnerability of a food system to global environmental change? *Ecology and Society*, 13(2): 14–24.

Fankhauser, S., Smith, J.B. and Tol, R.S.J. (1999) Weathering climate change: some simple rules to guide adaptation decisions. *Ecological Economics*, 30(1): 67–78.

FAO (1996) *Declaration on World Food Security*. World Food Summit. Rome: FAO.

Federalimentare (2010) L'industria alimentare italiana apre le porte al pubblico all'insegna del 'gusto sostenibile'. Available at: www.federalimentare.it (accessed 15 December 2014).

Folke, C. (2006) Resilience: the emergence of a perspective for social–ecological systems analyses. *Global Environmental Study*, 16(3): 253–267.

ISPRA (2014) *Italian Greenhouse Gas Inventory 1990–201*. Rome: ISPRA. Available at: www.isprambiente.gov.it/files/pubblicazioni/rapporti/Rapporto_198_2014.pdf (accessed 15 December 2014).

KESKO (2013) Viljelyohjelman tavoitteena on parantaa asiakkaan viljelyn kannattavuutta. Available at: www.kesko.fi/fi/Vastuullisuus/Ajankohtaista/Viljelyohjelman-tavoitteena-on-parantaa-asiakkaan-viljelyn-kannattavuutta/ (accessed 13 December 2014).

Lang, T. and Barling, D. (2012) Food security and food sustainability: reformulating the debate. *The Geographical Journal*, 178(4): 313–326.

Ministero dell'Ambiente (2009) Fifth National Communication under the UN Framework Convention on Climate Change. Available at www.minambiente.it/ (accessed 15 December 2014).

Ministero dell'Ambiente (2013) Elementi per una Strategia Nazionale di Adattamento ai Cambiamenti Climatici. Available at: www.minambiente.it/ (accessed 15 December 2014).

MMM (2011) Maa-ja metsätalousministeriön ilmastonmuutokseen sopeutumisen toimintaohjelma 2011–2015. Helsinki: MMM. Available at: www.mmm.fi/attachments/mmm/julkaisut/muutjulkaisut/5yZhPxNpC/MMM_n_ilmastonmuutoksen_sopeutumisen_toimintaohjelma.pdf (accessed 7 July 2014).

MMM (2014) Kansallinen ilmastonmuutokseen sopeutumissuunnitelma 2022. Helsinki: MMM. Available at: www.mmm.fi/attachments/mmm/julkaisut/julkaisusarja/2014/FJ0qKpCH7/2014_5_lmastonmuutos.pdf (accessed 28 December 2014).

Molarius, R., Keränen, J., Jylhä, K., Sarlin, T. and Laitila, A. (2010) Suomen elintarviketuotannon turvallisuuden haasteita muuttuvissa ilmasto-olosuhteissa. Tampere: VTT. Available at: www.vtt.fi/inf/julkaisut/muut/2010/VTT-R-2672-10.pdf (accessed 17 July 2014).

MTK (2014) Ilmastolaki jättää kysymyksiä ilmaan Tiedote 5.6.2014. Available at: www.mtk.fi/ajankohtaista/tiedotteet/tiedotteet_2014/kesakuu/fi_FI/ilmastolaki_jattaa_kysymyksia_ilmaan/ (accessed 28 December 2014).

Niemi, J., Knuuttila, M., Liesivaara, P. and Vatanen, E. (2013) Suomen ruokaturvan nykytila ja tulevaisuudennäkymät. Helsinki: MTT. Available at: www.mtt.fi/mttraportti/pdf/mttraportti80.pdf) (accessed 17 July 2014).

Norton, B.G. (1992) Sustainability, human welfare, and ecosystem health. *Environmental Values*, 1(2): 97–111.

Peltonen-Sainio, P., Jauhiainen, L., Hakala, K. and Ojanen, H. (2009) Climate change and prolongation of growing season: changes in regional potential for field crop production in Finland. *Agricultural and Food Science*, 18: 171–190. Available at: www.mtt.fi/afs/pdf/mtt-afs-v18n3-4p171.pdf (accessed 28 December 2014).

Rete Rurale Nazionale (2012) Sfide ed opportunità dello sviluppo rurale per la mitigazione e l'adattamento ai cambiamenti climatici. Available at: www.reterurale.it (accessed 15 December 2014).

Riches, G. and Silvasti, T. (2014) *First World Hunger Revisited: Food Charity or Right to Food*. Basingstoke: Palgrave Macmillan.

Schulz, T.M. (2009) Ilmastonmuutoksen vaikutukset Suomen maatalouteen. Available at: www.syke.fi/download/noname/%7B1FC49C12-19D2-48A9-B907-F5D118953497%7D/40626 (accessed 28 December 2014).

SDC (2009) Food security and sustainability: the perfect fit. Available at: www.sd-commission.org.uk/data/files/publications/SDCFoodSecurityPositionPaper.pdf (accessed 28 December 2014).

Sitoumus 2050 (2014) Available at: http://sitoumus2050.fi/fi/sitoumus/s-ryhm%C3%A4n-sitoumus-energiank%C3%A4yt%C3%B6n-tehostamiseksi-ja-tuulivoiman-lis%C3%A4%C3%A4miseksi (accessed 13 January 2015).

Statistics Finland (2012) *Suomen kasvihuonekaasupäästöt 1990–2010*. Helsinki: Statistics Finland.

Terveyttä Ruoasta (2014) Ravitsemusneuvottelukunta, Helsinki. Available at: www.ravitsemusneuvottelukunta.fi/files/attachments/fi/vrn/ravitsemussuositukset_2014_fi_web.3.pdf (accessed 5 July 2014).

UNEP (2009) The environmental food crisis. Available at: www.grida.no/files/publications/FoodCrisis_lores.pdf (accessed 12 August 2013).

Virtanen, Y., Kurppa, S., Saarinen, M., Katajajuuri, J-M., Usva, K. and Mäenpää, I. (2010) Carbon footprint of food: approaches from national input-output statistics and a LCA of a food portion. *Journal of Cleaner Production*, 19(2011): 1849–1856.

Wolf, T. and Menne, B. (2007) Environment and health risks from climate change and variability in Italy. Available at: www.euro.who.int/__data/assets/pdf_file/0007/95920/E90707.pdf (accessed 15 December 2014).

7 Climate change, vulnerability and the local adaptation strategies of food enterprises in Finland

Antti Puupponen

Introduction

Climate change is one of the greatest challenges to the sustainable development of societies. It also has a fundamental influence on food production, food supply chain management and eating habits (Tirado *et al.* 2010; Smith and Gregory 2013). In this context, some interesting questions are: How well can food chains adapt to climate change? What kind of strategies do food enterprises have for adapting to climate change? At the same time, there has been discussion about localised food systems (Allen 2010; Mount 2012). Furthermore, it is interesting to discuss how adaptation to climate change and emerging local food systems could be combined.

This chapter aims to present the benefits and challenges of food supply chain localisation in the current political and business environment of Finland. It also propounds some ideas about how local and proactive food supply chains – that aim to counter the predicted threats of climate change – could be created in the future. The structure is as follows: first, some discussion on how the concepts of vulnerability and adaptation strategy have been defined in research literature. Then the localisation of the Finnish food systems and how food enterprises operate in Finland are presented. Finally, some observations based on the case study are made and the discussion concludes.

Climate vulnerability and adaptation strategies

Societies, communities, organisations and individuals are vulnerable to the risks caused by climate change. Therefore, a key concept in climate change studies is vulnerability. Adger (1999: 249) defines vulnerability "as the exposure of individuals or collective groups to livelihood stress as a result of the impacts of such environmental change". Füssel (2007: 157) argues that there are four fundamental dimensions to be used when describing a vulnerable situation: system, attribute of concern, hazard and temporal reference. System can refer to any kind of system such as a human-environment system, a population group, an economic sector or geographical region. Attribute of concern refers to, for instance, the risk to human lives and health, income or the cultural identity of a community.

Hazard means some influence that may potentially damage the system. It is usually, but not always, external to the system. Temporal reference means the time period being considered. Risks to the system can be changing during the time horizon and that is why temporal reference is significant in the context of vulnerability (ibid.: 157).

Adger (1999) particularly highlights social vulnerability. Traditionally, climate change studies have concentrated on the physical dimensions and impacts of the issue, however, social vulnerability broadens this view to include societal and human dimensions. Based on this, vulnerability can be seen as a combination of social factors and environmental risk (ibid.: 252).

States, regional governments, municipalities, enterprises and other organisations have made strategic plans to adapt to climate change and reduce their vulnerability to it. Governing climate change demands multilevel politics (Bulkeley and Betsill 2013). Nevertheless, strategic planning is challenging because the impacts of climate change are unknown. Thus, despite the wealth of research, reports and scenarios related to the risks of climate change, it is not easy to recognise what the essential sources of information for the support of strategic planning are. As a result, uncertainty is always present in the context of climate change (Buuren *et al.* 2014).

There are several types of strategies that can be used to adapt to climate change. In the research literature, at least five different adaptation strategies can be found: (1) reactive adaptation; (2) anticipatory adaptation; (3) autonomous adaptation; (4) planned adaptation; and (5) pro-active adaptation (Fankhauser *et al.* 1999; Beermann 2011). Reactive adaptation means that measures are taken after some change has already occurred. Anticipatory adaptation refers to deliberate decisions that could prepare people for climate change's potential effects, for instance, using renewable energy sources instead of non-renewable energy. Autonomous adaptation can be characterised as natural and spontaneous adaptation to the threats of climate change. Planned adaptation requires conscious intervention. A pro-active strategy is the most demanding strategy. It aims to build resilience and take into account mitigation and adaptation requirements in a broader sense.

Regarding the limits of adaptation, Adger *et al.* (2009) especially examine the social limits of adaptation. They argue that discourse around the limits to adaptation is constructed by ecological, physical, economic and technological limits. Furthermore, they see climate change adaptation as being limited by societal factors that have not been adequately taken into account in academic research. These factors are significant for food enterprises and their adaptation strategies because creating local food networks, for example, is dependent on societal factors and community relations.

Local food and Finnish food enterprises

Academic research into local food has grown over the past 10–15 years. The research finds that the idea of local food has attracted many good features and it is claimed that local food can create new markets for farmers and food processing companies, can support family farming, reduce environmental degradation and create local jobs (Allen 2010: 296–297). In a wider sense, local food even enhances the social capital of a community (see e.g. Hinrichs 2003). However, local food does not have set standards or labels in Finland. On the contrary, the definition of local food is quite broad (Jokinen *et al.* 2009: 7–8). According to the Finnish Ministry of Agriculture and Forestry, the basic idea of local food is to promote the economy, employment and food culture of a region. Local food is produced, processed, marketed and consumed in the same region (MAF 2013). However, there are also some other definitions for local food, but usually the definitions do not take a position on exact distances and time between production and consumption. Nonetheless, local food aims to shorten the food supply chain.

Local food can be beneficial, in the sense of climate mitigation, due to fewer emissions stemming from the shorter transportation distances of local food products. However, according to Wallgren's (2006) study, the consideration of transportation distance is inadequate because the energy intensity of transportation depends on several parameters, such as distance, transport mode, quantity loaded and the vehicle. However, local products usually need less packaging and storage as well. In a wider sense, especially in developing countries, this has raised the question of food democracy. In this context, some researchers have argued that the localisation of food could create better opportunities for food democracy and sovereignty (see e.g. Quaye *et al.* 2010).

However, according to estimates, local food products have only an 8 per cent share in the Finnish retail food sector (MAF 2013). It is also well known that the Finnish food industry is highly polarised between just a few large companies and many small companies. In 2012, the Finnish food industry employed 39,400 persons in total. Seventy-one per cent of the firms employ fewer than five workers and many of those small firms are located in rural areas. The bakery industry and the meat processing industry are the most numerous food processing industries (Niemi and Ahlstedt 2014).

Centralisation is a strong trend in the Finnish retail market. In fact, Finland has the most centralised food retail structure in Europe. The Finnish food supply chains are dominated by two main companies: the S-Group and the Kesko Group (K-Group), together they have about an 80 per cent share of the Finnish retail market. In 2013, the S-Group's market share was 45.7 per cent and the K-Group's was 34 per cent (Niemi and Ahlstedt 2014). Their main competitors are Suomen Lähikauppa (7 per cent share) and the German company Lidl (6.6 per cent share), which is growing (ibid.). There are approximately 4,000 food retail outlets in Finland (Tike 2011). The whole food chain employs about 300,000 persons (Hyrylä 2012). Although the retail sector for food is centralised, globalisation is also a major trend in the Finnish food markets. In many cases, both production and processing are located outside Finland and that makes the food chain long and adds to the complexity of its structure.

Finnish agriculture has traditionally been based on small family farms. In 2013, there were about 57,600 farms in Finland. The number of farms is decreasing, but the average size of a farm is growing. At the moment, the average arable area of a farm is about 40 hectares (Niemi and Ahlstedt 2014). Plant production is important in the southern part of the country and dairy production in the north. Producer cooperatives have a significant position in the dairy and meat processing industries but there are long distances between Finland's countryside and residential centres. Thus, trucks move most of the domestically produced food and a well-functioning road network is important from the viewpoint of the Finnish food supply chain.

Findings of the case study

Data and methods

The findings are based on a qualitative case study that was conducted in three Finnish inland regions in 2012. For the study, 14 thematic interviews were conducted – nine interviews with food enterprises representing the dairy and the bakery industries and five interviews with professional associations. The research data consists of mainly individual interviews, but two interviews featured a couple and due to this there were 16 persons interviewed in total. The persons interviewed were food entrepreneurs, managers of food enterprises and representatives of professional organisations. The research regions were Central Finland, Pirkanmaa and South Savonia, all traditional Finnish provinces.

Approximately 500,000 inhabitants live in Pirkanmaa, 275,000 inhabitants in Central Finland and 152,000 inhabitants in South Savonia. In 2012, there was a total of 452 food enterprises in these three provinces (Ruoka-Suomi 2012). There are many livestock and vegetable producers in the research regions, but only a few milk processing enterprises. It is a characteristic of the Finnish food market that milk processing is done by two large companies (Valio and Arla).

All enterprises in the study were small and medium-sized enterprises (SMEs). Some of them could be defined as self-employed. However, they still had quite an established circle of customers and all of them operated mainly locally or regionally. I also interviewed representatives from the professional organisations of the provinces because I assumed that they would hold a holistic overview of the food industry in their own region. The professional organisations in the study were the Central Union of Agricultural Producers and Forest Owners (MTK) and the agricultural expert organisation ProAgria. The basic information concerning the interviewees' background is presented in Table 7.1. The interviews are presented by region, and were not conducted in that order.

In the beginning of the study it was quite difficult to find interviewees because many of them refused the request to be interviewed, citing a variety of reasons: a difficult subject to answer, the enterprise was committed to other studies, there was a generational change in the enterprise or the time was not good. Finally, ten

Table 7.1 Interviews undertaken in the study of vulnerabilities and adaptation strategies

Number of interview	*Interviewee(s)*	*Organisation type*	*Region*
1	Marketing Manager	Food Enterprise (Bakery)	South Savonia
2	Managing Director	Food Enterprise (Dairy)	South Savonia
3	Entrepreneur (couple)	Food Enterprise (Bakery)	South Savonia
4	Executive Manager	Professional Organisation	South Savonia
5	Managing Director	Professional Organisation	South Savonia
6	Entrepreneur (couple)	Food Enterprise (Dairy)	Central Finland
7	Entrepreneur	Food Enterprise (Bakery)	Central Finland
8	Managing Director	Food Enterprise (Bakery)	Central Finland
9	Project Leader	Professional Organisation	Central Finland
10	Office Manager	Food Enterprise (Bakery)	Pirkanmaa
11	Entrepreneur	Food Enterprise (Dairy)	Pirkanmaa
12	Production Manager	Food Enterprise (Dairy)	Pirkanmaa
13	Distribution Manager	Food Enterprise (Dairy)	Pirkanmaa
14	Executive Manager	Professional Organisation	Pirkanmaa

interviews were conducted face-to-face and four by phone due to the interviewees' busy timetables. There were three main themes in the interviews: the first theme covered the background information of the interviewee and the activity of their organisation; the second dealt with the interviewee's perceptions and experiences of climate change; and the third concerned foresight and adaptation to climate change in the future. The research data was analysed by using qualitative content analysis with the theory-bound and abductive approach (see e.g. Timmermans and Tavory 2012; Silvasti 2014). A more detailed analysis of the data is presented by Puupponen and Paloviita (2014).

Food enterprises and their attitudes to climate change

When the study started, it soon became clear that enterprises do not have very clear ideas about the issue of climate change. At the beginning of the study, there were many entrepreneurs who did not want to be interviewed, which was also a signal that dealing with the issue of climate change is experienced as difficult and challenging by food enterprises. There were also some doubts concerning the authenticity of climate change:

> Well, I don't have a clear idea of climate change. There are a lot of discussions about it, but I have a bit of feeling that there is some real change or transformation coming, or is it just normal that these weather conditions vary over time?
>
> (Interview 6, woman, enterprise, Central Finland)

Even this entrepreneur had noticed that some changes in climatic conditions are probably occurring. More precisely, according to the research data, it seems that the entrepreneurs and managers of the food enterprises take the risk of climate change seriously. However, it is considered a lower-level priority issue compared to other pressures.

One reason for this vagueness regarding climate change risks is certainly the time-period of climate change, which seems to be somehow indistinct from the food enterprises' viewpoint. In addition, it is not easy to identify the intensity of climate risks and the degree of one's own vulnerability (see Füssel 2007). Furthermore, according to earlier studies on climate change, we know that awareness of climate change does not necessarily lead to action (Wilson 2006). Based on my data, the reasons for that are also due to the other pressures of business, such as market competition and increased bureaucracy. The effects of these pressures seem to be much more concrete for food enterprises in comparison to climate change. Thus, these enterprises have a feeling that there is no time to think about climate strategies in their daily activities. In this regard, the adaptation strategies of food enterprises can be described as reactive, anticipatory or autonomous, but not planned or pro-active strategies.

It is obvious that state and transnational bureaucracy is experienced as an overwhelming burden by food enterprises. However, despite its good intentions, such bureaucracy can also increase vulnerability and even weaken adaptive capacity.

> This is becoming a really bureaucratic system and it is going to choke on its own impossibility, so that some are establishing the rules and others are trying to follow those rules. Then the mess is almost ready. The bureaucracy is even feeding itself. The good things are being crushed by the wheels of this system. Of course, there are a lot of good things, but there is a clear need to lighten the bureaucracy and the role of governance as well.
>
> (Interview 2, man, enterprise, South Savonia)

On the other hand, the information presented about and the reportage of climate change seems to be indefinite and even contradictory. Some researchers argue that the way the public is informed about climate change may cause concerns and qualms. The creation of negative feelings influences risk perception and may lead to the avoidance of the source of risk (Marx *et al.* 2007). Swim *et al.* (2011) note that concern about and the anticipation of climate change may even weaken the quality of life and have negative impacts for mental health at the individual level. This may lead to stress and passivity, because the effects may appear as fatal and inevitable. Swim *et al.* (2011: 242–244) argue, "Those who have the fewest social and economic resources are likely to be the most vulnerable to physical and psychological impacts." Thus, when taking into account the other pressures placed on enterprises, it is no surprise that climate change is easily given a back seat in the strategic planning of SMEs. Hence, action to combat future climate change demands time and support. It seems that enterprises are willing to adapt to climate change, but the indistinct time-span makes it difficult from their point of view.

Climate change and local food

What is the role of local food in terms of climate change adaptation? According to the results, food entrepreneurs and the managers of food enterprises see the localisation of food as a key climate change adaptation strategy for the whole food chain.

> Well, of course, it is good for the whole province and the food supply if there is, for instance, rye in stock for the needs of the next year. And if the sites of production are located in many places, the system is less vulnerable ... One could imagine that it would be more secure. And then it is, of course, a marketing advantage as well, like I said. So, I believe that an awareness of the risks of climate change increases people's willingness to use more local products.
>
> (Interview 3, male, enterprise, South Savonia)

Thus, a local or regional approach to food production can enhance the adaptive capacity and resilience of a food chain. However, according to the interviews, there are some obstacles to this development. One major obstacle is the structure of the retail markets in Finland. One interviewee pointed this out:

> When we are dependent on the two big retail chains – for which we produce [our goods]. And then again, they are fighting bloodily between themselves trying to make good profits. Honestly, their values are not really at the level they say they are, even though in their speeches they are something else.
>
> (Interview 2, male, enterprise, South Savonia)

The centralised structure of the food retailing industry creates unfavourable conditions for the competitive ability of small food enterprises, which can be problematic in the context of climate change adaptation too. For instance, if transport connections are broken due to climatic reasons, centralised stocks are more vulnerable compared to a situation in which production and stocks are decentralised and located in many places. Thus, a centralised structure can be seen as a social limitation for the adaptation described by Adger *et al.* (2009). Centralisation also causes economic losses for retail chains if the inventory cycle is disrupted due to storms, floods or other changes in weather conditions.

In the discussion of local food, one aspect is related to food security, which broadens the idea of local food. On the other hand, input production was seen as a vulnerability aspect, which should be developed on a more domestic, regional and local basis so that whole chains would be less vulnerable.

> So we are not very self-sufficient with regards to input production [here in Finland]. We should think about whether we can do something to improve it. Of course, all goals are dependent on energy and whether there is any

> renewable energy we can utilise. But we depend very much on imports of oil, fertilisers and, overall, how we use our machinery.
>
> (Interview 8, male, professional organisation, South Savonia)

However, many interviewees highlighted the strengths of small-scale local food production compared to global mass production. These strengths are related to the use of natural resources, such as cleaner air or clean water, which can also be seen as factors of production. These factors can be identified as marketing advantages for local or regional production because they have strong significance for local communities. Thus, they are more than just water and air; they are part of the local identity and well-being too. Adger *et al.* (2011) are therefore critical of climate policy that is only based on the material and instrumental reasons behind the problem. They think that it is necessary to highlight places as a context "in which people create their lives, and through which those lives derive meaning". Hence, they argue that place and identity provide a greater force for arguments based on values that people really care about (ibid.).

Future prospects

Even though the interviewees did not see climate change as the most urgent priority for their business, most of them had noticed fundamental and rapid changes in weather conditions, such as increasingly frequent windy and stormy periods. The interviewees thought that these changes will intensify in the future, but some of them thought that geographically Finland is not the most vulnerable country in the world.

Adaptation issues are mostly related to the discussion of energy from the viewpoint of food entrepreneurs. The interviewees believe that the price of energy has a crucial influence on the food chain. Hence, many enterprises have adopted solutions that enhance the eco-efficient use of energy. However, this is not primarily happening due to climate change, but rather is due to savings made through the reduction of production costs. It seems that energy-related issues are more concrete and easier to integrate as part of business than other measures about mitigating or adapting to climate change.

Global market competition is one of the pressures influencing the activities of SMEs, though they operate on the regional or local level. Increased competition also extends to an even wider range of stakeholders within the food chain, such as public procurement:

> Public administration is inviting us to tender for bakery products and for all the other products as well. So, price is the most important thing for them. There is no significance … when the price is the most important thing. These small enterprises producing goods through domestic raw materials and even organic products are never ever going to win those tenders. And we have not been successful either.
>
> (Interview 1, male, enterprise, South Savonia)

Thus, a focus on product prices restricts well-functioning local food systems. Folke (2006) believes that, in terms of climate change, the aim should be a system that allows an adaptive governance system, while supporting adaptive management at all levels – globally, nationally and locally. Hence, incentive schemes for adaptation and an integrated knowledge base that is available for different stakeholders in the food chain are needed. On the other hand, stakeholders may need support with their learning ability. Different actors within the food chain must find better ways to meet each other's needs and they should be able to create genuine interaction as well. So, according to Folke: "Social networks serve as the web that seems to tie together the adaptive governance system" (ibid.).

Governing global food chains is even more challenging, because the power in the chain is divided unequally. Fresco (2009: 384) argues that food production and distribution are more centralised and governed by fewer actors than ever before. A limited group of actors is producing food for a growing global population. Thus, there is a need for transparency regarding food-related knowledge, measures and political decisions, so that consumers could have better opportunities to make their own decisions. According to the research data, the interviewees thought that a more localised and decentralised food system would create better opportunities to achieve that transparency.

Conclusion

The localisation of food is seen in a positive light by food entrepreneurs and representatives of professional organisations. Most of the enterprises in the study were SMEs operating mainly in local and sub-regional markets. Thus, localisation and regionalisation are natural development paths for their business. However, representatives from the bigger companies and professional organisations also saw local and sub-regional markets as a very important target in the context of climate and rural policy. It seems that localisation is a clear trend in current food markets (Puupponen 2010; Pearson *et al.* 2011).

The case study indicates that the localisation of food chains can have a positive influence on enterprises, a local economy and food consumers. On the other hand, the centralised food system has been cost-effective and it will take time to create an equally cost-efficient localised system. However, in the Finnish context, operating at the sub-regional level could be a sufficient target for different stakeholders wishing to create a profitable business.

The discussion of the food industry seems to return often to the prices of products and the costs of production. Climate change is forcing food enterprises to operate eco-efficiently, because rapid changes in the environment may raise costs unexpectedly. Enterprises are anticipating these changes at some level, at least when the changes are related to energy-saving solutions or the rationalisation of logistics systems. In a wider context, these solutions are part of the new resource-efficient thinking in society, where saving, recycling and borrowing become virtues for enterprises and individuals alike. Local food production and the decentralisation of the food chain also follow this thinking.

Particularly in the near future, food enterprises will need to integrate energy efficiency into local food systems in order to achieve more benefits from their local system. Energy-efficient and climate-resilient local food systems will be attractive to consumers as well. According to this study, it is easy to agree with Wallgren (2006) who argues that it is possible to develop technologies that are more suitable for small-scale farmers and enterprises, for instance, by using biogas as a fuel for transport and as a heating energy as well. Such local and regional solutions could quite easily be integrated into local food systems. In order to make the local food business flourish, there is obviously a need for structural changes in food consumption culture and preferences. All these drivers will push local food systems forwards and perhaps make them become the mainstream system in the future – when climate risk is conceived of more clearly in people's minds, and thus tackled more comprehensively.

Acknowledgements

This research was funded by the Academy of Finland through the research project A-LA-CARTE (decision no. 140870).

References

Adger, W.N. (1999) Social vulnerability to climate change and extremes in coastal Vietnam. *World Development*, 27: 249–269.

Adger, W.N., Barnett, J., Chapin, F.S. and Ellemor, H. (2011) This must be the place: underrepresentation of identity and meaning in climate change decision-making. *Global Environmental Politics*, 11: 1–25.

Adger, W.N., Dessai, S., Goulden, M., Hulme, M., Lorenzoni, I., Nelson, D.R., Naess, L.O., Wolf, J. and Wreford, A. (2009) Are there social limits to adaptation to climate change? *Climatic Change*, 93: 335–354.

Allen, P. (2010) Realizing justice in local food systems. *Cambridge Journal of Regions, Economy and Society*, 3: 295–308.

Beermann, M. (2011) Linking corporate climate adaptation strategies with resilience thinking. *Journal of Cleaner Production*, 19: 836–842.

Bulkeley, H. and Betsill, M.M. (2013) Revisiting the urban politics of climate change. *Environmental Politics*, 22: 136–154.

Buuren, A., Driessen, P., Teisman, G. and Rijswick, M. (2014) Toward legitimate governance strategies for climate adaptation in the Netherlands: combining insights from a legal, planning and network perspective. *Regional Environmental Change*, 14: 1021–1033.

Fankhauser, S., Smith, J.B. and Tol, R.S.J. (1999) Weathering climate change: some simple rules to guide adaptation decision. *Ecological Economics*, 30: 67–78.

Folke, C. (2006) Resilience: the emergence of perspective for social-ecological systems analysis. *Global Environmental Change*, 16: 253–267.

Fresco, L.O. (2009) Challenges for food system adaptation today and tomorrow. *Environmental Science and Policy*, 12: 378–385.

Füssel, H-M. (2007) Vulnerability: a generally applicable conceptual framework for climate change research. *Global Environmental Change*, 17: 155–167.

Hinrichs, C.C. (2003) The practice and politics of food system localization. *Journal of Rural Studies*, 19: 33–45.

Hyrylä, L. (2012) Elintarviketeollisuus – toimialaraportti. Available at: www.temtoimialapalvelu.fi/files/2079/Elintarviketeollisuus_lokakuu_2012.pdf (accessed 8 Aug. 2014). [In Finnish.]

Jokinen, P., Järvelä, M. and Puupponen, A. (2009) Local food systems and rural sustainability initiatives by small scale rural entrepreneurs in Finland, *Maaseudun uusi aika, Finnish. Journal of Rural Research and Policy*, 17: 5–20.

MAF (2013) Lähruokaa – totta kai! Hallituksen lähiruokaohjelma ja lähiruokasektorin kehittämisen tavoitteet vuoteen 2020. Ministry of Agriculture and Forestry of Finland. Available at: www.mmm.fi/attachments/lahiruoka/6GeZ7N4oG/LahiruokaohjelmaFI.pdf) (accessed 23 Sept. 2014). [In Finnish.]

Marx, S.M., Weber, E.U., Orlove, B.S., Leiserowitz, A., Krantz, D.H., Roncoli, C. and Phillips, J. (2007) Communication and mental processes: experiential and analytic processing of uncertain climate information. *Global Environmental Change*, 17: 47–58.

Mount, P. (2012) Growing local food: scale and local food systems governance. *Agriculture and Human Values*, 29: 107–121.

Niemi, J. and Ahlstedt, J. (eds) (2014) Finnish Agriculture and Rural Industries 2014. *Maa- ja elintarviketalouden tutkimuskeskus*. Helsinki: Agrifood Research Finland, Economic Research.

Pearson, D., Henryks, J., Trott, A., Jones, P., Parker, G., Dumeresq, D. and Dyball, R. (2011) Local food: understanding consumer motivations in innovative retail formats. *British Food Journal*, 113: 886–899.

Puupponen, A. (2010) Lähiruoka nousevana trendinä elintarviketuotannon muutoksessa. *Maaseudun uusi aika*, 18: 56–60. [In Finnish.]

Puupponen, A. and Paloviita, A. (2014) Ilmastonmuutoksen sopeutuminen elintarvikeketjun hallinnan näkökulmasta. Tapaustutkimus kolmen maakunnan alueella. *Alue ja Ympäristö*, 43: 61–72. [In Finnish.]

Ruoka-Suomi (2012) Elintarviyritykset toimialoittain 6/2012. Available at: www.ruokasuomi.fi/tilastot/taulukko_elintarvikeyritykset_toimialoittain_2012.pdf (accessed 12 Nov. 2014). [In Finnish.]

Quaye, W., Jongerden, J., Essegbey, G. and Ruivenkamp, G. (2010) Globalization vs. localization: global food challenges and local solutions. *International Journal of Consumer Studies*, 34: 357–366.

Silvasti, T. (2014) Sisällönanalyysi. In I. Massa (ed.) *Polkuja yhteiskuntatieteelliseen ympäristötutkimukseen*. Helsinki: Gaudeamus Helsinki University Press, pp. 33–48. [In Finnish.]

Smith, P. and Gregory, P.J. (2013) Climate change and sustainable food production. *Proceedings of the Nutrition Society*, 72: 21–28.

Swim, J.K., Stern, P.C., Doherty, T.J., Clayton, S., Reser, J.P., Weber, E.U., Gifford, R. and Howard, G.S. (2011) Psychology's contributions to understanding and addressing global climate change. *American Psychologist*, 66: 241–250.

Tike-Maa-ja metsätalousministeriön tietopalvelukeskus (2011) *Pellolta pöytään 2010*. Helsinki: Edita. [In Finnish.]

Timmermans, S. and Tavory, I. (2012) Theory construction in qualitative research: from grounded theory to abductive analysis. *Sociological Theory*, 30: 167–186.

Tirado, M.C., Clarke, R., Jaykus, L.A., McQuatters-Gollop, A. and Frank, J.M. (2010) Climate change and food safety: a review. *Food Research International*, 43: 1745–1765.

Wallgren, C. (2006) Local or global food markets: a comparison of energy use for transport. *Local Environment*, 11: 233–251.

Wilson, E. (2006) Adapting to climate change at the local level: the spatial planning response. *Local Environment*, 11: 609–625.

8 Carbon footprinting

The clearest way to create a climate-friendly food consumption and food chain

Hanna Hartikainen, Hannele Pulkkinen, Juha-Matti Katajajuuri and Pirjo Peltonen-Sainio

Introduction

Food production and consumption have a significant impact on the environment. Agricultural production in particular generates substantial amounts of emissions, such as nitrogen and phosphorus leaching, ammonia and greenhouse gas (GHG). Consequently, a substantial share of emissions from private consumption originates from food consumption (see e.g. Tukker and Jansen 2006). For instance, in Finland, over half of the phosphorus and nitrogen emissions and one quarter of GHG emissions from private consumption originate from food (Seppälä *et al.* 2009; Regina *et al.* 2011).

However, agriculture is at a crossroads – as is the food system that it underpins. The human population is expected to increase from 6 billion to up to even 9 or 10 billion in the next couple of decades (UNEP 2010). As the rise in the standard of living in highly populated regions will continue to increase, as will the demand for animal products and consequently animal feed, global food availability will have to increase by 100 to 180 per cent to meet the demand. This should not, however, endanger the bearing capacity of our planet (Rockström *et al.* 2009; Foley *et al.* 2011). Nevertheless, climate change complicates food production challenges and is projected to jeopardise global food production capacities (IPCC 2014). Hence, there is a need to find effective solutions to adapt to the various interplaying global changes and challenges, and to concomitantly increase food production capacities without sacrificing the environment. This agrees with the recent study of Rockström *et al.* (2009), who argue that we have already crossed some biophysical thresholds, including climate change, and consequently have already exceeded humanity's safe operating space. Foley *et al.* (2011) highlight that reductions in GHG emissions are among the most critical environmental goals that food production needs to contribute to in the near future. Clearing forests to gain more arable land for food production – at the expense of carbon sinks (IPCC 2014) – is not a viable option, thus agricultural expansion needs to be halted (Foley *et al.* 2011). Taken as a whole, balancing the targets of increasing productivity and reducing environmental footprints is challenging. According to a recent FAO estimate, action to achieve current hunger reduction goals has so far been insufficient, despite some progress (FAO, IFAD and WFP 2013). Furthermore, the growth trends of the yields of the major staple crops have not increased as anticipated (Ray *et al.* 2012).

While there are few opportunities in food production chains to reduce the environmental impact of food production by adopting new technology, such as low carbon technology (Weidema *et al.* 2008), improvements in production to mitigate pressing environmental impacts, such as climate impacts, are still urgently needed. Agriculture is foremost a primary production system, which is expected to go through sustainable intensification that benefits from plant breeding and technological developments, as well as improved land use planning, for example, land sharing and land sparing. These are critical steps in providing environmental benefits (Peltonen-Sainio 2012; Soussana *et al.* 2012), making agriculture better able to meet the sustainable development goals (see e.g. Leach *et al.* 2012), and especially help to contribute to GHG emission reduction targets – though there is an evident need to concomitantly enhance production capacities per cultivated land area (Cassman 1999).

According to several studies (see e.g. Weidema *et al.* 2008; Carlsson-Kanyama and Gonzalez 2009), there is substantial potential to reduce the environmental impacts of food consumption by changing food consumption patterns. For instance, it is estimated that food-related climate impacts can be reduced by up to 25–50 per cent, even if energy and protein intake were to stay the same (Berners-Lee *et al.* 2012; Åström *et al.* 2013). Switching our diets to make them less meat-intensive would mean that more of the yields of major staple crops could be allocated directly to human consumption, instead of their current mix of uses, which includes animal feed. This would also correspond to about a 50 per cent increase in the delivery of food calories (Foley *et al.* 2011). Moreover, in comparison to choices regarding housing and transportation, food choices are different because they are personal, and therefore consumers have the opportunity to make environmentally friendly choices several times a day. However, consumers need to be informed as to how to make such choices.

Taken as a whole, there is a lot of pressure to make food production and consumption more sustainable. This chapter demonstrates that though carbon footprinting and carbon footprint communication still face challenges, and are often intended as a consumer-oriented climate policy tool, carbon footprinting itself is seen as pressuring food chain actors into reducing actual GHG emissions. Consequently, carbon footprinting can foster long-term commitment to reducing total GHG emissions, thus minimising future emissions. Accordingly, we suggest that – due to its comprehensiveness and practicality – carbon footprinting provides the clearest path to lead consumers and companies towards making GHG emission reductions via their consumption patterns and within the food chain. Moreover, we argue that carbon footprinting provides a solid foundation for improving the total sustainability of the food chain. However, it should be noted that emissions cannot be reduced to zero in food production, demand for food is increasing rapidly, we have already exceeded the safe operating space for humanity, climate change is already evident and, therefore, carbon footprinting should primarily be seen as a tool to both mitigate and to adapt to climate change.

Lifecycle assessment as a tool to reduce the impact of climate change

The environmental impacts of food production are based on complex causal relations and from time to time actions taken to improve the environmental impact of one part of the food chain lead to further impacts in other parts of the food chain. It is very likely that partial improvements, which are based on certain parts of the food chain, are not as resource-efficient as improvements that consider the whole chain and aim for the most resource-efficient solutions throughout the chain. This highlights the need for holistic lifecycle approaches, e.g. the need to make lifecycle thinking (LCT) part of the strategies and operations of food companies, including all types of actors of the food chain, such as primary producers, manufacturers, retailers, etc.

One of the most used LCT approach is lifecycle assessment (LCA) that "addresses the environmental aspects and potential environmental impacts throughout a product's life cycle from raw material acquisition through production, use, end-of-life treatment, recycling and final disposal" (ISO 14040 2006), and is based on the international ISO standard (ISO 14040 2006; ISO 14044 2006). In fact, many companies which claim to be environmentally responsible, such as Unilever and Nestlé, have carried out several LCA case studies of food products and entire brand volumes to identify hotspots in their chains and to enable continuous and optimised improvements.

LCA can be combined with economic and social impact assessments that are also based on LCT. Therefore, even if one initially conducts only an assessment of GHG emissions, it is easier to do more LCAs with other impact categories, plus it will also be easier to include economic and social assessments in any futures scopes and arrive at a whole sustainability assessment. For now, the assessment of GHG emissions is clearly one of the most methodologically developed impact categories (IPCC 2007; ISO 14040 2006), and thus it is one of the most viable environmental impact categories with which to assess and to communicate. Communication is also easier since climate impact is a global impact with worldwide impacts and consequently it is easy to discuss it. In contrast, many other environmental impacts are regional, such as nitrogen leaching into water, and therefore they are hard to standardise and very difficult to communicate. Furthermore, climate impact itself is widely perceived as one of the most important impact categories. Hence, environmentally pro-active food companies, including the Italian Barilla, the Swedish Lantmännen and the French retailer Casino, assess and communicate their climate impacts.

Even though climate impact is one of the most developed impact categories and its methodology has improved remarkably in recent years (Nemecek *et al.* 2014), there are still many methodological questions under discussion that need more work and specification. This is reflected in scientific and practical studies, but also in the guidelines trying to harmonise LCA methods. Consequently, even if the ISO standard for LCA provides a basis for LCA, it is commonly criticised as not being specific enough as it leaves too much room for various choices and interpretations (see e.g. Ekvall and Finnveden 2001). This ambiguity results in difficulties, especially when communicating and comparing the results of LCA studies. Therefore, there are several international specifications, such as the GHG Protocol (WRI/WBCSD 2011), PAS2050 (2011), the ILCD Handbook (2010) and the Dutch Horticulture specification (2009) that aim to provide more specific LCA guidelines. However, despite the efforts to specify LCA practices, the specifications fail to provide detailed enough guidelines for the variable and complex food sector (see e.g. Hartikainen *et al.* 2014b), leading to unnecessary ambiguity. Moreover, the number of different guidelines increases the ambiguity because there is no common agreement on which LCA specification should be used.

Despite the weaknesses of LCA, the progress is promising. For instance, LCA methodologies, particularly in the agricultural sector, such as the inclusion of emissions from direct land use changes or soil carbon changes, have advanced significantly during the past 10 years, and can be projected to advance in the future relatively rapidly, due to the vast scientific interest in the issue. In addition, several Environmental Product Declaration systems (ISO 14025 2006) have been established in different geographical areas, such as Europe (Environdec 2014a), the USA (IERE 2014) and Japan (JEMAI 2014), aiming at the harmonisation of the methodologies of specific product groups. Among these systems, a large number of Product Category Rules (PCRs) have been developed. It is expected that methodologies, specifications and, in particular, PCRs will be further developed to provide a better, common ground for assessing and communicating results.

Communication of the carbon footprints of food products began in 2008

In 2008, a Finnish food manufacturer, the Raisio Group, which produces plant-based products, published their first carbon emission label (carbon label) on a product package, becoming one of the first food companies in the world to do so. According to their 2014 website, the carbon label was a natural continuation of several years of assessment of the GHG emissions caused by some of their products. Since 2008, many other food companies around the world have added carbon labels to their product packages and now numerous food products are carbon-labelled. For instance, at least six Finnish food companies put carbon labels on their packaging. In addition, the EU is testing the voluntary Product Environmental Footprint Guide initiative and a French governmental initiative (Environmental Product Declaration) is ongoing – it has been piloted with the aim of having climate impact information on all products in the near future (PEF World Forum 2013).

The lack of a commonly agreed LCA methodology has been one of the main barriers to adequate consumer communication, consequently the existing carbon labels are different in appearance and companies have a poor understanding of how to conduct environmental assessments. Without methodological uniformity between different assessments, consumers cannot accurately compare different carbon-labelled products with each other. The lack of uniformity is also seen as a problem in companies because the ambiguity and miscellaneous messages undermine consumer understanding, reducing their ability to arrive at a deep understanding of the issue. Additionally, the forerunners of environmental issues seek to improve their processes and environmental performance, but also need adequate tools to study their environmental impact. The possibility of being accused of "greenwashing" also provides companies with a strong incentive to first fully understand how to do a high-quality LCA before communicating their environmental impact.

Many food chain actors have faced the complexity and challenges of producing and communicating the carbon footprints of food products. For example, in Finland, some food manufacturers have asked for practical guidance on conducting LCA for their own food products. Additionally, due to growing consumer interest in sustainability, food manufacturers are increasingly interested in climate impact communication and communicating the sustainability of their products. In fact, the Raisio Group was the first food company in the world to add a water footprint to its product packaging, indicating the total virtual water consumption of the product.

It is important to harmonise both the communication and the LCA methodology, and to make the LCA more accessible. At the moment, the method requires access to resources, which makes it most appropriate for large companies, though work is ongoing to make the LCA accessible to small and medium-sized enterprises (SMEs) (see e.g. Doublet *et al.* 2014). In the future, it is hoped that the LCA will become more accessible if data collection becomes more automated and decentralised in the food chain (see e.g. MTT 2014, as an example of such initiatives). However, for now, it is important to promote the LCT and a simplified LCA to SMEs.

Finnish guidelines for the assessment of the GHG emissions of food chains

Due to growing interest in climate communication and the need for harmonised and accessible LCA methodologies, there has been a need for more specific guidelines in the Finnish food industry. In 2009, a Finnish project started with the aim of producing more detailed food product climate impact assessment guidelines for the Finnish food sector (MTT 2012). The project was initiated at the request of the food industry and included case studies on the carbon footprints of different food items (e.g. sausage, canola oil). The project also tested the guidelines as they were used in practice. The aim was to harmonise calculation methods and consequently the communication of footprints in the food sector while taking into account international developments and best practices.[1] Additionally, other aims were to provide guidelines that are simultaneously practical but which also push actors to make available adequate amounts of primary data so that LCA practitioners will obtain a good idea of the actual food chain and its environmental impact, thus ensuring the assessments have greater potential to lead to real improvements in the production chain.

In the Finnish guidelines, the topic of using adequate data sources was dealt with by specifying which data was to be collected directly from a supply chain and which data could be collected from national statistics, databases and other possible sources. Additionally, the methodology specified problems areas as well, such as methodological imprecision, like system boundaries and allocation rules. In the end, the guidelines were recognised by the food industry and attracted a lot of interest among its members. That happened because, in comparison to an earlier situation, the guidelines set common rules for the industry and laid a better basis for expanding the guidelines into other impact categories. Time will tell whether the guidelines will be introduced into the strategic and operational planning of companies.

Consumers are confused about how to make climate-friendly choices

The most important issues in climate communication are how the target groups, especially consumers, perceive such communication and what kind of impact it has on them. Since climate communication on food products has only existed since 2008 and because only a few companies communicate the climate impacts of their products, consumer interest in climate communication is speculative to a certain extent. If more and more food companies were to communicate the climate impacts of their products, it is expected that consumer understanding would slowly increase – as consumer interest in nutritional content has. Although Finnish food companies have communicated their products' nutritional content for over two decades, consumers have only really understood the information within the past decade. Additionally, one should bear in mind that while interest in sustainability has been a growing trend, interest does not always automatically turn into actual behaviour. For instance, simultaneously with increased consumer awareness of nutrition, there are now more overweight people in Finland than ever before. Also, a study on organic food products found a large gap between the intention to buy organic products and the market share of organic products (Röös and Tjärnemo 2011).

Regarding adaptation to climate change, the links between the increasing awareness of consumers and the actual changing of behaviour are more complicated. Namely, a number of consumer studies have revealed the desire of consumers to reduce their negative impact on the climate (see e.g. European Commission 2009; Hartikainen *et al.* 2014a). However, the consumers' understanding of the subject is rather limited. Hartikainen *et al.* (2014a) noted that Finnish consumers have a lack of understanding regarding their potential to make climate-friendly choices when it comes to food consumption. For instance, most consumers did not know that they can reduce their climate impact significantly by changing what they eat. Additionally, Finnish consumers have trouble comprehending the factors that contribute most to the load placed on the climate and environment by food production. Therefore, there is a need to educate consumers and make the subject more familiar to them, enabling consumption patterns that have fewer impacts on the climate.

Harmonisation of environmental communication about food

The Finnish food industry has actively discussed the potential for communicating the climate impacts caused by food production, and there is consensus on cooperative strategies to harmonise communication. With a uniform message it would be possible to improve consumers' understanding of the climate impacts of food production and consumption. With that aim in mind, in 2013, nine large Finnish food chain companies and three other stakeholders (two ministries and one research centre) signed a *Communication Recommendation* document to harmonise communication on the impact of food products on the climate and environment (MTT 2013). The recommendation refers to the *Finnish Guidelines for the Assessment of the Life Cycle GHG Emissions of Food* (MTT 2012) and recommends that the guidelines be used when communicating the assessment results of GHG emissions. The recommendation also gives instructions on how to communicate the climate and environmental impacts of food production. For instance, it suggests some specific terms that should be used to harmonise communication.

On the whole, the *Communication Recommendation* is perceived as a good tool for helping environmentally pro-active food companies harmonise their environmental communication. Many Finnish food companies have stated that common rules promote a level playing field and harmonised messages deepen consumer understanding, increasing consumer interest in the issue in the long run. During the process of writing the *Communication Recommendation* the food companies and their stakeholders also indicated that they were willing to cooperate in the future to further harmonise climate and environmental communication. For instance, while the labels used to identify the carbon footprint of a food product are different from each other at the moment, the long-term goal is to agree on one type of carbon label that is similar in design and is based on common LCA methodology.

A practical way towards a climate-friendly food consumption and food chain

Overall, the environmental impacts of food production and consumption are substantial and are expected to increase in the future, especially because of the growing demand for food due to population growth. As a result, there is an urgent need for instruments that can adapt to this situation and direct consumption and production patterns in a more sustainable direction. To accomplish that potential improvement and reduce the environmental impact of the whole food chain, a holistic lifecycle approach is required. Currently, LCA is the method preferred by researchers and politicians as well as the most used. The method does, however, have drawbacks as it lacks methodological precision and harmonisation, among other problems. The hope is that those issues will be tackled in coming years through extensive efforts by LCA practitioners, LCA guidelines and PCR developers. However, for now, while LCA itself is helpful when environmentally proactive food chain actors seek to improve their environmental performance, the final output, for example, a carbon footprint, may not yet be fully comparable due to methodological challenges. Hence, at the moment, the environmental footprinting of food products does not provide sufficient information for government incentive systems, such as taxation. Despite the lack of adequate tools and data to assess a food product's environmental impact, voluntary policy instruments, such as carbon footprinting, still remain potential tools for improving the environmental performance of a company. These voluntary instruments are also a crucial step in enabling the successful implementation of other possible future climate policy instruments, such as taxes and subsidies.

It is also crucial not to dismiss the other environmental impacts of food production, such as biodiversity losses and the depletion of freshwater resources. However, the assessment of GHG emissions is clearly one of the most methodologically developed impact categories, and hence readily available to companies. Therefore, carbon footprinting can provide a way for companies working in the food chain to reduce their environmental impact. Moreover, when companies assess their climate impact, they also learn the LCA in practice and can introduce the LCT into their planning. This enables possible future environmental assessments and overall sustainability assessments – when economic and social impacts are included in an assessment. In other words, carbon footprinting is an already available gateway for companies that wish to introduce practical and tangible sustainability assessments into their strategies and operations.

Furthermore, since carbon footprinting is a concrete and practical method, it will likely pressure other food chain actors into making GHG emissions reductions. Through measurements practitioners will know their present GHG emissions and can set up targets to decrease their emissions. Additionally, the LCA enables lifecycle practitioners to identify hot spots where GHG reductions are the most effective, leading to overall, optimised improvements in the food chains' climate impacts. However, the LCA methodology still needs to be developed further and, in particular, harmonised in order to enable adequate communication.

Food companies can use product-level carbon footprint information and so can consumers, NGOs, politicians and authorities. Generally, carbon footprinting is intended as a consumer-oriented climate policy tool, and carbon labels on product packages are one of the most common examples of these. If consumer demand for carbon-labelled products increases, it will also create a clear driver for companies wishing to assess and communicate their carbon footprint and the need for clear rules regarding LCA. While companies seek to create more value for their products when using carbon labels, these labels can also direct consumer behaviour or, at least, make carbon footprints a customary thing for them, raising awareness of the fact that food has a substantial impact on climate. Communication about the climate impacts of food production and how consumers can contribute to reducing those impacts by changing their food consumption habits is important. This is because consumers are currently confused as to how to make climate-friendly food choices, though they have the potential to reduce their food-related climate impact to a great extent.

Conclusion

Carbon footprinting can foster long-term commitment to reducing total GHG emissions, thus minimising future emissions. Moreover, initiating footprinting now enables possible future climate policy instruments, such as taxes and subsidies. In addition, increased information on the climate impact of food production also raises public awareness of the issue. However, GHG emission reductions in food production and consumption are currently limited, while the demand for food is expected to increase. Consequently, carbon footprinting and climate communication should be seen first and foremost as tools to mitigate and to adapt to climate change.

The Finnish initiatives to provide food producers with more practical tools for assessing their GHG emissions, as well as the joint communication agreement between the food industry and its stakeholders, on how to communicate the impact of food production on the climate and environment, are good examples of action that could be taken in other countries, too. According to the Finnish experience, the initiatives have increased the food companies' knowledge of environmental issues and the ability to assess their environmental impact. The initiatives have also provided a better basis for improving consumer understanding of the issue via harmonised messages. They also set common rules for other stakeholders in the food chain, such as administrative organisations, NGOs and consulting firms, thus orienting and harmonising the whole communication of the environmental impact of a food product. Consequently, this is expected to deepen overall understanding on the issue. Time will tell whether the two initiatives will actually increase environmental assessment and the communication of the environmental impacts of food production. At the very least, such initiatives will help to set common rules for harmonising environmental assessments and communication.

Note

1 While the project was unique in Finland, it should be noted that projects to build LCA specifications (for food products, too) have existed in the past decade (see e.g. Environdec 2014b).

References

Åström, S., Roth, S., Wranne, J., Jelse, K. and Lindblad, M. (2013) *Food Consumption Choices and Climate Change*. Göteborg: Swedish Environmental Research Institute.

Berners-Lee, M., Hoolohan, C., Cammack, H. and Hewitt, C.N. (2012) The relative greenhouse gas impacts of realistic dietary choices. *Journal of Energy Policy*, 43: 184–190.

British Standards Institute (2011) PAS2050 Specification for the assessment of the life cycle greenhouse gas emissions of goods and services. England: BSI Group.

Carlsson-Kanyama, A. and Gonzalez, A.D. (2009) Potential contributions of food consumption patterns to climate change. *American Journal of Clinical Nutrition*, 89(5): 1704–1709.

Cassman, K. (1999) Ecologial intensification of cereal production systems: yield potential, soil quality, and precision agriculture. *Proceedings of the National Academy of Sciences of the USA*, 96: 2952–2959.

Doublet, G., Ingólfsdóttir, G.M., Yngvadóttir, E., Landquist, B., Jungbluth, N., Aronsson, A., Ramos, S., Keller, R. and Ólafsdóttir, G. (2014) Key Environmental Performance Indicators for a simplified LCA in food supply chains. Paper presented at 9th International Conference LCA of Food, San Francisco, 8–10 October 2014, Seminar presentation. Available at: www.senseproject.eu/images/publications/Oral246.pdf (accessed 8 January 2015).

Dutch Horticulture Specification (2009) Carbon footprinting of horticultural products for business to business communication: calculating greenhouse gas emissions of horticultural products as a specification of the PAS2050 protocol. Available at: www.tuinbouw.nl/sites/default/files/Protocol%20engles.pdf (accessed 6 December 2014).

Ekvall, T. and Finnveden, G. (2001) Allocation in ISO 14041: a critical review. *Journal of Cleaner Production*, 9: 197–208.

Environdec (2014a) The International EPD System: A Communications Tool for International Markets. Available at: www.environdec.com/ (accessed 7 November 2014).

Environdec (2014b) Product Category Rules (PCR). Available at: www.environdec.com/en/PCR/ (accessed 30 October 2014).

European Commission (2009) Europeans' attitudes towards the issue of sustainable consumption and production. Analytical report, Flash EB Series 256. EC.

FAO, IFAD and WFP (2013) *The State of Food Insecurity in the World, 2013: The Multiple Dimensions of Food Security by FAO, IFAD and WFP*. Rome: FAO.

Foley, J.A., Ramankutty, N., Brauman, K.A. *et al.* (2011) Solutions for a cultivated planet. *Nature*, 478: 337–342.

Hartikainen, H., Roininen, T., Katajajuuri, J.M. and Pulkkinen, H. (2014a) Finnish consumer perceptions of carbon footprints and carbon labeling of food products. *Journal of Cleaner Production*, 73: 285–293.

Hartikainen, H., Silvenius, F. and Katajajuuri, J.M. (2014b) Critical review of allocation rules: the case of Finnish rainbow trout. Paper presented at 9th International Conference LCA of Food San Francisco USA 8–10 October 2014, Seminar presentation. Available at: http://lcafood2014.org/papers/233.pdf (accessed 30 October 2014).

IERE (2014) Earthsure. Available at: http://iere.org/programs/earthsure/ (accessed 7 November 2014).

ILCD (2010) *Handbook of International Reference Life Cycle Data System: General Guide for Life Cycle Assessment: Detailed Guidance*, First edition, Brussels: JRC, European Union.

IPCC (2007) *Climate Change 2007: The Physical Science Basis: Contribution of Working Group I to the Fourth Assessment Report of the Intergovernmental Panel on Climate Change*. ed. S. Solomon, D. Qin, M. Manning *et al.* Cambridge: Cambridge University Press. Available at: www.ipcc.ch/publications_and_data/publications_ipcc_fourth_assessment_report_wg1_report_the_physical_science_basis.htm (accessed 30 October 2014).

IPCC (2014) *Summary for Policymakers: IPCC Fifth Assessment Synthesis Report* 40. Available at: www.ipcc.ch/pdf/assessment-report/ar5/syr/SYR_AR5_SPM.pdf (accessed 30 October 2014).

ISO 14025 (2006) Environmental labels and declarations. Type III environmental declarations. Principles and procedures, Standard. Geneva: International Organization for Standardization.

ISO 14040 (2006) Environmental management. Life cycle assessment. Principles and framework, Standard. Geneva: International Organization for Standardization.

ISO 14044 (2006) Environmental management. Life cycle assessment. Requirements and guidelines, Standard. Geneva: International Organization for Standardization.

JEMAI (2014) EcoLeaf Environmental Label. Available at: www.ecoleaf-jemai.jp/eng/ (accessed 7 November 2014).

Leach, M., Rockström, J., Raskin, P., Scoones, I., Stirling, A.C., Smith, A., Thompson, J., Millstone, E., Ely, A., Arond, E., Folke, K. and Olsson, P. (2012) Transforming innovation for sustainability. *Ecology and Society*, 17: 11.

MTT (2012) *Guidelines for the Assessment of the Life Cycle Greenhouse Gas Emissions of Food*. Helsinki, 7 November 2012. Available at: www.mtt.fi/foodprint (accessed 30 October 2014). [In Finnish.]

MTT (2013) Recommendations for communication of the environmental impacts of food products. Helsinki 2 October 2013. Available at: https://portal.mtt.fi/portal/page/portal/mtt/hankkeet/climate-communication-I-II/Elintarvikkeiden%20ilmastoviestint%C3%A4%20Suomessa%20-seminaari%202.10.2013/Etenemissuositus.pdf (accessed 30 October 2014). [In Finnish.]

MTT (2014) EcoModules: connecting partners and improving environmental performance with empowered LCA. Available at: https://portal.mtt.fi/portal/page/portal/mtt_en/projects/bioconvention%202014/ecomodules (accessed 8 January 2015).

Nemecek, T., Schnetzer, J. and Reinhard, J. (2014) Updated and harmonised greenhouse gas emissions for crop inventories. *International Journal of Life Cycle Assessment*. DOI: 10.1007/s11367-014-0712-7.

PEF World Forum (2013) Environment Product Declaration, France. Available at: www.pef-world-forum.org/initiatives/country-governmental-initiatives/france/ (accessed 8 January 2015).

Peltonen-Sainio, P. (2012) Crop production in a northern climate. In A. Meybeck, J. Lankoski, S. Redfern, N. Azzu and V. Getz (eds) *Proceedings of a Joint FAO/OECD Workshop, Building Resilience to Climate Change in the Agriculture Sector*, pp. 183–216. Available at: www.fao.org/agriculture/crops/news-events-bulletins/detail/en/item/134976/ (accessed 30 October 2014).

Raisio (2014) Company website. Available at: www.raisio.com/www/page/mainpage (accessed 30 October 2014).

Ray, D.K., Ramankutty, N., Mueller, N.D., West, P.C. and Foley, J.A. (2012) Recent patterns of crop yield growth and stagnation. *Nature Communications*, 3: 1293.

Regina, K., Lehtonen, H. and Perälä, P. (2011) [The role of agriculture as a greenhouse gas emissions producer and as a part of climate policy.] Maatalouden rooli kasvihuonekaasupäästöjen tuottajana ja osana ilmastopolitiikkaa, Selvitys Maa-ja metsätalousministeriölle, Maa-ja elintarviketalouden tutkimuskeskus MTT. [In Finnish.]

Rockström, J., Steffen, W. and Noone, K. (2009) A safe operating space for humanity. *Nature*, 461: 472–475.

Röös, E. and Tjärnemo, H. (2011) Challenges of carbon labelling of food products: a consumer research perspective. *British Food Journal*, 113: 8.

Seppälä, J., Mäenpää, I., Koskela, S., Mattila, T., Nissinen, A., Katajajuuri, J.M., Härmä, T., Korhonen, M.R., Saarinen, M. and Virtanen, Y. (2009) [The environmental impact assessment of material flows of Finland's national economy with the ENVIMAT-model]. Suomen kansantalouden materiaalivirtojen ympäristövaikutusten arviointi ENVIMAT-mallilla Suomen Ympäristö 20/2009 Suomen ympäristökeskus SYKE. [In Finnish.]

Soussana, J.F., Fereres, E., Long, S., Mohren, F.M.J., Panday-Lorch, R., Peltonen-Sainio, P., Porter, J.R., Rosswall, T. and von Braun, J. (2012) A European science plan to sustainably increase food security under climate change. *Global Change Biology*, 18: 3269–3271.

Tukker, A. and Jansen, B. (2006) Environmental impacts for products. *Journal of Industrial Ecology*, 10(3): 159–182.

UNEP (2010) *Assessing the Environmental Impacts of Consumption and Production: Priority Products and Materials, A Report of the Working Group on the Environmental Impacts of Products and Materials to the International Panel for Sustainable Resource Management.* Ed. E. Hertwich, E. van der Voet, S. Suh, A. Tukker, M. Huijbregts, P. Kazmierczyk, M. Lenzen, J. McNeely and Y. Moriguchi. UNEP. Available at: www.greeningtheblue.org/sites/default/files/Assessing%20the%20environmental%20impacts%20consumption%20and%20production.pdf (accessed 6 December 2014).

Weidema, B.P., Wesnæs, M., Hermansen, J., Kristensen, T., Halberg, N., Eder, P. and Delgado, L. (2008) Environmental improvement potentials of meat and dairy products. European Commission Joint Research Centre (JRC) – Institute for Prospective Technological Studies (IPTS) Report No. EUR 23491 EN 2008. Available at: http://ftp.jrc.es/EURdoc/JRC46650.pdf (accessed 6 December 2014).

WRI/WBCSD (2011) Greenhouse Gas Protocol, Product Life Cycle Accounting and Reporting Standard. Washington, DC: World Resources Institute/WBCSD.

Part III

Sustainable livelihood, community and farm resilience

9 Good farmers, good adapters? How a cultural understanding of good farming affects the adaptive capacity of farmers

Suvi Huttunen, Hanna Mela and Mikael Hildén

Introduction

The ability to adapt to external pressures forms an essential part of farming and its ability to survive (Darnhofer *et al.* 2010; Milestad *et al.* 2012). In this sense, adaptation to climate change differs little from fluctuating commodity prices, changing policies and environmental demands, for example. There are a few studies on the adaptive capacity of farmers to alter farming practices according to climate change in industrialised countries. In contrast, changes in farming trajectories under general external pressures and the design of suitable policies to support the movement of farming systems in a desirable direction have been well studied (e.g. Wilson 2008; Sutherland *et al.* 2012; de Sainte Marie 2014). These studies provide important insights that are relevant for the adaptive capacity related to climate change and form the basis for the development of studies that can achieve a deeper understanding of the socio-cultural factors influencing adaptation (Wise *et al.* 2014).

Studies of the transition of farms to more sustainable production practices have revealed difficulties that involve conflict with farming culture, such as local norms, identity and cultural capital (Burton *et al.* 2008; Sutherland *et al.* 2012). On a more systemic level, the organisation of the agri-food sector and the institutional context greatly influence farming practices (e.g. Spaargaren *et al.* 2012). Furthermore, the changes observed at the farm level (farming trajectories) do not proceed linearly, but are often complex, inconsistent and highly influenced by farm household specificities (Wilson 2008). Studies related to climate change adaptation, on the other hand, recognise the need to increase the understanding of the interdependencies between adaptation and, for example, norms, values and knowledge cultures (Adger *et al.* 2013; Wise *et al.* 2014). In this chapter, we focus on the cultural understanding of good farming, and explore its relationship to adaptive capacity in the context of Finnish agricultural policy and climate change.

An interest in good farming derives from studies related to the adoption and efficiency of agri-environmental schemes in the EU, which have demonstrated that social norms and cultural capital related to the perception of good farming practices can create significant barriers to the success of agri-environmental measures (e.g. Burton *et al.* 2008). Similarly, the perceptions related to good farming may affect the ability to adapt to climate change. In particular, we are interested in the following questions: (1) how does good farming relate to the ability to adapt to climate change, and (2) how do agricultural policies affect the adaptive capacity of Finnish farms from the viewpoint of good farming?

We approach this by identifying three essential dimensions of adaptive capacity and examine how they are mapped onto four commonly identified elements of good farming, allowing us to examine the interrelated role of social norms, socio-cultural capital and identity in influencing farmers' adaptive capacity in the form of good farming. Furthermore, this enables us to study how these are likely to be played out in concrete policies, which is exemplified by the new Rural Development Programme (RDP) for the years 2014–2020 (MAF 2014). We start by examining the need to adapt from the perspective of the most likely changes that climate change will bring about in Finland. Then we explore the concepts of adaptive capacity and good farming, which provide us with the analytical framework through which policies can be examined.

Adaptation needs

Climate change is likely to significantly alter the conditions under which agriculture is practised in Finland. By the end of the century, the thermal growing season is projected to be 1–1.5 months longer than in the period 1971–2000 (Ruosteenoja *et al.* 2011). As a result of average temperature rise, it will be possible to grow crops further north and a marked growth in potential yields is expected. Winter cereals that have a higher yield potential are likely to replace spring cereals when their over-wintering capacity becomes sufficient for a particular region. Furthermore, crops that are currently of little importance in Finland, such as oilseed rape, pea and fava bean, can be grown on larger areas in the future, meaning the potential for a significant increase in protein feed self-sufficiency (Peltonen-Sainio *et al.* 2009).

However, the realisation of these potentials is uncertain. For example, new plant varieties are needed to achieve the higher yields (Peltonen-Sainio *et al.* 2009, 2011). Climate change will also increase the risk of adverse weather events that can hamper the potential growth in the production of Finnish agriculture. Extreme weather events such as heatwaves, drought in the summer or heavy rainfall are projected to become more frequent. Increased temperatures and humidity as well as milder winters are likely to increase the occurrence of various pests and diseases, which adds to the uncertainty of production. Less snow cover and frost in wintertime will mean wetter soil and a poorer carrying capacity with risks related to soil compression, leaching and erosion. On the other hand, the increased cultivation of winter cereals can help to protect against these adverse developments (Peltonen-Sainio *et al.* 2009).

Important adaptation needs in Finnish farming include the development of new control methods for pests and plant disease; plant breeding for the development of plants suitable for the future climate; the maintenance of soil quality;

developing risk control methods related to agricultural production and income, especially those related to extreme weather events; and animal nutrition and health risk control (MAF 2011). The security of supply and the potential to increase self-sufficiency in protein feed need to be maintained. Environmental demands require the reduction of the eutrophication of waters, which will require new cultivation techniques for the changing climate.

At the farm level, these changes would require a readiness to adopt new plant breeds, changes in timing and methods of cultivation and related practices and an increased commitment to maintaining soil condition and water management. They also raise questions about the adaptive capacity of farms and the whole farming system, but are also connected to the perception of good farming.

Linking adaptive capacity to good farming

Adaptive capacity

The IPCC has defined adaptation to be "the process of adjustment to actual or expected climate and its effects. In human systems, adaptation seeks to moderate or avoid harm or exploit beneficial opportunities" (IPCC 2014: 5). Adaptation can be incremental, requiring only small modifications to current practices, or transformational, in which case more fundamental changes are required (Nelson *et al.* 2007). Adaptive capacity (or adaptability) means the ability of a system, region, community or an individual to respond and adjust to the stresses caused by climate change (Gallopin 2006). It involves both resilience to changes and the ability to transform farming methods in a desired direction while demonstrating the potential for implementing adaptations (Engle 2011).

In studies on farming systems, adaptive management has emerged as a way to better respond to uncertainty and surprises in the farming environment, while recognising change and diversity in farmers' goals and perceptions (Milestad *et al.* 2012). Adaptive management aims at building adaptive capacity on farms and is seen as helping farmers because climate change can be seen as a core factor causing uncertainty and adaptation needs (Marshall *et al.* 2012). Darnhofer *et al.* (2010) have suggested that a farming system's strategies should increase its adaptive capacity to include greater learning ability, flexibility and diversification. We will use those ideas to examine the adaptive capacity of Finnish farms to cope with climate change.

Through *learning*, the farmer sees new perspectives and perceives new opportunities related to climate change – understanding how and when to adapt. Evidence of learning includes the use of extension services, experiments with new practices and the active monitoring of change.

Flexibility is an indication of a farmer's ability to adapt both in the short term and more strategically in the long term. It implies an ability to adjust farming activities to cope with or benefit from climate change. Evidence of flexibility includes the active building of the capacity to react to different conditions or extreme events, for example, dealing with drought or becoming familiar with a wider range of cultivars.

Diversification of resources increases the options to act and do a variety of things in the face of change. For example, the capacity for irrigation when faced with drought allows a wider set of crops than a pure rain-fed agriculture and the existence of resources for non-agricultural activities can stabilise income. Evidence of diversification can be found in the variety of crops and the production units and lines of a farm.

The scale of adaptation needed determines the relevance of the adaptive capacity (Marshall *et al.* 2012), though it should be recognised that individuals have different adaptive capacities. Adaptive capacity is not static, it can change and it can also be influenced by policies. The primary goal of adaptation policies is often to enhance adaptive capacity at individual, community and societal levels because predicting actual adaptation needs well in advance is difficult. Furthermore, the various policies of different domains have direct and indirect effects on adaptive capacity, stressing the importance of the ability to integrate adaptation policies with other policy domains.

Cultural factors are likely to affect adaptive capacity in many ways. For example, place attachment and occupational identity among farmers have been observed to reduce the capacity to make radical changes, which might be necessary for long-term transformational adaptation (ibid.). However, in the short term, the same factors can be an asset because they motivate adaptation through a wish to continue farming. Similarly, social and cultural capital can function as important reinforcing assets for adaptive capacity (Pelling and Hing 2005), but they can also have counter-effects as, for example, social networks can reduce the feeling of risk related to the climate (Wolf *et al.* 2010).

Good farming

Numerous studies have found that the perception of good farming plays an important role in determining farming practices (e.g. Silvasti 2003; Burton 2004; Singleton 2012; Sutherland 2013). Perhaps the most widely adopted theoretical framing of good farming derives from Pierre Bourdieu's conceptualisation of social and cultural capital (e.g. Burton *et al.* 2008). In the farming context, being a good farmer is valued in the community and it means the possession of cultural capital. Good farming is demonstrated via symbols, which in farming typically include tidy fields, quality livestock and high yields (Sutherland 2013). Presenting these symbols brings acceptance in the eyes of the local farming community, making the issues related to good farming difficult to change. Good farming is often connected to traditional farming community values, which differ from entrepreneurial farming. However, it seems that core values are quite persistent as they are embedded in farming practices (Sutherland and Darnhofer 2012). The core features of good farming in Western, industrialised farming systems have been found to be productivity, independence, continuity and stewardship.[1]

Productivity implies that farmers aim at *efficiently producing food*, which is seen to require healthy and productive animals and tidy fields directly related to the appearance of the farm as well as skill in producing high yields (Silvasti 2003; Burton 2004; Vanclay *et al.* 2007; Niska *et al.* 2012). A farmer is a steward and untended land can even be regarded as the sign of an immoral farmer (Silvasti 2003; Vanclay *et al.* 2007). The emphasis on productivity is also visible in the observation that farmers have found it difficult to accept subsidies that are unrelated to production volumes, which seems to suggest that it is unacceptable to "pretend to produce food" (Silvasti 2009; Hangasmaa 2011). The production of mere environmental or scenic values is consequently easily labelled "quasi-farming" (Huttunen 2015). Some policies, such as those demanding the establishment of protective strips along water courses, have also clashed with the idea of tidy, high-yielding fields (Burton *et al.* 2008).

Independence means the ability to make autonomous decisions and it implies, for example, ownership of a sufficient number of machines so that decisions on what to grow and when to harvest can be made independently of other farms (Sutherland and Burton 2011). According to a recent farmer survey, the most important values for Finnish farmers are autonomy and economic profitability (Niska *et al.* 2012).

Farm continuity has been identified as a central value for farmers (e.g. Silvasti 2003; Stock 2007). Continuity primarily means that the time-frame of thinking extends over generations: the things I do now affect future generations. That can lead to conservatism and thus older farmers in particular may be unwilling to launch changes which tie the hands of their successor (Ingram *et al.* 2013). Farm continuity is closely linked to family farming. In Finland, recent survey results have not strongly emphasised continuity: continuing a family tradition or the work of one's parents was important for about half of the respondents (Niska *et al.* 2012). This can partially be explained by the difficulty of making an income from farming and the reduced pressure on children to take over the farm (Silvasti 2009). Continuity generally means enabling future generations to continue farming, not forcing them to do so (Hangasmaa 2011).

Stewardship means taking good care of the land and animals (Singleton 2012). Caring involves observation, the accumulation of tacit knowledge and skills and an ability to adapt. A good farmer is able to pass the farm to the next generation in good condition (Stock 2007). Silvasti (2003) identified stewardship by observing that the most valued land is that which is made productive. This also included living in harmony with nature in terms of not exploiting the land, but maintaining it for the next generation in terms of continuity. Social responsibility in the form of rural viability and respect for nature were important for over 75 per cent of Finnish farmers responding to a survey (Niska *et al.* 2012). Singleton (2012) has, however, suggested that the technical monitoring and rules related to current EU agricultural policies hamper the realisation of caring practices inherent in good farming.

Combining adaptive capacity and good farming

Based on a review of the relevant literature, we can link the good farming elements with the characteristics of adaptive capacity (Table 9.1). This cross-tabulation shows that good farming has both positive and negative implications for adaptive capacity. It seems that the positive links are more numerous and stronger. This can be regarded as a natural consequence of both adaptive capacity and good farming aiming at continued farming and economic viability. The positive implications are mostly realised through learning and flexibility.

The most important challenges to the adaptive capacity of farms are likely to arise from productivist values. They can narrow the perspective of development to merely increasing productivity, which can reduce diversification and increase vulnerability to particular aspects of climate change, such as extreme weather events or the increased frequency of pests. Additionally, too strong an emphasis on historical farm continuity may hamper the recognition of new emerging risks or opportunities and the ability to see the broader changes occurring in the future.

Overall, it seems that good farming strengthens short-term adaptive capacity, but its implications for longer-term transformative adaptation are not so clear. The comparison suggests that policy measures are needed, especially to overcome the potentially too simplistic focus on productivity and provide ways to find a balance between short-term coping and long-term adaptive capacity.

Policies influencing adaptation in agriculture

Policies for adaptation

In Finland, the National Adaptation Strategy of 2005 (revised in 2014) has provided guidance on adaptation. The Ministry of Agriculture and Forestry (MAF) has prepared a more specific action plan for the implementation of the adaptation strategy in the agricultural sector (MAF 2011). Beyond the 14 actions described in the action plan, the most important document steering agriculture is the new Rural Development Programme (RDP) for the years 2014–2020 (MAF 2014). It is therefore of interest to see how it relates to the adaptive capacity as identified above.

The RDP broadly aims at promoting a sustainable bio-economy, including agriculture, and diversifying the economic structure in rural areas and increasing rural viability. It includes a wide set of measures providing financial support for activities ranging from advisory services and educational projects to investments and environmentally friendly farming practices. Looking at these measures through the lens of adaptive capacity, we identified how the measures included in the programme are likely to influence learning, flexibility and diversity (Table 9.2).

Measures likely to affect all dimensions of adaptive capacity can be identified (Table 9.2). However, it seems that the most directly influential measures and also the measures with most of the funding are geared towards the diversification

Table 9.1 How the characteristics of good farming influence adaptive capacity

Characteristic of adaptive capacity	*Learning (Knowledge of what to change)*	*Flexibility (Capabilities/skills for how to change)*	*Diversification of resources (Resources to change)*
Meaning of good farming			
Productivity	– Can narrow the perspective of learning to increasing productivity, which can result in the neglect of environmental effects and emerging changes + Encourages the search for ways to benefit from climate change	– Can narrow the focus on skills development to only a particular production type, leading to a low capacity for transformative change and vulnerability to specific climate-related impacts + Provides incentives for the continuous development of farming practices, for example, by adopting new cultivars or varieties	– Focusing on the production of a specific product decreases the availability of resources for change + Successful increase of productivity increases farm income and thus the overall resources available for change and diversification
Independence	+ Encourages the search for new knowledge about how to cope with or benefit from climate change	+ Encourages the development of skills	– May limit opportunities for diversification if co-ownership or other cooperation is limited + Makes the farm more capable of autonomously using available resources
Continuity	– Can hamper the recognition of new risks or downplay their importance + Provides a strong motivation for maintaining the family farm and thus for acquiring new knowledge for farm management	– Restricts flexibility in terms of large changes to the farm-based income and may reduce willingness to make changes close to retirement + Provides high motivation to maintain the family farm and thus for acquiring new skills for farm management	+ Encourages the maintenance and improvement of farm resources, e.g. soil condition and farm buildings
Stewardship	+ Encourages the observing and understanding of changes related to nature on the farm	– Can hamper the ability and willingness to change practices towards a less maintained natural environment + Encourages the development of skills related to maintaining the productivity of the natural environment	+ Encourages the maintenance of productive natural resources

Table 9.2 RDP measures influencing farmers' adaptive capacity

	Learning	*Flexibility*	*Diversification of resources*
Direct effect	Knowledge transfer and information actions (M01) Advisory services, farm management and farm relief services (M02) Cooperation (M16)	Knowledge transfer and information actions (M01) Cooperation (M16)	Investments in physical assets (M04) Farm and business development (M06) Agri-environment-climate (M10) Cooperation (M16)
Indirect effect	Agri-environment-climate (M10) Organic farming (M11) Support for local development (the so-called LEADER, M19)	Investments in physical assets (M04) Farm and business development (M06) Agri-environment-climate (M10) Organic farming (M11) Support for LEADER local development (M19)	Basic services and village renewal in rural areas (M07) Organic farming (M11) Payments to areas facing natural or other specific constraints (M13) Animal welfare (M14) Support for LEADER local development (M19)

Note: Numbers in brackets refer to the number given to the measure in the RDP.

of resources. About a quarter of the funding originating from the EU is allocated to the agri-environment-climate measure, with investments in physical assets and farm and business development receiving about 6–7 per cent each. The relatively high emphasis on diversification is partially explained by the focus of the RDP on subsidies as enabling resources to be paid to farmers.

Most of the subsidies appear to support adaptation. However, some can also result in maladaptation. For example, investment support can reduce diversification and increase risks on farms as it tends to encourage farmers to focus on the production of one particular product. The support provided under agri-environment measures and less favoured areas (LFA) measures may counteract long-term diversification if they maintain short-term quasi-farming with no encouragement to develop farms or farming livelihoods.

There are fewer measures that can directly support learning and especially flexibility and they are financially less important than the subsidies. They support knowledge transfer in educational or information transfer-related projects, advisory services and cooperative activities. In the few measures directly influencing flexibility, actual skill transfer plays a minor role. Education to improve skills is supported, but the RDP does not specify how large a share of this will be focused on actual skills rather than just providing information.

Indirectly agri-environment-climate measures can support learning, for example, through the compulsory monitoring of soil fertility. The agri-environment-climate measures can also encourage farmers to try different actions and thus contribute to learning and skills. Furthermore, support for farming experiments (included in M06) and support for investments in the development of agricultural products (included in M04) can indirectly contribute to skill creation.

Despite the rather wide range of available measures, the descriptions of climate change adaptation remain vague in the RDP. Adaptation or adaptive capacity is seldom explicitly mentioned under the measures, even if they could directly affect adaptive capacity. This increases the risk for maladaptation and means that the RDP misses opportunities to actively strengthen adaptive capacity.

How does good farming fit in with adaptive capacity in agricultural policies?

A farmer's perception of good farming interferes with the effect of policies that can support adaptive capacity. As indicated in Table 9.1, the perception of good farming can strengthen adaptive capacity, especially in relation to learning and flexibility. This suggests that the cultural perception of good farming can support somewhat weak policy efforts in the areas of flexibility and learning (Table 9.2). Good farming is also likely to reduce the risk of quasi-farming that the RDP otherwise partly encourages.

The fact that the RDP is virtually silent on adaptation means that it can accentuate the problems that good farming can cause for adaptive capacity. The RDP can encourage interpretations – especially of productivity and continuity – that are non-adaptive by focusing on what has worked in the past rather than on future changes. Such a narrow focus can partially be strengthened by agri-environmental measures or by extension services. For example, agri-environmental measures that aim at compensating for the costs imposed by adopting specific measures, instead of encouraging diversification for future conditions, miss an important way of providing incentives for adaptation.

The ideals of good farming seem to focus on shorter-term adaptation with farm continuity rather than wider transformation in mind. For example, Australian farmers have adjusted to short-term risks by themselves as these risks involved the farm's current operation (Raymond and Robinson 2013). Long-term risks, on the other hand, are more difficult to prepare for. The preparation for long-term risks would require policy support. In Finland, the RDP could become such a policy instrument. It would require adaptation-based selection criteria for activities to be supported under the RDP.

Another method could be developed by encouraging a gradual change in the perception of good farming towards being adaptable. This would require activities supporting adaptation and the explicit recognition of the adaptive role of the activities. In this way, both skills and the meanings related to farming practices could foster adaptation and its desirability. This could build on the result-based agri-environmental measures, where farmers are compensated on the basis of environmental results obtained, such as increasing biodiversity or better adaptation to extreme events, instead of receiving compensation for the costs of predefined measures (e.g. Burton and Paragahawewa 2011; de Sainte Marie 2014). Such a pathway could lead to the greater appreciation of the environmental goods that are beneficial for adaptation, even if they do not necessarily support short-term farm income. Besides supporting policies, the appreciation of adaptability could also be promoted by other actors in the food supply chain.

Conclusion

In the agricultural context, it is generally acknowledged that besides modelling, participatory approaches are needed to identify the most suitable farming adaptation strategies relevant for stakeholders (e.g. Webb and Stokes 2012; Mitter *et al.* 2014). Our study points to the need to expand these enquiries to include the role of cultural factors and shows that there are fruitful lessons to be learned from general farming system change studies with regard to climate change adaptation. In order to truly acquire that level of understanding regarding the current cultural barriers and enablers for adaptation in Finnish agricultural systems, the implementation of the Rural Development Programme should recognise adaptation to climate change and actively promote it. The monitoring and evaluation of the programme could then provide a vehicle for policy learning.

Acknowledgements

The research was funded by the Ministry of Agriculture and Forestry (Project Polkeva) and the Academy of Finland (decision no. 277896).

Note

1 It should be noted that the details of good farming are likely to be regionally specific (Sutherland 2013), subject to continuous slow change (Sutherland and Burton 2011) and may also differ between different groups of farmers in the same region, for example, between organic and conventional farmers (Stock 2007; Hunt 2010).

References

Adger, W.N., Barnett, J., Brown, K., Marshall, N. and O'Brien, K. (2013) Cultural dimensions of climate change impacts and adaptation. *Nature Climate Change*, 3: 112–117.

Burton, R. (2004) Reconceptualising the "behavioural approach" in agricultural studies: a socio-psychological perspective. *Journal of Rural Studies*, 20: 359–371.

Burton, R., Kuczera, C. and Schwarz, G. (2008) Exploring farmers' cultural resistance to voluntary agri-environmental schemes. *Sociologia Ruralis*, 48: 16–37.

Burton, R. and Paragahawewa, U. (2011) Creating culturally sustainable agri-environmental schemes. *Journal of Rural Studies*, 27: 95–104.

Darnhofer, I., Bellon, S., Dedieu, B. and Milestad, R. (2010) Adaptiveness to enhance the sustainability of farming systems. *Agronomy for Sustainable Development*, 30: 545–555.

de Sainte Marie, C. (2014) Rethinking agri-environmental schemes: a result-oriented approach to the management of species-rich grasslands in France. *Journal of Environmental Planning and Management*, 57: 704–719.

Engle, N.L. (2011) Adaptive capacity and its assessment. *Global Environmental Change*, 21: 647–656.

Gallopin, G. (2006) Linkages between vulnerability, resilience, and adaptive capacity. *Global Environmental Change*, 16: 293–303.

Hangasmaa, L. (2011) Maanviljelyn kulttuurinen kestävyys – määrittelyn ja mittaamisen haasteita. *Maaseudun Uusi Aika*, 1: 61–70.

Hunt, L. (2010) Interpreting orchardists' talk about their orchards: the good orchardists. *Agrculture and Human Values*, 27: 415–426.

Huttunen, S. (2015) Farming practices and experienced policy coherence in agri-environmental policies: the case of land clearing in Finland. *Journal of Environmental Policy & Planning*. DOI: 10.1080/1523908x.2014.1003348.

Ingram, J., Gaskell, P., Mills, J. and Short, C. (2013) Incorporating agri-environmental schemes into farm development pathways: a temporal analysis of farmer motivations. *Land Use Policy*, 31: 267–279.

IPCC (2014) Summary for policymakers. In *Climate Change 2014: Impacts, Adaptation, and Vulnerability. Part A: Global and Sectoral Aspects. Contribution of Working Group II to the Fifth Assessment Report of the Intergovernmental Panel on Climate Change*. Cambridge: Cambridge University Press, pp. 1–32.

MAF (2011) *Action Plan for the Adaptation to Climate Change of the Ministry of Agriculture and Forestry 2011–2015. Security of Supply, Sustainable Competitiveness and Risk Management*. Ministry of Agriculture and Forestry. Memorandum. Available at: www.mmm.fi/attachments/mmm/julkaisut/muutjulkaisut/5yZhPxNpC/MMM_n_ilmastonmuutoksen_sopeutumisen_toimintaohjelma.pdf (accessed 24 October 2014) [In Finnish with an English abstract].

MAF (2014) Esitys Manner-Suomen maaseudun kehittämisohjelmaksi 2014–2020. Available at: www.mmm.fi/attachments/maaseutu/mZu0GyoRB/Luonnos4_Manner-Suomen_maaseudun_kehittamisohjelmaksi_2014-2020_15.4.2014.pdf (accessed 24 October 2014) [In Finnish].

Marshall, N.A., Park, S.E., Adger, W.N., Brown, K. and Howden, S.M. (2012) Transformational capacity and the influence of place and identity. *Environmental Research Letters*, 7: 034022.

Milestad, R., Fedieu, B., Darnhofer, I. and Bellon, S. (2012) Farms and farmers facing change: the adaptive approach. In I. Darnhofer, D. Gibbon and B. Dedieu (eds) *Farming Systems Research into the 21st Century: The New Dynamic*. New York: Springer, pp. 365–385.

Mitter, H., Kirchner, M., Schmid, E. and Schönhart, M. (2014) The participation of agricultural stakeholders in assessing regional vulnerability of cropland to soil water erosion in Austria. *Regional Environmental Change*, 14: 385–400.

Nelson, D.R., Adger, W.N. and Brown, K. (2007) Adaptation to environmental change: contributions of a resilience framework. *Annual Review of Environment and Resources*, 32: 395–419.

Niska, M., Vesala, H.T. and Vesala, K.M. (2012) Peasantry and entrepreneurship as frames for farming: reflections on farmers' values and agricultural policy discourses. *Sociologia Ruralis*, 52: 453–469.

Pelling, M. and Hing, C. (2005) Understanding adaptation: what can social capital offer assessment of adaptive capacity? *Global Environmental Change*, 15: 301–319.

Peltonen-Sainio, P., Jauhiainen, L. and Hakala, K. (2011) Crop responses to precipitation and elevated temperatures in cool growing conditions at high latitudes according to long-term multi-location trials. *Journal of Agricultural Science*, 149: 49–62.

Peltonen-Sainio, P., Jauhiainen, L., Hakala, K. and Ojanen, H. (2009) Climate change and prolongation of growing season: changes in regional potential for field crop production in Finland. *Agricultural and Food Science*, 18: 171–190.

Raymond, C.M. and Robinson, G.M. (2013) Factors affecting rural landholders' adaptation to climate change: insights from formal institutions and communities of practice. *Global Environmental Change*, 23: 103–114.

Ruosteenoja, K., Räisänen, J. and Pirinen, P. (2011) Projected changes in thermal seasons and the growing season in Finland. *International Journal of Climatology*, 31: 1473–1487.

Silvasti, T. (2003) The cultural model of "the good farmer" and the environmental question in Finland. *Agriculture and Human Values*, 20: 143–150.

Silvasti, T. (2009) Giving up the family farm: an alternative story of the structural change in agriculture in Finland. *Maaseudun uusi aika*, 2(2009): 21–32.

Singleton, V. (2012) When contexts meet: feminism and accountability in UK cattle farming. *Science, Technology & Human Values*, 37: 404–433.

Spaargaren, G., Oosterveer, P. and Loeber, A. (2012) Sustainability transitions in food consumption, retail and production. In G. Spaargaren, P. Oosterveer and A. Loeber (eds) *Food Practices in Transition*. New York: Routledge, pp. 1–34.

Sutherland, L-A. (2013) Can organic farmers be "good farmers"? Adding the "taste of necessity" to the conventionalization debate. *Agriculture and Human Values*, 30: 429–441.

Sutherland, L-A. and Burton, R. (2011) Good farmers, good neighbours? The role of cultural capital in social capital development in a Scottish farming community. *Sociologia Ruralis*, 51: 238–255.

Sutherland, L-A., Burton, R., Ingram, J., Blackstock, K., Slee, B. and Gotts, N. (2012) Triggering change: towards a conceptualization of major change processes in farm decision-making. *Journal of Environmental Management*, 104: 142–151.

Sutherland, L-A. and Darnhofer, I. (2012) Of organic farmers and "good farmers": changing habitus in rural England. *Journal of Rural Studies*, 28: 232–240.

Stock, P.V. (2007) "Good farmers" as reflexive producers: an examination of family organic farmers in the US Midwest. *Sociologia Ruralis*, 47: 83–102.

Vanclay, F., Sivasti, T. and Howden, P. (2007) Styles, parables and scripts: diversity and conformity in Australian and Finnish agriculture. *Rural Society*, 17: 3–8.

Webb, N.P. and Stokes, C.J. (2012) Climate change scenarios to facilitate stakeholder engagement in agricultural adaptation. *Mitigation and Adaptation Strategies for Global Change*, 17: 957–973.

Wilson, G.A. (2008) From "weak" to "strong" multifunctionality: conceptualising farm-level multifunctional transitional pathways. *Journal of Rural Studies*, 24: 367–383.

Wise, R.M., Fazey, I., Stafford Smith, M., Park, S.E., Eakin, H.C., Archer Van Garderen, E.R.M and Campbell, B. (2014) Reconceptualising adaptation to climate change as part of pathways of change and response. *Global Environmental Change*, 28: 326–336.

Wolf, J., Adger, W.N., Lorenzoni, I., Abrahamson, V. and Raine, R. (2010) Social capital, individual responses to heat waves and climate change adaptation: an empirical study of two UK cities. *Global Environmental Change*, 20: 44–52.

10 Framing resilience in relation to territorialisation

Elena Battaglini, Marija Babović and Natalija Bogdanov

Introduction

In rural studies, resilience is defined as the capacity of a rural region to adapt to changing external circumstances in such a way that a satisfactory standard of living is maintained. As Heijman *et al.* (2007) claim, it can be described by the extent to which a rural area can simultaneously balance its ecosystem and its economic and cultural functions to cope with internal weaknesses and external threats, including institutional and policy mismatches. The question of how to build up the resilience of urban and rural areas in order to mitigate and adapt to the challenges of climate change is attracting great interest, especially in policy documents. It has, therefore, become a "pervasive idiom of global governance", being "abstract and malleable enough to encompass the worlds of high finance, defence and urban infrastructure" (Walker and Cooper 2011: 144).

Another crucial notion in environmental policy – the idea of sustainable development, introduced in 1987 by the Brundtland Commission (WCED 1987) – is commonly framed as the need to preserve the quality of natural resources for present and future generations. It has featured on international policy agendas since the 1972 Stockholm Conference. For some, however, the concept is now so broad as to be meaningless (Marshall and Toffel 2005; Baker 2006). The economist Pearce (Pearce *et al.* 1990) writes, in this regard, that it is hard to disagree with the basic assumptions of sustainable development because, like "motherhood and apple pie", they seem like something we should all agree with. If resilience is the capacity of an ecological or social system to adapt to external pressures while maintaining its functions and identity, sustainable development is the capability of these systems to undertake long-lasting socio-cultural, economic and environmental paths of development (Folke *et al.* 2002; Walker *et al.* 2004).

In terms of sustainability, a "resilient social-ecological system in a 'desirable' state has a greater capacity to continue providing us with the goods and services that support our quality of life while being subjected to a variety of shocks" (Walker and Salt 2006: 32). In this regard, the concept of resilience is inevitably normative (Duit *et al.* 2010), as is the concept of sustainable development. Both bad and good resilient systems can persist (Pisano 2012) in parallel with the institutional mainstreaming of particular systems. Accordingly, farm resilience and sustainable development trajectories depend upon the specific forms in which the local community "reinterprets and transforms" (Battaglini 2005) local heritage for its own use. Building on the definition given by Turco (1988, 2009, 2010), we will define farm resilience as an inner dimension of "territorialisation". Hence, farm resilience is understood as a process in which the communities settling in a place perceive the specific nature of that place, attributing symbols to its resources and to its local peculiarities, and thus reifying, structuring and organising the space.

"Territoriality" and "territorialisation" are crucial concepts in making sense of resilience and sustainable development because territorialisation is placed in relation to regimes of property rights that reflect complex historical and political processes. These divide the territories under state control into economic and political zones, rearranging people and resources within such units, and regulating who can and cannot use the resources (Vandergeest and Peluso 1995; Buch-Hansen 2003; Kumar and Kerr 2013). In our chapter, territorialisation reflects the concept of "human territoriality" that has been studied by the Swiss geographer Claude Raffestin since the 1970s. Referring to the works of Soja, Deleuze, Guattari and, above all, Lefebvre, he defines territoriality "as the ensemble of relations that a society maintains with exteriority and alterity for the satisfaction of its needs, towards the end of attaining the greatest possible autonomy compatible with the resources of the system" (Raffestin 2012: 121).

In this chapter, we deal with sustainable development and resilience as complex matters and with reference to space/time frames and to the cultural specificities of local communities in how they tackle either the endogenous potential of their local heritage or the external pressures of the market and globalisation. The main hypothesis proposed here is that resilience is driven by means of perceptions and values and that – on the basis of the different values attributed to different resources – decisions are made and farming practices implemented to make innovations based on these resources or to simply conserve, neglect or destroy them. Our contribution refers to a rural study in the Zlatibor region of Serbia. We pay special attention to the contextual changes that have occurred, to the coping and adaptive practices and to the perception of the effects of the changes in dairy chains and raspberry production.

Framing territorial farm resilience

Both the environment and society, through their dynamic interaction, act and drive the quality and the direction of territorial development. As argued elsewhere (Battaglini 2014; Battaglini and Babović 2015), we understand this process to take shape as an embodiment of territorialisation through which a "space" becomes a "place" – a "place to live in" – and thus a "territory" orienting the socio-territorial tides among local communities and their natural hybrids. The process of territorialisation alludes to the dynamic nature of the processes of perception (the symbolisation stage), settlement (reification stage) and the structuration of space (institutional stage). Hence, the conceptualisation of a territory should be understood as a relational and procedural concept as well as the main analytical instrument for studying the processes of transformation that space undergoes (Mubi Brighenti 2010).

Our approach is focused on the meso and micro levels – on small local communities (villages), farms, rural households and families engaged in agricultural production. It stems from our conviction that the resilience of communities primarily depends on the resilience of such groups, households, farms and, ultimately, individuals and their capability to adjust to more or less sudden changes and to preserve functions, structures, and satisfactory living standards. Therefore, our study focuses on the coping and adaptive mechanisms of the farms that enable resilient rural communities.

In our understanding, coping and adaptive responses to external challenges are a set of actions that arise from the symbolisation and reification stages of the patterns of territorialisation developed on the local level. More analytically, we would argue that such practices could be defined as being driven, first, by perceptions and symbols. This means that individuals and communities attribute specific possibilities to the conformation of the soil, the watershed, the morphological structures, the vegetation, location and climate on a local level and, in this way, give meaning to the use of the available assets: this is the symbolisation stage of territorialisation. Second, the practices are driven by the values and meanings attributed to assets in relation to the uses that can be made of them and the consumables that are available, accessible and cultivated at the local level.

Coping and adaptive practices, driven thus by perceptions, meaning and values, are patterns of action that aim at adjusting farm management practices to the changing natural, economic, social and cultural environment, in order to enable viable farm incomes and a satisfactory quality of life, thus providing answers to the challenge of how to use existing limited stocks in the long term. We refer to values as a "conception of the desirable, expressed or implied, distinction of an individual or characteristic of a group, which affects the action selection between modes, means and aims available" (Kluckhohn 1951: 395). In this regard, we relate values to three dimensions: (1) affective, relationships and internalised feeling of belonging; (2) cognitive, an actor's awareness of the specific choice; and (3) selective, choices posed by the affordances of local resources (Sciolla 2012; Battaglini and Babović 2015). From this perspective, we argue that coping and adaptive responses are the means through which resilience is achieved.

Our study of resilience will be anchored in the subjective perception of our respondents in the following economic and socio-ecological aspects: regular and satisfactory incomes, improved living standards, innovation, greater investment in production, the diversification of production, the multi-functionality of farms, adaptations in the use of land, soil preservation, the prevention of village depopulation, the development of social capital, improvement in the quality of life and in subjective and objective socio-economic status.

Community case study: changes and structural challenges

In our case study, we focus on the development of a community of small rural households in Sirogojno, a small village of 630 inhabitants located between Užice and Zlatibor in Serbia. Through the biographies of 14 farmers, mainly devoted to raspberry cultivation and dairy production, we look at the way they have faced structural challenges since the socialist era. The mechanisms employed by farmers to develop farming practices and satisfactory living standards are diverse and are simultaneously shaped by changes in the broader socio-economic environment and by the internal capacities of the actors.

Sirogojno fits into the typical picture of a mountain village in the prevailing model of extensive agricultural production. A major tourist destination is located nearby; its image is based on healthy air and beautiful surroundings, as well as on the high quality and recognisability of its local food. These characteristics of the area provide many opportunities for farms to diversify their incomes, shortening the value chain of food production through direct sales, reducing hidden unemployment and significantly contributing to the resistance of farms to market and transitional shocks. Farms in Sirogojno are small in size and a significant area of meadows and pastures are present in the structure of the agricultural lands, furthermore, significant areas are covered by forests. The incomes of family farms, according to the importance of income sources, are dependent on a combination of wages, pensions and earnings from agriculture (Statistical Office of Republic of Serbia 2013). In this area, a large part of a farm's agricultural products is consumed on the farm, providing the family with some of its food and nutritional resilience. The income from agriculture is largely derived from the sale of traditional local products that are processed on the farm.

The post-socialist transformation of agriculture and rural areas in Serbia has brought great challenges to family farms. The liberalisation of the land market and the abolition of the maximum farm size led to the emergence of a dual farm structure, with a large number of semi-subsistence farms and a small number of large farms. Trade liberalisation exposed farmers, for the first time, to the global food market and global competition. At the same time, the deregulation of food prices, the reduction of state intervention in agriculture, and the decrease in budgetary support for agriculture all acted together to increase farmers' income risks, changing the overall business environment in the agricultural sector. The dismantling of traditional food supply chains and the setting up of new chains took time. Additionally, the emergence of new actors in the food supply chain was not legally regulated – with the result that many farmers suffered heavy losses. Finally, privatisation and the slow transformation of the non-agricultural sector in rural areas led to a loss of jobs and an increase in hidden unemployment among farm labourers. In fact, this development resulted in the growing dependence of rural areas on agricultural income (Bogdanov *et al.* 2012).

In addition, the growing impact of the changing climate has meant that six out of the past 15 years have had extreme weather conditions. There is also a lack of overall human, technical, infrastructural and institutional capacity held by the stakeholders in their provision of logistical support to farmers. This is further observed in the rudimentary institutions for knowledge transfer, networking, marketing and promotion, social capital and business networks. New circumstances have brought great challenges to the family farms, which need to build adaptive strategies and the capacity to anticipate changes, while shaping new forms and models of partnerships and more efficient farming patterns (Berkum and Bogdanov 2012). Typical barriers to the emergence of a resilient agricultural system in transitional countries usually include difficulties in accessing information, knowledge, new technologies, new markets and financial markets.

The changes have also brought new opportunities: a local ethno village (described as an "open air museum") opened during the 1990s and gave impetus to the development of rural tourism in the area; new restaurants opened, a local entrepreneur who had purchased a sweater company moved into the raspberry trade and the production of frozen berries; the state introduced some new subventions for agricultural production – some from the central government and some from the local government.

The transitional changes described above are reflected in the local economy in a number of ways. The greatest shock of the post-socialist transformation was felt in the local community with the disbanding of the local cooperative in early 2000. Beyond that, the marketisation of food chains and the privatisation of the local sweater company took place. Besides these socio-economic challenges, climate threats – in the form of consecutive droughts and flood – produced yet more challenges. The following section describes how our respondents reorganised and adjusted to the new situation, and to what extent they were innovative and made use of new opportunities to develop their households, farms and the broader local community.

The reconstructing of dairy chains as a coping response

During the socialist period, the dairy farms in the village and in the local area sold their dairy products to the local cooperative. The cooperative purchased their products at a relatively fair price, on time, providing additional incentives for quality milk. The terms of trade were transparent and reliable. After the breakdown of socialism, the cooperative began to face liquidity problems; cooperative property was partially privatised and a gap in the dairy chain appeared. Instead of selling dairy products (mostly cream and cheese), the farmers decided to start selling milk to private companies, such as the distribution intermediaries and resellers that emerged in the dairy product market. However, given the low average production of milk per farm, farmers were not able to secure beneficial trade conditions. In the beginning, they obtained contracts with a relatively large dairy company and each morning the company's truck would collect the milk from each farm. Yet the newly introduced law on quality standards increased the requirements in terms of equipment, hygiene and quality of milk. Since this required a significant investment for small local dairies and milk collection systems, this form of trade was ultimately abandoned.

After the withdrawal of the large dairy company from the local community and given the lack of alternative retailers, the farmers decided to jointly seek another solution. As they were all small producers (up to six cows), it was hard to find a new buyer who would be interested in collecting the milk from the individual farms. They managed to find a retailer somewhat further away from the village and organised the milk transportation themselves. They drew up a schedule and each morning one of them would collect milk from the farms in the hamlet and deliver it to the dairy company:

> We struggled hard during that time to maintain the production of milk. Many others in the village gave up. We succeeded due to cooperation. During this time, the core of this informal dairy cooperative was formed and it is still going today.
>
> (Male respondent, 52 years old)

Eventually, in 2005, a new retailer appeared in the local community, offering to provide a milk-cooling tank for the hamlet. The farmers accepted immediately and once again reorganised the milk supply chain. The farm on which the milk-cooling tank was placed belonged to the biggest producer, but was also in a good position that was accessible throughout the year. In addition to this, since the state introduced bonuses for producers that could sell at least 40 litres of milk per day, they decided to organise in specific way. Only one farmer (the 'key farmer') formally sells the milk. In this way, the group can obtain and share the milk premium.

For 10 years, this cooperation has been maintained with several rules and the same practices: the milk-cooling tank is positioned on the farm of the key farmer, the milk collection point is always open and each farmer brings milk and puts it in the tank, recording the amount in the record book. Every morning, the dairy company comes to collect the milk and checks the quality. Payments are made twice per month, while milk premium is paid by the state once every few months. All payments go to the key farmer, who distributes the income and bonuses to the individual famers in accordance with their contributions. He also provides them with concentrated food for the livestock because he has subsidies for this as a producer.

Through this method of organisation, the farmers dealt with the lack of a cooperative in the dairy chain and adjusted to the new market conditions. Although their cooperation is not formalised and remains limited to milk production, it has the key features of a cooperative:

> We've practically created a cooperative; it's not legally a cooperative, but it functions based on mutual trust and honest interpersonal relations. We share the risks and benefits. If somebody's milk is not of good quality, we all feel the consequences. Nobody is privileged or negatively treated.
>
> (Male respondent, 52 years old)

This cooperation is economically significant in several ways. It leads to an inflow of €1500 to €2000 to the hamlet each month. For farmers, who are focused on farming and agricultural production, this form of cooperation brings a regular, solid income. A farm with four cows can provide a monthly income of 400–500 euros, which is about the level of the average salary in Serbia. A few farms that combine milk and raspberry production are well off due to this combination of income-generating activities. For some retired elderly farmers, this income is an important additional extra to their very low pensions (of 70€), and prevents them from falling below the poverty line. For those who are employed off-farm, this cooperation offers the possibility of keeping some milk for consumption and selling the surplus, which is too little for regular retail but too much for domestic use:

> A cow means life for a peasant. If you have a cow, you have always something to eat ... We, who are employed, also like to have clean, healthy milk. We like to produce it for ourselves, for our children. But today families are small, so we have a surplus of milk. For me, this is the best way. I give that surplus away, leaving a bit for the family, and this is perfect.
>
> (Female respondent, 53 years old)

The key to the effectiveness of this informal cooperative lies not only in how the financial aspects are organised, but also in the flexibility of the social organisation. The openness and the kind of self-service approach provide a more suitable framework for the producers. While some other milk retailers in the region require farmers to deliver the milk during certain hours, small producers in this informal cooperative can be more flexible:

> If we're picking raspberries, I can't manage to bring the milk until the late evening. But this way, I am relaxed. When we finish with the raspberries, I milk the cows, go to the delivery station, pour the milk in and record the amount. It's never locked.
>
> (Female respondent, 53 years old)

In order to understand how this kind of cooperation came to be established, it is important to bear in mind two significant factors: the affordances that the morphology of the village enables, and the social territorial belonging that we comprehend in the sense of Pollini (2005). The village is scattered across several hills. Our respondents live in one part of the village that is physically separated from the central part and from some other hamlets closer to the centre. Their hamlet is harder to access, due to narrow roads, and sharp ascents and descents that could be problematic during wintertime. This puts more pressure on farmers from the hamlet to show solidarity and to be cooperative and innovative in their organisation. Second, the social network among the farmers in the hamlet is dense, woven by double kinship and neighbourly relations. As a consequence, the levels of trust and solidarity were relatively high, enabling more successful coping practices.

Although the most visible benefits of this informal cooperative are of the financial kind, the regular delivery of milk is also an opportunity to socialise, to exchange information and to spend some time together. Due to this, cooperation further strengthens the social territorial belonging within the community by increasing trust, solidarity and cooperation. All the respondents are aware of the benefits that this cooperation brings and they all consent in the assessment that this kind of cooperation is possible due to the loyalty, solidarity and sense of affinity that exists between them:

> This cooperation is grounded in trust and honesty. If I bring 5.5 litres of milk, I will not record six, but only five.
>
> (Female respondent, 53 years old)

> We behave seriously, as if we have signed a formal contract, but we are not responsible to anybody except to each other – when we look each other in the eye. It works based on trust and it has worked for 10 years.
>
> (Male respondent, 52 years old)

In this way, the informal cooperative represents not only an example of an organisational form that was adjusted in response to a changing socio-economic environment, enabling individual farms and households to be more resilient to these changes, but it also contributes to the overall resilience of the community as it maintains an economic activity that was threatened, protects the living standards of the individuals and families and builds new forms of social capital that can be used to invest in various developmental processes in the broader community.

Raspberry production as an innovative adaptive response

Unlike the milk supply chains, which were an example of an adjustment in cooperation, raspberry production is an example of the innovation of individual local farmers as an adaptive response to structural changes in their livelihood strategies. Although wild berries have always been important in this region for nutrition and trade, raspberries are a relatively new product that became important in the 1990s.

At the start of the 1990s, with the first signs of transition and economic crisis, farmers for the first time faced problems such as the uncertainty of jobs in other sectors, the difficulties of accessing agricultural markets and the low competitiveness of small farms. Larger farms opted for the purchase of machinery, leasing or buying new land, while small farms chose the strategy of structural adjustment in niche markets, which provided an attractive opportunity with faster turnover and smaller initial investment. The challenge was to find a product or service to provide an alternative income for households of a small size, which would not entail a big investment and which would contribute to the greater involvement of the farm labour force. Many found it in raspberry production, and today almost all households with working-age members have at least a small raspberry yard while large producers pick 3–5 tons in the season. The whole region has become famous for raspberry production. Research indicates several important factors for this development: the tradition of wild berries, the character and the affordances of local natural resources, economic and market factors. However, deeper insight reveals the importance of cultural factors – the values and the symbolisation attributed to raspberry production by the farmers.

The most important economic factor is the proximity of the raspberry market in the form of a large buyer of fresh raspberries. This emerged, as has been mentioned above, following the privatisation of the local socialist sweater company, which oriented itself towards the production of frozen raspberries and wild berries. This family company became in time a major exporter of frozen raspberries. This stimulated local producers to increase raspberry production in order to gain immediate economic benefits. Our respondents perceive the buyer as fair and reliable as he pays on time, gives bonuses and provides cheaper fertilisers for producers. With this opportunity, many landowners with small holdings decided to start raspberry production and, due to the fact that it can provide a high income from a small area, raspberries became greatly appreciated:

> My 10 acres growing raspberries are worth more than somebody else's 10 hectares growing something else. From the production of such an area, I can receive an income equivalent to the present annual salary for me and my wife.
>
> (Male respondent, 32 years old)

Although all respondents primarily emphasised the economic values of raspberry production, there are other important reasons for raspberry cultivation. The raspberry yard is a symbol of household prosperity, thus symbolising a successful family business. Therefore, social status values are also attributed to the raspberry production. Finally, the respondents attribute aesthetic values to the raspberry plant. For them, a raspberry yard is a place of beauty. They are proud when their yards are tidy and in order:

> In the raspberry yard, a man gets a lust for life. Of all types of work, I like most to work in the raspberry yard. It's such a nice feeling when you see how it becomes more beautiful every year. It grows, it's all in rows, orderly, green and red … beautiful.
>
> (Male respondent, 48 years old)

> I like doing everything on the farm. But when I enter the raspberry yard, it's relaxation for me. It is not hard work, it's beautiful and the scent is nice.
>
> (Female respondent, 69 years old)

Older respondents hope that the improvement in living conditions they introduced, particularly based on raspberry production, will motivate the younger generation to stay in the village. The strong depopulation trends that are typical of the vast majority of rural areas in Serbia can be noticed in this village as well. However, the improvement in living conditions and the better economic opportunities in the village, brought about especially by raspberry production, coupled with poor opportunities in urban areas during the years of the economic crisis and the high unemployment levels among young people, have probably contributed to the fact that the youngest members of the families of our respondents have mostly remained in the village. Some have found off-farm employment in nearby towns, but continue to live in the village and to participate in agricultural production on the farm. Their decisions to remain in the village are also of crucial importance for sustainable raspberry production in the future because this is a labour-intensive activity:

> It's better here for the young people. They have no job or accommodation in the city. Here, at least, they won't go hungry. They have everything they need, and they can always go to earn some income. Living conditions are satisfactory … We do not have theatre, or cinema, but we do have the Internet. We also have something that they don't have in the city – fresh air, healthy food, and some independence, because you can provide for yourself.
>
> (Male respondent, 52 years old)

From the interviews with the younger respondents, the desire to use opportunities to move to the city is not insignificant. However, in the present period, the pull factors are not as strong, bearing in mind the years of economic crisis and stagnation in Serbia; the push factors are also relatively weak in the community where the research was conducted. Both milk and raspberry production are important factors in these circumstances, obviously making this community more resilient to negative economic cycles.

Conclusion

Two aims were pursued in this study: first, to define farm resilience as an inner dimension of territorialisation. The territorial bonds between nature and culture drive the quality and the direction of resilient local development, which we understand to be a process of territorialisation. By reconstructing the dairy and the raspberry chains as coping and innovative adaptive responses to external pressures, our study attempted to give evidence showing how adaptive capacities to the changing climate rely on the relationship between the settling community and the settled land in relation to its specific positions, resources and climates. Second, the main question of our research was related to the factors that contribute to the resilience of farming households in the context of turbulent socio-economic changes and environmental challenges.

In the case of milk supply chains, we discovered that the coping mechanism included the successful reorganisation of the milk supply chains, which was possible due to the social territorial ties that enabled networks of trust, and solidarity in the small community. Reorganising the milk supply chain in the form of an informal cooperative allowed the farming households to maintain milk production, to increase their economic resilience and to further develop new forms of social capital. The case of raspberry production was an example of innovation as a mechanism for dealing with changes and challenges. The key factors in the development of raspberry production that appeared were the natural environment, favourable economic circumstances – particularly in the form of the presence of a large raspberry exporter in the village – and non-economic drivers related to the aesthetic and symbolic values attributed to raspberry production.

Both cases represent alternative insights into farm management. The dairy practices responded to short-term efficiency needs, while the raspberry production complemented that orientation with a long-term transformability pattern, balancing, as Darnhofer (2014) puts it, exploitation and exploration – the alternative ways to build on the equilibrium that relates a farmer's agency to the environmental specificities when navigating change. As the cases show, the local natural environment is an important factor in orienting these practices, particularly in terms of how the local hybrids afford them: altitude (a bit less than 900 m), terrain morphology (hills, sometimes with very steep slopes that are hard to access and cultivate), good quality air, rich forests and plenty of wild herbs, berries and mushrooms.

Territorialisation has the conceptual strength to frame and identify place-based trajectories as it is grounded in the enduring features of human experience and life-trajectory patterns (Battaglini *et al.* 2015). Further research is needed to answer the following questions: to what extent, and in what way, can local farmers' trajectories meet national priorities and strategies related to the risks of extreme weather? How can the Serbian government benefit from the territorialisation process and the endogenous practices developed here? Given the trajectories implemented by the farmers to date, what are the implications for the policies underpinning the changing climate? We expect that a deeper analysis of the institutional stage of the territorialisation patterns that occurred in the region after the year 2000, and of the local configurations of the market, state and society can provide further tools to tackle these issues.

Acknowledgements

This chapter was written as part of a IS1007 COST Grant. The case study is based on the research supported by the Italy and Serbia Bilateral Scientific Cooperation Agreement and fostered by the effective encouragement of ABT-ISF-IRES.

References

Baker, S. (2006) *Sustainable Development*. London: Routledge.

Battaglini, E. (2005) Enhancing local sustainability: the role of social capital in the value attribution of a territory. In M. Järvelä, P. Jokinen and A. Puupponen (eds) *Kestävän kehityksen paikalliset verkostot* [Local Sustainability Networks]. Jyväskylä: Jyväskylän yliopistopaino, pp. 197–207.

Battaglini, E. (2014) *Sviluppo territoriale. Dal disegno di ricerca alla valutazione dei risultati* Milan: Franco Angeli.

Battaglini, E. and Babović, M. (2015) Nature and culture in the territorialisation processes towards sustainability. In J. Dessein, E. Battaglini and L. Horlings (eds) *Cultural Sustainability and Regional Development: Theory and Practice of Territorialisation*. London: Routledge.

Battaglini, E., Horlings, L. and Dessein, J. (2015) Conclusion: territorialisation, a challenging concept for framing regional development. In J. Dessein, E. Battaglini and C. Horlings (eds) *Cultural Sustainability and Regional Development: Theory and Practice of Territorialisation*. London: Routledge.

Berkum, S. and Van Bogdanov, N. (2012) *Serbia on the Road to EU Accession*. Wallingford: CABI.

Bogdanov, N., Rodi , V. and Vittuari, M. (2012) Structural change in transitional agriculture: evidence from Serbia. Paper prepared for presentation at the 132nd Seminar of the EAAE "Is transition in European agriculture really over? New dimensions and challenges of transition and post-transition processes in agriculture and food sectors in the European Union and EU acceding and neighbouring countries", Skopje, 25–27 October. Available at: http://ageconsearch.umn.edu/bitstream/139490/2/Bogdanov.pdf (accessed 8 January 2015).

Buch-Hansen, M. (2003) The territorialisation of rural Thailand: between localism, nationalism and globalism. *Tijdschrift voor economische en sociale geografie*, 94(3): 322–334.

Darnhofer, I. (2014) Resilience and why it matters for farm management. *European Review of Agricultural Economics*, 41(3): 461–484.

Duit, A., Galaz, W., Eckerberg, K. and Ebbesson, J. (2010) Governance, complexity and resilience. *Global Environmental Change*, 20(3): 363–368.

Folke, C., Carpenter, S., Elmqvist, T., Gunderson, L., Holling, C.S. and Walker, B. (2002) Resilience and sustainable development: building adaptive capacity in a world of transformations. *Ambio*, 31(5): 437–440.

Heijman, W., Hagelaar, G. and Heide, M.V.D. (2007) Rural resilience as a new development. Concept paper presented to EAAE seminar Serbian Association of Agricultural Economists, Novi Sad, Serbia. Available at: http://portal.zzbaco.com/mojo_baco/Data/Sites/1/docs/mono/EAAE/C/52%20SC%20Heijman_Wim.pdf (accessed 4 July 2014).

Kluckhohn, C. (1951) Values and value-orientations in the theory of action: an exploration in definition and classification. In T. Parsons and E. Shils (eds) *Toward a General Theory of Action*. Cambridge, MA: Harvard University Press, pp. 388–433.

Kumar, K. and Kerr, J.M. (2013) Territorialisation and marginalisation in the forested landscapes of Orissa, India. *Land Use Policy*, 30(1): 885–894.

MacKinnon, D. and Derickson, K.D. (2013) From resilience to resourcefulness: a critique of resilience policy and activism. *Progress in Human Geography*, 37(2): 253–270.

Marshall, J.D. and Toffel, M.W. (2005) Framing the elusive concept of sustainability: a sustainability hierarchy. *Environmental Science & Technology*, 39(3): 673–682.

Mubi Brighenti, A. (2010) On territoriology. Towards a general science of territory. *Theory. Culture & Society*, 27(1): 52–72.

Pearce, D.W., Markandya, A. and Barbier, E.B. (1990) *Blueprint for a Green Economy*. London: Earthscan.

Pisano, U. (2012) Resilience and sustainable development: theory of resilience, systems thinking and adaptive governance. *ESDN Quarterly Report*, 26.

Pollini, G. (2005) Elements of a theory of place attachment and socio-territorial belonging. *International Review of Sociology: Revue Internationale de Sociologie*, 15(3): 497–515.
Raffestin, C. (2012) Space, territory, and territoriality. *Environment and Planning D: Society and Space*, 30: 121–141.
Sciolla, L. (2012) *Sociologia dei processi culturali*. Bologna: Il Mulino.
Statistical Office of Republic of Serbia (2013) Household Budgetary Survey. Available at: http://pod2.stat.gov.rs/ObjavljenePublikacije/G2014/pdf/G20145583.pdf (accessed 8 January 2015).
Turco, A. (1988) *Verso una teoria geografica della complessità*. Milan: UNICOPLI.
Turco, A. (2009) Topogenèse: la généalogie du lieu et la constitution du territoire. In M. Vanier (ed.) *Territoires, territorialité, territorialisation. Controverses et perspectives*. Rennes: Presse Universitaires de Rennes, pp. 37–44.
Turco, A. (2010) *Configurazioni della territorialità*. Milan: Franco Angeli.
Vandergeest, P. and Peluso, N.L. (1995) Territorialisation and state power in Thailand. *Theory & Society*, 24(3): 385–426.
Walker, B., Holling, C.S., Carpenter, S.R. and Kinzig, A. (2004) Resilience, adaptability and transformability in social-ecological systems. *Ecology and Society*, 9(2): 5. Available at: www.ecologyandsociety.org/vol9/iss2/art5/ (accessed 4 July 2014).
Walker, B. and Salt, D. (2006) *Resilience Thinking: Sustaining Ecosystems and People in a Changing World*. Washington, DC: Island Press.
Walker, J. and Cooper, M. (2011) Genealogies of resilience: from systems ecology to the political economy of crisis adaptation. *Security Dialogue*, 43: 143–160.
WCED (1987) *Our Common Future*. Oxford: Oxford University Press.

11 Balancing climate change mitigation and adaptation with the socio-economic goals of farms in Northern Europe

Heikki Lehtonen, Xing Liu and Tuomo Purola

Introduction

Two response strategies related to the risks associated with climate change are well known as mitigation and adaptation. While the key issue of mitigation is to reduce the emissions of greenhouse gases (GHGs), adaptation aims to adjust the food system to altered production conditions resulting from climate change and to moderate the potential harmful effects and the risks of further climate change. Adaptation to climate change may also include the adjustments necessary for improved productivity and other gains. Interactions between mitigation and adaptation strategies that have been progressively implemented by farmers can be both positive and negative. Farm management is significantly affected by distinct local level socio-economic characteristics and pressures as well as global market developments (Tubiello and van der Velde 2012; Kanellopoulos *et al.* 2014).

Future projected trends in European agriculture include the northward movement of crop suitability zones and increasing crop productivity in Northern Europe (Easterling *et al.* 2007; Peltonen-Sainio *et al.* 2009). However, uncertainty on both the market and the production side may present significant challenges for farmers in the Nordic countries (Hakala *et al.* 2011). As an important contributor to GHGs, agriculture can also contribute to climate change mitigation through multiple efforts such as carbon sequestration, organic soil and other land use management as well as changes in livestock diets and manure management (Regina *et al.* 2009, 2014). Some adaptive management choices, such as the more judicious use of fertilisers, soil improvements and increased land use diversity may lead to increased resilience and thus decrease the vulnerability of a farming system to the impact of climate change.

Crop rotation is the practice of growing dissimilar crop species on the same land in consecutive seasons. It is also considered essential for the maintenance of soil fertility as well as sustained and relatively stable yields (Maynard *et al.* 1997; Hennessy 2006; Dury *et al.* 2011). Crop rotation has been an important agricultural practice since the beginning of agriculture and recently it has regained attention due to the observed problems of short rotations and monocropping, such as increasing pest and disease pressure, declining soil quality and increasing environmental degradation. Crop rotation that is diverse may also mitigate farm income risk by reducing the negative impacts of extreme events and by hedging volatile commodity prices (Di Falco and Perrings 2005). In addition, diverse rotations could decrease the intensive usage of synthetic chemicals inputs and mitigate GHGs (Meyer-Aurich *et al.* 2006; Cai *et al.* 2012).

However, such developments are dependent on market and policy incentives affecting farm-level decision-making. Van Wijk *et al.* (2014) showed that long-term integrated analyses at the farm level (over 20 years) – that can combine dynamic mathematical programming and decision models – are urgently needed to deal with complex climate change issues. Thus, one aim of this study is to provide an integrated analysis.

The practical objective of our study is to evaluate the adaptation and mitigation choices for two different farm types possessing different socio-economic characteristics. We incorporate both social and biophysical factors into the rational decision-making process at the farm-level over the long term. We evaluate how different farms, when incentivised for GHG mitigation, can adopt mitigation measures together with different farm management options. The mitigation measure selected in this study is the management of organic soils, due to their proven effectiveness with respect to national GHG abatement targets (Regina *et al.* 2009, 2014).

The next section shows the agricultural features of our empirical study area, the North Savonia region of Finland, and the farm types we focus on. The GHG reduction targets for Finnish agriculture as well as the most important adaptation challenges in North Savonia are then briefly introduced. After that, the main structure, principle and purpose of the model employed in the farm level management analysis are introduced. Next, we present the key issues raised by the model's implementation and frame the market scenarios and other necessary assumptions. The results section provides the main results regarding the farm-level production decisions in the case of specific price scenarios. We conclude by interpreting the results in the context of the case study region, and from the point of view of policy design and the synergies and conflicts between climate change adaptation and mitigation.

Background and context

Specialised cereal crop farms and other crop farms with different land allocations are the focus of this study. The reason for this selection is that they provide a simple example regarding the balance between adaptation and mitigation. The main difference between these farm types is that specialised cereal crop farms mainly cultivate cereals and some grassland, such as dry hay, while other crop farms are smaller and mainly cultivate grasslands for dry hay and silage and have less cereal crops. Both farm types allocate 10–20 per cent as set-aside, especially on the other crop farms, due to the high costs of production (Table 11.1). North Savonia in Finland is the area we examine.

Table 11.1 Agricultural land use on dairy, beef, cereal crop and other crop farms in Northern Savonia, 2013 (%)

	Dairy	*Beef*	*Cereals*	*Other crop farms*
Wheat	0.5	0.8	3.3	0.7
Rye	0	0.1	0.7	0.5
Barley	16.4	13.5	33.4	10.5
Oats	5.9	4	19.1	6.9
Mixed grain	2.9	3.1	0.6	1.1
Oilseeds	0.4	0.3	2.4	0.7
Silage/hay	53.5	52.3	20	52.5
Pasture grass	11	9.3	1.5	6.4
NMF	2.8	2.6	8.4	10.2
Set-aside	2.4	2.6	6.8	7
Other crops	1.4	2.7	3.9	3.6

Source: Luke (2015).

North Savonia has 248,000 inhabitants and accounts for 4.6 per cent of Finland's total population. There are 4200 farms in the region with 148,000 hectares (ha) of farmland (6.4 per cent of the total farmland used in Finland in 2011). Farmland is composed of dairy farms (46 per cent), beef farms (16 per cent), specialised cereal crop farms (19 per cent) and other crop farms (12 per cent) (TIKE 2012). The length of the growing season varies between 150 and 170 days and the effective temperature sum is mostly around 1200–1300 °C days. This means that the growing season is significantly shorter and the temperature sum smaller than in South-Western Finland. These conditions also mean there are greater risks regarding yield and quality with respect to cereal crop and oilseed cultivation, especially when compared to the most feasible growing regions in the country, though such risks do exist everywhere in Finland. Hence the production conditions restrict the crops that can be selected for cultivation. The area allocated to fodder grass was 56 per cent of all farmland in the region in 2012 (ibid.). Feed barley was the most important cereal. However, 24.7 per cent of farms are classified as "Other plant production" and 21 per cent of the farms are cereal crop farms.

Farm size has been increasing both in Finland and North Savonia. The rate of structural change in dairy farming in the region has been rapid – the number of farms has halved in the last 10 years despite a small increase in production. The rapid increase in the size of dairy and beef farms has, together with increased land-specific EU CAP payments per hectare and increasing cereal crop prices during the last 10 years, resulted in a rise in land prices. This has resulted in an increase in costs for expanding farms. However, there has been a 7 per cent increase in the number of cereal crop farms in North Savonia.

Dairy and beef farms managing the largest share of the total farmland in the region are specialised livestock farms with intensive feed and land use operations driven by cereal-grassland rotation. This means renewing grasslands by cultivating cereals every 3–4 years as a shelter crop, allowing grass cultivars to grow without much competition from weeds. Since dairy and beef farms have been increasing rapidly in size, they often face a scarcity of land (Lehtonen *et al.* 2013). Consequently, farms, and especially many livestock farms, intensify their crop cultivation in order to harvest high yields locally. The increases in farm size and the intensification of production are considered (by farmers) the most important means of maintaining farm viability (ibid.).

For this reason, dairy and beef farms allocate only a small amount of land for Nature Management (NMF) and set-aside (Mavi 2014). NMF is, according to its specification in the Agri-environmental Support Scheme, a specific kind of set-aside that aims for higher biodiversity compared to cereal crop and intensive grassland cultivation. This is done by establishing grass vegetation that can be maintained for several years. Fertilisation is allowed only when sowing a specific type of grass seed. Cutting the grass is only allowed in late summer to avoid endangering the nesting of birds and other wildlife. NMF implies higher costs for a farmer than other set-aside due to its specific conditions. NMF is paid at 170 euro/ha, a higher subsidy than other set-asides but a farmer cannot allocate more than 15 per cent of the farmland area to NMF (ibid.). Set-aside land, on the other hand, must also be established as grassland, but cannot be fertilised or harvested. Nevertheless, NMF and set-aside are ideal for carbon sequestration and organic soil management. However, livestock farmers have expressed their dissatisfaction with policy conditions aiming for more extensive production (Lehtonen *et al.* 2013). The farm subsidies with specific conditions are important, as the average farm household income in North Savonia has been decreasing since 2004.

Both farm types in this study are important feed producers in North Savonia. Their land use decisions are more flexible than livestock farms, which are more restricted in their land use due to the need for feed, specific restrictions on manure spreading, i.e. limits imposed on (manure) phosphorus and nitrogen fertilisation by the Agri-environmental Support Scheme as well as the specific environmental permits imposed on large livestock farms (MMM 2007; Mavi 2014).

Greenhouse abatement targets and adaptation challenges

Greenhouse gas emissions from agriculture in Finland have been included in overall emissions since 1990 due to the United Nations Framework Convention on Climate Change and the Kyoto Protocol. Emissions that can be identified as belonging to agriculture are 20 per cent of all GHGs. Methane and nitrous oxide emissions from agriculture are also reported as belonging to agriculture. In Finland, GHGs accounted for 5.9 Mt of the carbon dioxide equivalents for the year 2011, or 9 per cent of Finland's total emissions. In the energy sector, emissions from agriculture were 1.5 Mt CO_2 equivalents in 2011 (Statistics Finland 2013). In the land use sector, emissions from agricultural land area use accounted for 6.8 Mt CO_2 equivalent in 2011 (ibid.), 6 Mt of these were emissions from organic soils.

A 13 per cent reduction in GHGs was the target imposed on the "agriculture" sector (not including land and energy use, as specified above) for 2005–2020 by the National Climate and Energy Strategy of Finland, based on the EU's effort-sharing decision. This should be achieved without restricting domestic production. However, that is very difficult if attempted in terms of methane and nitrous oxide, but could be attempted in terms of direct CO_2 emissions from organic soils (Regina *et al.* 2009, 2014). The Agri-environmental Scheme 2007–2013 (Mavi 2014) included a premium of 100 euros/ha, which was paid for organic field parcels if they were kept under grass for 10 years without tillage.

However, specialised livestock farmers are rather unwilling to participate in such an agreement since the nutritive quality of grass feed decreases fast if the grass is not renewed using tillage and cereals are not cultivated as a shelter crop (Lehtonen *et al.* 2013). Intensive livestock farms also have restrictive obligations for manure spreading. In practice, intensive grass silage production, within the nitrogen and phosphorus fertilisation limits imposed by the Agri-environmental Support Scheme, is the most feasible and profitable option in areas where land supply is weak and land prices and livestock production have been increasing, such as in North Savonia. Hence there is a need to analyse how cereal crop farms and other crop farms could adopt such no-tillage agreements, i.e. keep organic land parcels permanently under no-tillage grassland, instead of cereal crop cultivation and tillage.

The mitigation of GHG needs to be combined with simultaneous adaptations to climate change. The main expected direct effects of climate change in North Savonia are various over-wintering problems associated with grasslands, and an increase in early summer droughts, which are especially harmful to cereals but also to grasslands. Relieving the increasing disease and pest pressure (Hakala *et al.* 2011) will require more diverse crop rotation. However, the increasingly volatile markets for crops and other agricultural commodities will restrict medium- and long-term investment in agricultural productivity and adaptation to a changing climate. For example, it has already been observed that liming and drainage investments carried out since the early 1990s are not sufficient to maintain land fertility in the long run, even if climate change were not taken into consideration (Myyrä *et al.* 2005). Higher market prices for agricultural commodities may be required to cover the extra costs of such adaptation measures.

The model

Our aim is to evaluate the willingness of specialised cereal farms and other crop farms to adopt permanent (no-tillage) grass cover on their organic soil farmlands, while at the same time making economically rational management decisions in terms of adaptation. For this evaluation, we use an economic farm-level model to produce economically rational management choices at the crop and field parcel level, optimal crop rotation paths for the next 30 years, and we explicitly consider farmers' risk aversion behaviour.

We use a dynamic optimisation framework for the following reasons. First, it can accommodate truly dynamic inter-temporal decisions, but without excluding short-term decisions affecting only one year. The optimisation framework is flexible enough to accommodate various technical data and response functions, such as a change in crop yield due to nitrogen fertilisation, the shown empirical impacts of liming (soil pH) on crop yields, the impacts of fungicide treatment on plant disease spread and implied yield changes.

The model parameters are validated using existing data and by comparing the simulation results with published studies. However, we are fully aware of the obvious normative character of this kind of dynamic optimisation model, which may be an exaggeration of the ability of farmers to make long-term rational decisions under uncertainty. We are also aware of the difficulties of finding empirically validated values for risk aversion parameters, a problem frequently encountered in the vast literature on economic risk modelling (Hardaker *et al.* 1997). Hence, we use the risk aversion parameter as a calibration parameter.

We formulate and solve our dynamic model of optimal crop rotation via non-linear programming. Farmers plant individual crops on an annual basis, assuming that a farmer is a rational utility maximiser, i.e. he/she seeks to maximise the present discounted value of the future profit stream, while minimising the variance of expected profits by choosing the sequence of crops planted every year over a period of 30 years. Output and input prices are exogenous for the model. Five crops and two types of set-aside land are included in our model. Nitrogen fertilisation and the implied crop yield response are included, based on the validated approach (Lehtonen, 2001). The crop yield levels are obtained by determining the optimal fertilisation at the farm level. In addition, crop yields are also affected by two other agri-management options of the model: fungicide use for barley and liming treatment for field parcels, affecting the yields of all crops. Furthermore, the land use decisions of the previous five years affect crop yields because monoculture is assumed to imply yield loss. A transition matrix determines a yield loss of some percentage carried over five successive years as described in Liu *et al.* (2014).

Overall, we see our approach as a relevant normative framework to analyse economically rational land use and management at the farm level. It is also capable of showing the likely direction of differences in future management as farmers respond to exogenous parameter changes (prices and disease pressure). We separately address the validation of the model, especially land use outcomes, which are affected by the risk aversion coefficient, in comparison with the realised land use patterns.

Model implementation and data

Data on yields, fertilisation and cost in two selected farm types

We implemented the model to fit a typical, average-sized, cereal-producing farm in North Savonia. Five typical crops cultivated in this region were chosen for the simulation. In addition, set-aside and NMF land use types are included. The data consist of 17 years (1995–2012) of the crop yield, variable cost and subsidy data available for the region from various statistical sources in the public domain. The averages of the variable costs and the subsidies of the study crops are derived from a recent version of a dynamic regional sector model of Finnish agriculture, DREMFIA (Lehtonen 2001, 2013), which provides validated approximations of the average use of inputs per crop in each region.

Two representative farm types are selected for the scenario analysis: a specialised cereal crop farm of 50 ha. and a smaller "other crop farm" with 30 ha. of farmland. Based on the difference in farm size and the farm-level crop-specific calculations employed by Seppälä *et al.* (2014), we calculated the costs of the production of cereals to be 9 per cent higher on other crop farms compared to the cereal crop farms. This is partly due to the smaller farm size resulting in higher machinery maintenance and labour costs per hectare. The main reason for this is the assumed 30 per cent higher opportunity cost of labour on other crop farms. This assumption is supported by the higher share of off-farm income on the other crop farms (74 per cent), compared to the cereal crop farms (68 per cent). Nevertheless, the other crop farm purchases services from other farms or contracts operators when managing set-aside lands and harvesting hay crops, or silage. This means that the costs per hectare for the set-aside and NMF are 4 per cent lower than the costs on the cereal crop farms. The costs of hay production are 30 per cent lower on other crop farms than on cereal crop farms. Other crop farms also often cooperate with livestock farms to maintain efficient machinery (Lehtonen *et al.* 2013).

The fields of both farm types are split equally into 10 parcels and the distances of the parcels to the farm centre vary between 0 and 7 km, with an average distance of 2.9 km for the region (Hiironen and Ettanen 2013). One field parcel of organic soil type was assumed to be located at a median distance (3 km) to the farm centre on both farm types. The decision to cultivate a crop in each field parcel thus implies logistic costs dependent on the distance.

The discount rate used in this study was 2 per cent. This small discount rate was chosen due to the long time span (30 years) and in order to avoid very significant discounting impacts on the results produced by the model. Higher discount rates would mean lower gross margins and less production, especially in the latter part of the simulation period. However, small changes in the discount rate do not change the main patterns of the results since the discount rate similarly affects the costs and prices of all crops.

Price scenario setting

To be able to evaluate the role of prices on farm management, we include three price scenarios. Our baseline price scenario is the moderate price scenario – with prices very close to the average cereal prices observed in Finland between 2009 and 2013 – which is in line with the price range of predictions given by OECD-FAO (2012) and Hertel *et al.* (2010). By increasing and decreasing 20 per cent of the moderate price (MP) level, we set up the high price (HP) and low price (LP) scenarios (Table 11.2). Modelling different cereal price scenarios is important because price levels affect the willingness of farmers to change tillage practices.

Parameter calibration: disease pressure and risk aversion

The disease pressure parameters represent the yield loss due to monoculture. One per cent yield loss is assumed for wheat and barley if wheat or barley were cultivated in the same field parcel in the previous year. The yield loss is smaller, 0.5 per cent, in the case of oats as a pre-crop for wheat and barley since the diseases that affect oats are partly different. In the case of oilseeds, one may expect up to a 20 per cent yield loss due to plant diseases if the pre-crop was also oilseeds. When calculated over a five-year period of monocultures of wheat and barley, this implies a 5 per cent yield loss. The model, when assuming average prices, replicates the observed crop yields and land use in the region (see Liu *et al.* 2014 for details).

Current and future land use and input use decisions are coupled and affected by expected prices and risk aversion. We chose the risk aversion parameters that statistically provide the best fit with the simulated land use with respect to the observed land use for two different farm types. The comparison with 2009–2013 was chosen as the basis for evaluation because NMF was introduced in 2009. The model outcome does not match the observed average land use perfectly, but is still very close to the realised land use decisions of the two farm types (see Table 11.3 in the Results section on p. 141). Given that the differences between the observed land use and the simulated farm plans under various risk aversion coefficients are small, $\theta = 0.02$ clearly provides the best statistical fit with the cereal crops farms, and $\theta = 0.0165$ provides the best fit for other crop farms.

As the risk aversion coefficient is lower in the case of other crop farms, they are slightly more willing to take risks in agricultural production decisions than specialised crop farms due to the higher opportunity cost of labour, the lower

Table 11.2 Price settings in the scenario analysis

Crops (average price €/ton observed at the national level, 2009–2013)	*Low price €/ton –20% of moderate price*	*Moderate price €/ton*	*High price €/ton +20% of moderate price*
Spring wheat (174)	134	167	200
Winter wheat (174)	134	167	200
Barley (155)	124	155	186
Oats (145)	116	145	174
Hay	96	120	144
Oilseed (385)	248	310	372
Set-aside	–	–	–
NMF	–	–	–

share of agricultural income to total income and higher production costs per hectare in the cultivation of cereals compared to specialised cereal crop farms. The values of the risk aversion parameters are kept in the following simulations where the model is run at two other price scenarios, assuming other parameters and the plant disease scenario remain unchanged.

Results: adaptation and mitigation in the price scenarios

In the following we focus on the model's results regarding land use and other farm management choices on the two farm types when different price scenarios are applied. Only after reviewing the results are we able to draw any conclusions on the feasibility of incentivising climate change mitigation and what the implications for climate change adaptation would be as well as how different farm types could respond to such mitigation incentives.

Table 11.3 presents the simulated results of the specialised cereal crops farm and other crop farms. Both farm types adopt similar crop/field parcel specific management decisions in the different price scenarios, but the overall land use distribution remains different. The price scenarios are low price (LP), moderate price (MP) and high price (HP). Liming is sufficient to keep the average pH values of the soil at a reasonable level under MP and HP scenarios. The cereal farms keep the soil pH values of the field parcels at a slightly higher level than the other crop farms. This is because the cereal farms see better returns on liming, which can be considered a soil improvement investment for the next 10–15 years. On the other hand, on the basis of the risk aversion parameter calibration of this study, cereal crop farmers are slightly more risk averse than other crop farms.

Regarding nitrogen fertilisation, which depends largely on the given prices of crops and fertilisers, there is no difference between the two farm types since the same crop cultivars are assumed to be used on both farm types. There is a slightly more difference in the liming decisions between the farm types, but there are no significant differences in the cereal yield levels that are affected by the fertilisation and liming decisions. The simulated crop yields are thus rather close to each other in all price scenarios studied (Table 11.3). Hence there is reason to conclude that despite the rather different opportunity cost of labour and risk aversion, these two farm types will take roughly the same adaptation options in response to the price scenarios studied. In spite of that, their initially different land use decisions at the whole farm level remain different because of their different production costs, the opportunity cost of labour and risk aversion.

If GHGs are to be reduced significantly, it is important to keep organic soils constantly under grassland instead of cereal crop production. The model was used in calculating the premium levels necessary to keep cereals off organic soil (Table 11.4). Premiums are necessary since organic soil was assumed to be located at a median distance from the farm centre in both farm types. Hence the commitment to keep the organic soil parcel always under grass cover restricts

Table 11.3 Simulated average yields, fungicide usage, pH value and GHG emissions over the next 30 years

		Specialised cereal crop farms			*Other crop farms*		
		LP	MP	HP	LP	MP	HP
Average yields	Spring wheat [3068]	2670 (−13.0%)	3190 (4.0%)	3364 (9.6%)	–	–	–
	Winter wheat [3066]	–	–	–	–	–	–
	Barley [3000]	2555 (−14.8%)	2958 (−1.4%)	3203 (6.8%)	2704 (−9.9%)	2942 (−1.9%)	3207 (6.9%)
	Oats [2786]	2469 (−11.4%)	2898 (4.0%)	3034 (8.9%)	2538 (−8.9%)	2855 (2.5%)	3036 (9.0%)
	Hay [3615]	3191 (−11.7%)	3795 (5.0%)	3963 (9.6%)	3138 (−13.2%)	3634 (0.5%)	3886 (7.5%)
	Oilseed [1305]	1106 (−15.2%)	1368 (4.8%)	1452 (11.3%)	–	–	–
Share of fungicide-treated barley		0	0	116	0	0	97
Average pH		5.59	6.50	6.63	5.59	6.28	6.61
GHG emissions overall tons CO_2 eq./year (normalised per 10 ha./year)		23.49	28.75	31.52	16.90	22.00	24.34
GHG emission from organic soils tons CO_2 eq. (normalised per 1 ha.)/year		18.21	19.30	19.34	15.60	17.01	17.07

Note: Square brackets show the actual average yields in Northern Savonia, Finland, 1995–2012; round brackets represent the difference between the simulated yield and the actual average yield in percentages. Winter wheat does not appear in the solution in price scenarios and hence no simulated yields are available.

Table 11.4 Premium needed to prevent any grain crop being cultivated on organic parcels and the corresponding emission changes in different scenarios

	Specialised farm type			*Other crop farm*		
	LP	*MP*	*HP*	*LP*	*MP*	*HP*
Premium needed €/ha	150	280	300	45	120	210
GHG emission overall tons CO_2 eq./year (normalised per 10 ha.)	20.14	24.58	27.41	16.26	20.29	22.00
CO_2 eq. from organic soils (normalised per 1 ha./year)	15.03	15.03	15.69	15.03	15.03	15.03

the farmer's crop rotation and other choices, imposing logistic and other costs. The premium levels in Table 11.4 reflect the farm-level opportunity costs of foregone net income on the two farm types. Farm incomes are unaffected by the GHG abatement measures on organic soils due to the paid premium. This is because the model does not accept the allocation of organic soils under grass unless a sufficient premium is paid. Thus, the abatement cost is equal to the paid premium.

The simulated premium levels implicitly reveal the net income loss of GHG abatement. It seems that the net income loss from mitigation (the premium level) is slightly higher on a cereal farm than on other crop farms. Nevertheless, it seems that the other crop farm can be incentivised for GHG mitigation with a rather low premium level, compared to the overall level of agricultural subsidy payments in the region, 550 euros/ha. Also the cereal crop farms in the region can be incentivised for GHG abatement with a payment of 250–300 euros/ha., even in the high crop price scenario. The GHG abatement of 3.3 to 4.1 tons of CO_2 equivalent can be achieved, but is dependent on the expected crop prices. The abatement cost is close to 62–73 euros/ton CO_2, but only 45 euros/ton CO_2 at low crop prices. However, low crop prices are not realistic according to Hertel (Hertel *et al.* 2010) and OECD-FAO (2012). Other crop farms produce GHG reductions at the same abatement costs per ton of CO_2. This is because other crop farms allocate most of their farmland and also organic soils on grass already without the abatement scheme and the premium.

For cereals farms, a compensation of 150–300 euros/ha., depending on the +/– 20 per cent range of expected future prices, is needed to keep organic soils under permanent grass cover. Already, moderate prices require at least a premium of 250 euros/ha to keep organic soils under permanent grass cover. This is almost 50 per cent of the total value of existing agricultural subsidies paid per hectare. For other crop farms, a compensation of 45–210 euros/ha is needed to keep organic soils under permanent grass cover. However, other crop farms, if they behave in an economically rational way, will consider permanent grassland restrictive in terms of crop rotation and other farm management. For this reason, they also require a significant premium to keep organic soils permanently under grass. Since the resulting GHG emission abatement is relatively smaller on other crop farms than on specialised cereals farms, the abatement costs per ton of CO_2 equivalent is almost equal in these farm types.

What is important to note in this context is that NMF fields are allocated as organic soil parcels as soon as the paid premium is sufficiently high. This means that the results are significantly linked to NMF policy. If such measures were not in place, somewhat higher compensation levels would be required for both farm types. Hence GHG abatement measures may work in good synergy with other agri-environmental policy measures promoting extensive land use. Nevertheless, organic soils do not seem to provide an inexpensive way of decreasing GHG emissions because the GHG abatement of 0.6 to 4.1 tons of CO_2 equivalent/ha/year was achieved according to the expected crop prices. The abatement cost calculated in the simulations is close to 39–73 euros/ton CO_2.

Conclusion

Agriculture in northern Europe is characterised by increased agricultural input prices, which have led to rapid structural change in the Nordic countries. Increasing production and increased farmland prices are not the best context to find a balance between climate change mitigation, keeping agriculture competitive and promoting the adaptation of agriculture to combat likely climate and market changes. A recent trend at the livestock farms is intensification due to the weak supply of farmland and increased production costs. Thus GHG abatement requiring more extensive land use is difficult for livestock farms. Climate change has affected farmers, resulting in more volatile yield levels and prices, and increased costs. In this study, we focused on two specific farm types, cereal crop farms and other crop farms, and evaluated how they are able to cope with the simultaneous challenges of adaptation and mitigation.

Our study provides interesting insights to balance climate change adaptation and mitigation according to the different socio-economic characteristics of these two farm types. First, our results show that significant abatements in GHGs can be achieved, if farm-level abatements are sufficiently realised on many farms. However, the required incentive, a premium for organic soil management, is highly dependent on the expected market prices of crops, as well as on the production orientation of the farm. A premium is worth considering for farms with high production costs for cereals and which already allocate a significant area to be left under grass or as set-aside. However, higher compensation is required for the management of organic soils if crop prices increase above the estimated moderate prices. Overall, inexpensive GHG abatement cannot be expected to be realised on these farm types.

Our second main result is that policy measures meant to promote other targets, such as biodiversity promotion, may work as important complements to measures aiming at GHG abatement. NMF and other set-asides were already common in the studied farm types, even more so if incentivised for GHG abatement. The required premium for GHG abatement is likely to be significantly higher without such biodiversity payments, at least on production-oriented farms.

Our third main result is that seemingly very different crop farms may make rather similar management decisions at the crop and field parcel level. Land use decisions, management and their adaptation are dependent on production costs, the opportunity cost of labour, the share of agricultural income to total household income and risk aversion. These related factors sum up the way that crop and field parcel-specific management decisions, such as liming and nitrogen use, may be rather similar. However, the whole farm-level land use decisions of cereal crop and other crop farms are likely to remain different in the future. Nevertheless, by cooperating with more intensive and production-oriented farms, the analysed farm types may provide significant benefits not only in feed production but also in GHG abatement. This is encouraging since more than 60 per cent of farmland in the region is used by ambitious, production-oriented full-time farmers. This means that GHG mitigation, while constraining farm management and decreasing the farm-level benefits of adaptation, is not completely contradictory to climate change adaptation.

Acknowledgements

This research was funded by the Academy of Finland, through the following projects: A-La-Carte (decision no. 140870) and Marisplan (decision no. 140840), both belonging to the FICCA programme; and NORFASYS (decision no. 268277). We also acknowledge funding from the MTT strategic projects MODAGS (www.mtt.fi/modags) and SUSINTENSE.

References

Cai, R., Mullen, J.D., Wetzstein, M.E. and Bergstrom, J.C. (2012) The impacts of crop yields and price volatility on producers' cropping patterns: a dynamic optimal crop rotation model. *Agricultural Systems*, 116: 57–59. DOI http_//dx.doi.org/10.1016/j.agsy.2012.11.001.

Di Falco, S. and Perrings, C. (2005) Crop biodiversity, risk management and the implications of agricultural assistance. *Ecological Economy*, 55: 459–466.

Dury, J., Bergez, J.E., Schaller, N., Garcia, F. and Reynaud, A. (2011) Models to support cropping plan and crop rotation decisions: a review. *Agronomy Sustainability Development*, 32(2); 567–580.

Easterling, W., Aggarwal, P., Batima, K., Brander, J., Bruinsma, L., Erda, M., Howden, F., Tubiello, J., Antle, J. and Baethgen, W. (2007) *Food, Fibre and Forest Products. Climate Change 2007: Impacts, Adaptation and Vulnerability Contribution of Working Group II* Cambridge: Cambridge University Press.

Hakala, K., Hannukkala, A., Huusela-Veistola, E., Jalli, M. and Peltonen-Sainio, P. (2011) Pests and diseases in a changing climate: a major challenge for Finnish crop production. *Agricultural and Food Science*, 20(1): 3–14. Available at: www.mtt.fi/afs/pdf/mtt-afs-v20n1p3.pdf (accessed 4 September 2014).

Hardaker, J.B., Huirne, R.B.M. and Anderson, J.R. (1997) *Coping with Risk in Agriculture*. Wallingford: CAB International.

Hennessy, D.A. (2006) On monoculture and the structure of crop rotations. *American Journal of Agricultural Economics*, 88: 900–914.

Hertel, T.W., Burke, M.B. and Lobell, D.B. (2010) The poverty implications of climate-induced crop yield changes by 2030. Working Paper 59, Global Environmental Change, Global Trade Analysis Project. West Lafayette: GTAP.

Hiironen, J. and Ettanen, S. (2013) Peltoalueiden tilusrakenne ja sen parantamismahdollisuudet Maamittauslaitos Publication No. 113. Available at: www.maanmittauslaitos.fi/sites/default/files/Peltoalueiden%20tilusrakenne%20ja%20sen%20parantamismahdollisuudet.pdf (accessed 4 September 2014).

Kanellopoulos, A., Reidsma, P., Wolf, J. and van Ittersum, M.K. (2014) Assessing climate change and associated socio-economic scenarios for arable farming in the Netherlands: an application of benchmarking and bio-economic farm modeling. *European Journal of Agronomy*, 52: 69–80.

Lehtonen, H. (2001) Principles, structure and application of dynamic regional sector model of Finnish agriculture. PhD dissertation, Helsinki University of Technology.

Lehtonen, H. (2013) Sector-level economic modeling as a tool in evaluating greenhouse gas mitigation options. *Acta Agriculturae Scandinavica, Section A: Animal Science*, 62(4): 326–335. DOI: 10.1080/09064702.2013.797011.

Lehtonen, H., Kässi, P., Niskanen, O. and Huttunen, S. (2013) Yhteenveto ja muistiinpanot ryhmäkeskusteluista työpajasta Nivalassa 26.11.2013, MTT internal document. [A summary on workshop discussions in Nivala, upper central part of Finland, November]. [In Finnish].

Liu, X., Lehtonen, H., Purola, T., Pavlova, Y., Rötter, R. and Palosuo, T. (2014) Dynamic economic modelling of crop rotation choice with farm management practices under future pest pressure challenges. Submitted for evaluation in *Agricultural Systems*.

Luke (2015) Finnish official statistics. Structure of agricultural and horticultural enterprises. Available at: www. maataloustilastot.fi/en/structure-of-agricultural-and-horticultural-enterprises (accessed 25 May 2015).

Mavi (2014) Hakuopas. Available at: www.mavi.fi/fi/oppaat-ja-lomakkeet/viljelija/Hakuopas/Documents/Hakuopas_2014.pdf (accessed 4 September 2014).

Maynard, L.J.J., Harper, K. and Hoffman, L.D. (1997) Impact of risk preferences on crop rotation choice. *Review of Agricultural and Resource Economics Review*, 26(1): 106–114.

Meyer-Aurich, A., Weersink, A., Janovicek, K. and Deen, B. (2006) Cost efficient rotation and tillage options to sequester carbon and mitigate GHG emissions from agriculture in Eastern Canada. *Agricultural Ecosystem of Environment*, 117: 119–127.

MMM (2007) Manner-Suomen maaseudun kehittämisohjelma, 2007–2013 [Rural Development Programme for Continental Finland, 2007–2013]. Available at: www.maaseutu.fi/attachments/6BQPIuj8V/Manner-Suomen_maaseudun_kehittamisohjelma_2007-2013_090114.pdf (accessed 4 September 2014).

Myyrä, S., Ketoja, E., Yli-Halla, M. and Pietola, K. (2005) Land improvements under land tenure insecurity: the case of pH and phosphate in Finland. *Land Economics*, 81(4): 557–569.

OECD-FAO (2012) Agricultural Outlook 2012–2021. Available at: www.agri-outlook.org (accessed 4 September 2014).

Peltonen-Sainio, P., Jauhiainen, L., Hakala, K. and Ojanen, H. (2009) Climate change and prolongation of growing season: changes in regional potential for field crop production in Finland. *Agricultural and Food Science*, 18: 171–190.

Regina, K., Lehtonen, H., Nousiainen, J. and Esala, M. (2009) Modelled impacts of mitigation measures on greenhouse gas emissions from Finnish agriculture up to 2020.

Agricultural and Food Science, 18(3–4): 477–493. Available at: www.mtt.fi/afs/pdf/mtt-afs-v18n3-4p477.pdf (accessed 4 September 2014).

Regina, K., Lehtonen, H., Palosuo, T. and Ahvenjärvi, S. (2014) Maatalouden kasvihuonekaasupäästöt ja niiden vähentäminen. *MTT Raportti*, 127. Available at: http://jukuri.mtt.fi/bitstream/handle/10024/481727/mttraportti127.pdf (accessed 4 September 2014).

Seppälä, A., Kässi, P., Lehtonen, H., Aro-Heinilä, E., Niemeläinen, O., Lehtonen, E., Höhn, J., Salo, T., Keskitalo, M., Nysand, M., Winquist, E., Luostarinen, S. and Paavola, T. (2014) Nurmesta biokaasua liikennepolttoaineeksi. Bionurmi-hankkeen loppuraportti. *MTT Raportti*, 151.

Statistics Finland (2013) Greenhouse gas emissions in Finland 1990–2011. National Inventory Report under the UNFCCC and the Kyoto Protocol, 15.4.2013. Available at: www.stat.fi/greenhousegases (accessed 3 November 2014).

Statistics Finland (2014) Maa-ja metsätalousyritysten taloustilasto. Available at: www.stat.fi/til/mmtal/index.html (accessed 31 October 2014).

TIKE (2012) Finnish Official Statistics: Average farmland area per farm (ha/farm) at different farm types. Available at: www.maataloustilastot.fi/node/3153 (accessed 4 September 2014).

Tubiello, F.N. and van der Velde, M. (2012) Land and water use options for climate change adaptation and mitigation in agriculture, SOLAW Background Thematic Report – TR04A, FAO. Available at: www.fao.org/fileadmin/templates/solaw/files/thematic_reports/TR_04a_web.pdf (accessed 4 September 2014).

von Wijk, M.T., Rufino, M.C., Enahoro, D.D., Parsons Silvestri, S., Valdivia, R.O. and Herrero, M. (2014) Farm household models to analyse food security in a changing climate: a review. *Global Food Security*, 3(2): 77–84. DOI: 10.1016/j.gfs.2014.05.001.

12 Coping with climate change

Rural livelihoods, vulnerabilities and farm resilience

Marja Järvelä and Teea Kortetmäki

Introduction

The permanence and stability of the livelihoods of farms are vital for the continuation of agriculture. Traditionally, a farmer's livelihood was usually directly connected to yields but – due to modernisation – livelihoods have become more complex. Agricultural incomes and farm livelihoods no longer depend solely on annual yields, but also are based on many other factors, such as technological standards, production branches and the present social status of the farmer and his/her family. Coping with climate change is one further aspect adding to both the uncertainty and complexity of a farm and agricultural livelihood.

In a traditional rural village, wealth might have been distributed quite unevenly. Yet, agricultural prosperity was, in most cases, reflected throughout an entire village. Agriculture was labour-intensive and successful cultivation on bigger farms provided labour opportunities for the smallholders as well. In fact, bigger farms were often dependent on smallholders for their labour force.

In the past, a family farm was arguably the most prevalent social model for agricultural production. The most important asset for farming was land, and owning land was generally presumed to guarantee the permanence and stability of a farm livelihood. However, the predominance of land-owning family farms seems to be fading in many places, resulting in a major reorganisation of the social system in farming regions. Important parts of agriculture have been modified, more or less, into industrial production branches where family farms do not play as important a role as they used to. However, in many countries, family farms are still important suppliers, and thus key actors in the food supply chain. This chapter discusses rural livelihood issues and the main focus is on how family farms cope with modernisation and climate change (see Meert *et al.* 2005; Rønning and Kolvereid 2006).

Due to agricultural modernisation, the family farm is increasingly associated with smallholdings and/or some kind of alternative modes of production, such as organic production, local food or pluriactivity (e.g. Rønning and Kolvereid 2006). Although this tends to minimise the importance of the family farm in some situations, it also highlights the potential for innovation, which is important in coping with climate change. Thus, increasing the size of farms is not necessarily the main option for coping with climate change – as has been argued with reference to competitiveness in the global markets and the securing of farm livelihoods. However, one can ask if any signs indicate that alternative modes of agriculture can seriously challenge the economics produced by economies of scale and still simultaneously reduce the vulnerability of farms to climate change.

A further question concerns a more pervasive rural development. What is the impact of different agricultural models on the creation of a vital rural livelihood? This has been discussed, for example, in the productive versus post-productive rural development debate (e.g. Ilbery and Bowler 1998; Vesala and Vesala 2009). Rural modernisation has radically reduced the number of independent farms. Consequently, alternative sources of livelihood have been in high demand in rural areas. Concerning overall rural livelihood, it is important to consider how new methods of production and services in rural areas are connected to farms (Ploeg *et al.* 2000; Jokinen *et al.* 2008) and to ask if they function quite independently within the food chain. This "post-productivism" debate has mainly addressed the rural areas of industrialised countries, with many important observations being made in the EU. Moreover, EU countries have jointly composed major regulative mechanisms with the aim of guaranteeing the permanence and stability of rural development.

The main interest of this chapter is to revisit some issues concerning sustainable farm livelihoods from the perspective of farms trying to cope with climate change. Agriculture is an economic branch that continues to experience seemingly continual transitions. Generally these transitions are considered in terms of the challenges of maintaining competitiveness within the global markets and the subsequent socio-economic and socio-cultural changes in rural areas. However, competitiveness can also be conceived from the alternative perspective of food security and local resilience, especially when climate change is recognised as one of the major societal challenges of the twenty-first century. Farmers have an important role regarding their land use and are also key actors in the entire food supply chain. In fact, all other actors in the food chain depend on their provisions. However, in the modern food chains, farmers seldom have a dominant position (Jackson *et al.* 2006). An interesting question is how the interdependences between food chain actors are organised in order to deliver food eco-efficiently and in a flexible manner. In general, a farm's sustainable livelihood seems to correlate with good networking, adequate knowledge, skills and the transferable assets of individual farms (e.g. Ploeg and Renting 2000). However, a local cultural context may have even more meaning for the enhancing of a sustainable livelihood and adaptive capacity. These can be related to the spatial aspect of living and working space (Hinrichs 2011). This chapter will give one example of such embeddedness by using a case study in Finland for the analysis.

The chapter is structured as follows. First, some relevant approaches to rural sustainability and a climate-resilient farm livelihood are introduced. In addition to the literature review, some indicative questions will be proposed with a view to addressing the subsequent case study. We then display the case study research design and address some country profile issues regarding agriculture and the rural countryside in Finland. Next, we illustrate the thematic results of the main research issues, namely vulnerability, resilience and emerging assets for coping with climate change. We conclude with a brief discussion on the significance of the case study results from a more general point of view.

Climate-resilient farm livelihood and rural sustainability

Climate change research has developed the concept of resilience. This concept is based originally on ecology and refers to the capacity of the ecosystems to "withstand without changing self-organized processes and structures" when facing major disturbances (Gunderson 2000). In the social sciences, resilience usually refers to *social resilience* as the adaptive capacity of social systems. Specific meanings, such as community or rural resilience, have also been given. However, when considering the permanence of livelihood, the concept of resilience should not take us too far from the widely espoused concept of sustainability. Hence, we can ask how social sustainability translates into social resilience regarding agriculture, farm livelihood and community.

Looking at the sustaining of rural livelihoods from the farm resilience point of view, it is important to address the social embeddedness of local activities. In the food chain this embeddedness is emphatically embodied by reconnecting the food producer and the consumer (e.g. Jackson *et al.* 2006). Thus, the resilience of the entire food chain depends, first on all, on the capacity of farms to deliver the product to the next actor in all circumstances, and, second, on the other actors' capacity to complete their role in the chain. Furthermore, the supply chain needs to be integrated and managed efficiently from field to table in order to minimise vulnerabilities in food provision.

Five approaches were identified that can be called current coping strategies due to their capacity to increase permanence and the stability of the livelihoods of farms as well as rural livelihoods. Basically some of these strategies can be combined in rewarding ways (Meert *et al.* 2005). Nevertheless, the real impact of local strategies may be blurred if more than two strategies are combined simultaneously. The five approaches for coping, i.e. the sustainability strategies, are introduced below.

1 *Diversity of activities and pluriactivity on farms*: This coping strategy refers to the very general comprehension of systems in terms of their diversity, a characteristic inherent of a resilient system. When applied to agriculture and farm livelihood, this would mean that, instead of narrow specialisation and monoculture, a farm should strive to diversify its agri-economic efforts. Also external sources of livelihood may play an important role (Meert *et al.* 2005). Moreover, pluriactivity may even be associated with part-time farming (Fuller 1990; Eikeland and Lie 1999).
2 *Community and territorial food system as part of rural development model*: This strategy sees local networks and reciprocity as the key to rural development.

Thus, there is a strong emphasis on creating assets with a view to the entire community and the ameliorated livelihood of its population. This has much in common with the prevalent EU rural development strategy and the EU CAP policy, highlighting the consumption aspect within rural spaces. Therefore, a multiplicity of service activities, e.g. tourism and the maintenance of ecosystem services, can be understood as essential for rural sustainability and social resilience (see also Vesala and Vesala 2009). This strategy may also be linked to promoting provincial or local food brands and, in this way, enlarging the market for commerce from local areas to areas further afield, such as the EU, and, in some cases, even to global markets. Reciprocity not only means social networking for immediate *horizontal* provisions and delivery but even includes the idea of enhancing sustainability through long-term community learning (Meppem and Gill 1998; Marsden and Smith 2005; Kelemen *et al.* 2008).

3 *Vertical dependency model with special issues of reciprocity and trust*: The vertical dependency model highlights the issue of negotiations and power between possibly very unequal partners. Trust is necessary for these links and negotiations to operate in a way that guarantees an efficient delivery from field to table. In modern societies the setting of unequal partners in a vertical relationship often creates tensions and conflict (Jackson *et al.* 2006). However, these tensions may also lead to a dynamic situation regarding organising and re-organising the internal relationships of food chains in creative ways.

4 *Survival strategies with a short food supply chain*: Food chains in global markets tend to become continually more complex and spatially more extensive. This creates new risks and vulnerabilities regarding delivery. Therefore, one strategy proposed to enhance resilience and local sustainability is simply to reduce the complexity and the distances in the supply chain. From the individual farm standpoint, it might make sense to reduce the number of partners in the food chain in order to avoid sharing the value produced with too many other actors, such as the food industry and the retail sector. The logical extreme of this strategy is direct sales from farms. However, this kind of truncated supply chain is often associated with the "survival strategy" of family farms and even "marginal farming" (Meert *et al.* 2005). However, some community-based models, such as selling directly to consumers via farmers' markets, CSA arrangements or over the internet, have been recognised as more promising alternatives.

5 *Social safety net with macro-arrangements, such as social security schemes*: In this strategy a farm's livelihood depends strongly on social security arrangements. Each family farm has a generational lifecycle, thus the intensity of farming may alter depending on the age of the farmer. A generation shift on a farm is an important issue in many countries where rural to urban migration has been significant in recent decades. This has happened to the extent that food security might be in doubt both globally and locally. On the other hand, the EU in particular has identified the problem of abandoned rural development in its social policy and developed its own CAP strategy to

secure farm livelihood through integrated welfare state measures (see Vesala and Vesala 2009). This is an important support both for ageing farmers and to ensure the generation shift on farms.

All these strategies have been found not only in academic discussion but also in attempts to enhance farm livelihoods and rural development. We argue that the five strategies above are relevant, even with regard to coping with climate change. This is due simply to the fact that without major new regulative measures, it is likely that the transitions begun by farmers would have been the same.

Furthermore, we can presume most farms are looking at models that would guarantee the sustainability of their livelihood in the immediate future. Many individual family farms and farm households are currently in such a vulnerable position that closing down the business can be considered an alternative, especially at handover from one generation to the next. The reason to shut down can be, obviously, a lack of interest in farming. Yet, often the decisive factor behind closure is the poor prospects of earning an income from agriculture.

Before discussing the case study, a few concluding remarks will bridge the strategic issues and questions concerning farm resilience and income in Finland. As argued above, farm resilience is embedded in local activities. Therefore, it is natural to refer to the literature on case studies that are similar to rather than extremely different from Finland. For example, Rønning and Kolvereid (2006: 413) found, in their study on income diversification in Norwegian farm households, that young farmers have a higher income than those of the older generation. This is a simple statistical fact, yet in the local and regional context it reveals something about the current transition. Perhaps, younger farmers – those still working the farms after so many have moved to urban centres – have improved their ability to tackle the topical challenges of sustainable farming, including climate change. Simultaneously, older farmers may have adopted a more down-shifting strategy leading to insufficient plans for coping with climate change and other current challenges.

Case study: farming in Finland

Agriculture in Finland mainly produces food for the domestic market. Furthermore, people in Finland have quite a high respect for the quality of domestic food products in value terms (Järvelä *et al* 2009). Nevertheless, consumption statistics show that price is an important factor and despite the appreciation of domestic food, the majority of consumers choose the cheaper product in most cases. Thus, considering the negotiation terms along the food chain, there seems to be a constant issue of low payment at the start of the primary production line. Moreover, agricultural production is a highly regulated business. This is partly due to EU membership, but only partly because Finland has traditionally upheld a comprehensive national system of setting norms and incentives, and of providing public advice on agriculture.

The main reason for doing a case study of Finland is to illustrate some of the possible farm-level responses to the demand to adapt to climate change. To do so, we review the empirical investigations we have completed over several years during the past decade.[1]

We will refer more specifically to one set of interview data, which is used systematically (see below), while other data sets and secondary sources are used as general points of reference. We have had a long-term interest in understanding the circumstances and prerequisites for sustainable farm livelihoods in small North European countries, where the climate sets serious limits on agriculture. However, due to climate change the disadvantageous position of countries like Finland is no longer so obvious. Instead, it has been proposed that there are particularly good reasons to develop agriculture in the northern countries e.g. in Finland, to compensate for the eventual losses induced by climate change in the south of Europe.

Agriculture in Finland has gone through a profound transition since World War II. This has resulted in a considerable increase in farm size and the radical reduction of the number of farms. Nevertheless, the most typical farm still follows the family farm model and the average farm size remains fairly modest in comparison to other Western European countries. The number of farms has been halved from 110,000 to 55,000 in about two decades. Even so, many farms are presently under threat as the continuity of their business is endangered for many reasons, such as unprofitable production, a lack of means or the interest to invest, old age, the lack of a successor, etc. Furthermore, economies of scale have been the main reference point for agriculture. This applies both to the more traditional agricultural policy and to the environmentally orientated rural policy, including adaptation to climate change.

The resources and vulnerabilities are examined below through a content analysis applied to 12 interviews performed in 2013 with farmers working on their family farms. The investigation was performed under the aegis of the Finnish Climate Panel and was funded by the Ministry of the Environment. The main aim was to map out the perceptions of farmers regarding the social acceptability of the national climate policy. Each interview included a discussion on the resources for and constraints on current activities on farms, including livelihood issues. In the following analysis, livelihood issues are the main focus, while the legitimacy of the climate policy is mostly not discussed.

Coping with climate change: alternative farming, social vulnerabilities and emerging assets

The voice of Finnish farmers is heard in the following summary of the case study. Obviously, this demonstration is based on a small qualitative sample and might be biased because more active and knowledgeable people were probably selected for this inquiry rather than the average individual. This is because we carried out a consultation in farming communities, whereby the respondents were suggested by people who knew them. On the other hand, the group that was selected includes farmers from the main agricultural branches, from different age groups, and geographically covers most of Finland, except for the Arctic region. So the respondents are reasonably representative of national diversity.

The interviewees were predominantly full-time farmers who rely mainly on an agricultural income for their family's livelihood. Their arable land is usually less than 100 hectares, which is typical of functioning family farms in Finland. Consequently, in most cases, the farms do not hire regular external labour. Instead, the family members seem to be quite flexible about making themselves available when extra labour is needed. For example, the common-law wife of a farmer, who has a regular job in a city, joins in farm work at the weekend. Often, however, both spouses work on a farm, especially if the farm practises animal husbandry. It seems that in most cases a farm's household budget is tight, setting a high threshold for hiring an external labour force. This obviously constrains major investments regarding the extension of arable lands or the building of new facilities. In these circumstances continuation is still, however, largely guaranteed by passing ownership of the farmlands from father/mother to son/daughter.

Even if there are some pronounced limits for economic growth, current farmers seem clearly more business-minded than earlier generations. Various kinds of calculations concerning the profitability of their business, whether concerning the cultivation of new species or new crop combinations, are of great interest. This is an important change as previous research on Finland's agrarian population had pointed more towards how it aimed to preserve cultural continuity (see e.g. Silvasti 2003). However, with the shift in generations, we can clearly identify that younger farmers often have a much higher education than the previous generation, helping them to consider new alternatives within farming.

Alternative farming

Despite the remarkable agricultural transition in Finland, there is a relatively steady basis for the family farm type of land ownership and agriculture, which is further supported by many farms owning forests in addition to arable land. Even if forestry is seldom a major source of regular family income, it contributes to the overall stability of the economic situation. Combining agriculture and forestry on farms also opens up an interesting view on the issue of pluriactivity as a new paradigm for securing farm livelihoods. One could even argue that Finnish farms are multifunctional by tradition, since they have always more or less combined agriculture and forestry. In the past, this practice had an interesting impact on the gender division of labour. Before machines took over logging, men gained a livelihood for families through hard manual work in the forests, while women took care of the cattle and other animals on the farm. However, today's cattle herds are bigger and both spouses are often needed on a farm's premises. The fact that spouses now work closer to one another makes the gender division of labour more flexible.

Although there is a strong tradition of multifunctionality on Finnish farms, it does not necessarily imply a mindset appropriate to the options of alternative farming being proposed in the academic literature. Many pluriactivity options are connected to service branches that diverge considerably from traditional farming, e.g. eco-tourism. Based on the interviews, in Finland it can be argued that farm activities are combined more easily with paid work – even with long-distance commuting – than with novel on-farm services. Moreover, when speaking of *alternatives*, farmers tend to concentrate their efforts on their core agricultural production, thus they are more likely to consider alternative concepts of agriculture than the extension of business into other industries or services. For example, organic food and especially local food concepts have relatively high support among farmers. Yet they are quite cautious about fully committing themselves to setting up a business with these alternative concepts.

Finnish consumers have lately been putting increasing pressure on agriculture to increase and adopt alternative production modes. This is also reflected in their readiness to pay higher prices. Although this group of consumers is not the majority, they still tend to be more numerous than what is conventionally identified as niche market consumers. Conclusively, we can say there is a tendency towards moving to alternative agriculture on Finnish farms, even if it is a cautious tendency with many reservations related not only to profitability and family livelihoods but also to the eco-technological efficiency of these new alternatives.

Vulnerabilities

The main vulnerabilities with a view to climate change and farm livelihood stem from the prospects related to the three dimensions of sustainability. The ecological dimension of the future of farming includes both positive and negative perspectives for Finnish farmers. The respondents generally agree that – with the eventual warming of the climate – the change could bring some comparative advantages to farms in Finland. Some signs of an extended growing season have already been observed. However, risks related to climate change have already been noticed, such as an increase in storms. And, even if the immediate consequences are often felt more in the forestry sector (falling trees), the sense of risk is heightened and tentatively connected to livelihood prospects. Many respondents mentioned that climate change will probably increase the risk of pests, harmful insects and plant diseases. Moreover, depending on the location of the farm, it was anticipated that fields would be endangered by seasonal floods.

Although the farmers considered the ecological impacts of climate change that will affect the economic sustainability of Finnish farms, there was great uncertainty about whether the overall impact would be positive or not. Farmers themselves are used to making their own calculations about profitability on grounds other than the emerging climate change. Furthermore, they openly admit that their economies are quite restricted, meaning that a large investment, e.g. building a modern cow barn, needs careful consideration. A lack of capital also apparently leads to cautious steps being taken in the renewal of their crop selection and investment in new machinery. In this sense, the farmers saw their business as more vulnerable to climate change than resilient to it.

Economic vulnerabilities are perceived to be linked with social vulnerabilities, even if this connection is often difficult to articulate in concrete terms. With a view to the operative farm, the element of social vulnerability most often mentioned concerns the generational shift. It is not at all obvious that all farms will continue once the current farmer retires. This was emphatically heard in the considerations of the oldest generation still working. In their case, there were clear signs of reducing farm work as well as incentives and investment. Moreover, climate change as a topic was not necessarily tackled by them as a practical challenge, but more as an issue of general interest.

Finally, social vulnerability is intertwined with rural development in broader terms. As more people abandon the rural regions, the more farms are likely to become socially isolated. However, the impact of rural to urban migration also depends on the region. Parallel to the emptying of parts of the countryside, there are also rural or semi-rural areas near the urban agglomerations where the population density is actually growing rapidly. Hence, the most aggravated vulnerabilities remain for the most depopulated regions, while those areas gaining a new population are acquiring but also require new options to create alternative activities, such as truly local food.

Emerging assets

As a Nordic country, Finland is known for its highly developed welfare state measures, which are designed to avoid social exclusion. Furthermore, farming is highly regulated by EU standards and norms. To make public advocacy and steering even more complete, Finland has also created quite an impressive national agricultural policy. One important aspect of the emerging professionalism among farmers has been to cope with the high complexity of regulations. In contrast to previous times, it seems that most farmers today have sufficient skills to deal with all the regulative measures and endorsement schemes. Nevertheless, the complexity of the public schemes causes uncertainty and makes it difficult to assess the combined effects of the various environmental, economic and social security schemes on the productivity and economic viability of farms. This perplexity was reflected sometimes in the phrasing of the respondents when they tried to indicate which schemes they participated in but were not able to give them their proper name.

It is common knowledge among rural people that societal support has a reverse side and, in the worst case, might impede innovation and entrepreneurship in agriculture. Nonetheless, farmers are demonstrating an emerging modern entrepreneurial mind in the reorganisation of their family farms. For example, they might establish a new form of joint enterprise, most often with either close relatives or some neighbouring farmers. This seems to add a great deal to the perceived resilience of their farms since these arrangements help them to minimise the disadvantages related to the constant shortage of capital. They may share, for example, the investment costs of new building, machinery, or even rotate their labour forces between their farms. However, as mentioned by some of the respondents, there are quite clear limits to the practicality of these arrangements – since many activities are seasonally determined and require completing within a single brief period.

Horizontal networking may also increase resilience even in more modest modes, as in establishing networks to procure seeds, animals or fertilisers. Also reciprocal help for seasonal work might be on the agenda for otherwise independent farmers living in the same area. Today it is not easy to speak of traditional villages due to considerable outflow migration. Consequently, the landscape around the farms may be perceived more as productive space or ecosystem services for wider, more mobile populations than the villages in the traditional sense. Thus, the village as such is no longer considered a primary resort for resilience, therefore farmers need to cooperate as individuals when selecting their partners.

Finally, horizontal networking may empower farmers, even with regard to vertical relationships and these relationships may contribute to the supply chain at large by giving the farmers more voice in negotiating with the food industry, and both wholesale and retail agents. Horizontal relations can also empower farmers in their direct relations with the end-users of food, whether we are talking about restaurant businesses or individual consumers choosing their daily food from supermarkets or by purchasing directly from farms or a local farmers organisation.

Conclusion

At first sight, the family farm in Finland may seem more vulnerable than resilient when facing the challenge of coping with climate change. This seems to hold true both with respect to their immediate livelihood as well as the more long-term prospects for economic and social sustainability. However, the Finnish family farm is also quite flexible and perhaps has the best chance to efficiently use the local assets and local networks. Hence, the reasons for the suggested current vulnerabilities and risks to farm livelihoods should be identified and reduced in order to enhance resilience and food security. Much of the positive potential for Finland that is being brought about by climate change – regarding farming – requires the securing of sustainable farm livelihoods on the family farms that are currently in operation. That can be attained in a variety of ways: by diversifying farm activities and by the reorganisation of food chain management through bottom-up initiatives to enhance resilience.

Acknowledgements

This study was supported by the Academy of Finland, through the project A-LA-CARTE (decision no. 140870) and the Finnish Ministry of the Environment.

Note

1 These investigations were mainly performed within the framework of two different research projects funded by the Academy of Finland, namely Sustainable Development and Pioneering Small-Scale Rural Entrepreneurs (SUSMARU), 2007–2009 and Assessing the Limits of Adaptation to Climate Change and Opportunities for Resilience to be Enhanced (A-LA-CARTE), 2011–2014.

References

Eikeland, S. and Lie, I. (1999) Pluriactivity in rural Norway. *Journal of Rural Studies*, 15(4): 405–415.

Fuller, A.M. (1990) From part-time farming to pluriactivity: a decade of change in rural Europe. *Journal of Rural Studies*, 6(4): 361–373.

Gunderson, L. (2000) Ecological resilience: in theory and application. *Annual Review of Ecology and Systematics*, 31: 425–439.

Hinrichs, C. (2011) Sideline and lifeline, rural studies, the cultural economy of maple syrup production. *Rural Sociology*, 63(4): 507–532.

Ilbery, B. and Bowler, I. (1998) From agricultural productivism to post-productivism. In B. Ilbery (ed.) *The Geography of Rural Change*, Harlow: Longman, pp. 57–84.

Jackson, P., Ward, N. and Russell, P. (2006) Mobilising the commodity chain concept in the politics of food and farming. *Journal of Rural Studies*, 22(2): 129–141.

Järvelä, M., Jokinen, P., Huttunen, S. and Puupponen, A. (2009) Local food and renewable energy as emerging new alternatives of rural sustainability in Finland, *European Countryside*, 1(2): 113–124.

Jokinen, P., Järvelä, M., Puupponen, A, and Huttunen, S. (2008) Experiments of sustainable rural livelihood in Finland. *International Journal of Agricultural Resources, Governance and Ecology, (IJARGE)*, 7(3): 211–228.

Kelemen, E., Megyesi, B. and Kalamász, I. (2008) Knowledge dynamics and sustainability in rural livelihood strategies: two case studies from Hungary. *Sociologia Ruralis*, 48(3): 257–273.

Marsden, T. and Smith, E. (2005) Ecological entrepreneurship: sustainable development in local communities through quality food production and local branding. *Geoforum*, 36(2005): 440–451.

Meert, H., Huylenbroeck van, G., Gent, U., Vernimmen, T., Bourgeois, M. and Van Hecke, E. (2005) Farm household survival strategies and diversification on marginal farms. *Journal of Rural Studies*, 21: 81–97.

Meppem, T. and Gill, R. (1998) Planning for sustainability as a learning concept. *Ecological Economics*, 26(2): 121–137.

Ploeg, van der, J. and Renting, H. (2000) Impact and potential: a comparative review of European rural development practices. *Sociologia Ruralis*, 40(4): 529–543.

Ploeg, van der, J., Renting, H., Brunori, G., Knickel, K., Mannion, J., Marsden, T., Roest de, K., Sevilla-Quzmán, E., Ventura, F. (2000) Rural development: from practices and policies towards theory. *Sociologia Ruralis*, 40(4): 391–408.

Ronning, L. and Kalvereid, L. (2006) Income diversification in Norwegian farm households: reassessing pluriactivity. *International Small Business Journal*, 24(4): 405–420.

Silvasti, T. (2003) The cultural model of "the good farmer" and the environmentel question in Finland. *Agricultural and Human Values*, 20(2): 143–150.

Vesala, H.T. and Vesala, K.M. (2009) Enterpreneurs and producers: identities of Finnish farmers in 2001 and 2006. *Journal of Rural Studies*, 26(1): 21–30.

Part IV

Climate-resilient supply chain management

Upstream and downstream

13 Managing food systems to enhance resilience

Helena Kahiluoto, Karoliina Rimhanen, Miia Kuisma and Hanna Mäkinen

Introduction

Food systems are comprised of food chain (network) actors (Figure 13.1), input providers, waste managers and actors of various support systems including authorities and policy-makers. Food systems are social-ecological systems and, as such, vulnerable to shifts both in the ecological preconditions such as climate but also to market, financial and political instability. For example, the currently developing effects of climate change and the resultant weather extremes may affect fodder yield, while the effects of certain changes, such as more powerful storms than before, can be to interrupt the energy supply. The mitigation of climate change necessarily causes shifts in energy prices and consequently in fertiliser and fodder prices affecting profitability and increasing risks regarding long-term investments. Furthermore, new competitors currently are entering the globalising market, abruptly altering the operational environment. All of which suggests that food systems are facing increased uncertainty and volatility both in ecological and socio-economic terms.

The development of increased turbulence in the operational environment of food systems has created the need to develop increased resilience: "the capacity of a system to absorb disturbance and reorganise while undergoing change so as to still retain essentially the same function, structure, identity, and feedbacks" (Walker *et al.* 2004). When critical thresholds are crossed, and thus the adaptive capacity is exceeded, the capacity to transform becomes an essential quality – if the system operations are to be maintained (Folke *et al.* 2010). The subsequent transformation – due to shifts in climate, market or policies – can be dramatic, even implying a re-location of farming or processing.

For centuries, the dairy industry has been the most important production line and the main pillar of livelihoods in the Finnish and Russian rural regions around the Baltic Sea. It still is important for regional economies, but is now facing shifts and disturbances that are threatening its functions, its extent and even its existence. The dairy system relies on having self-sufficient forage production, which makes the system highly dependent on natural resources and very vulnerable to climate change. Furthermore, dairy systems have become globally networked, e.g. through market competition and procurement of protein

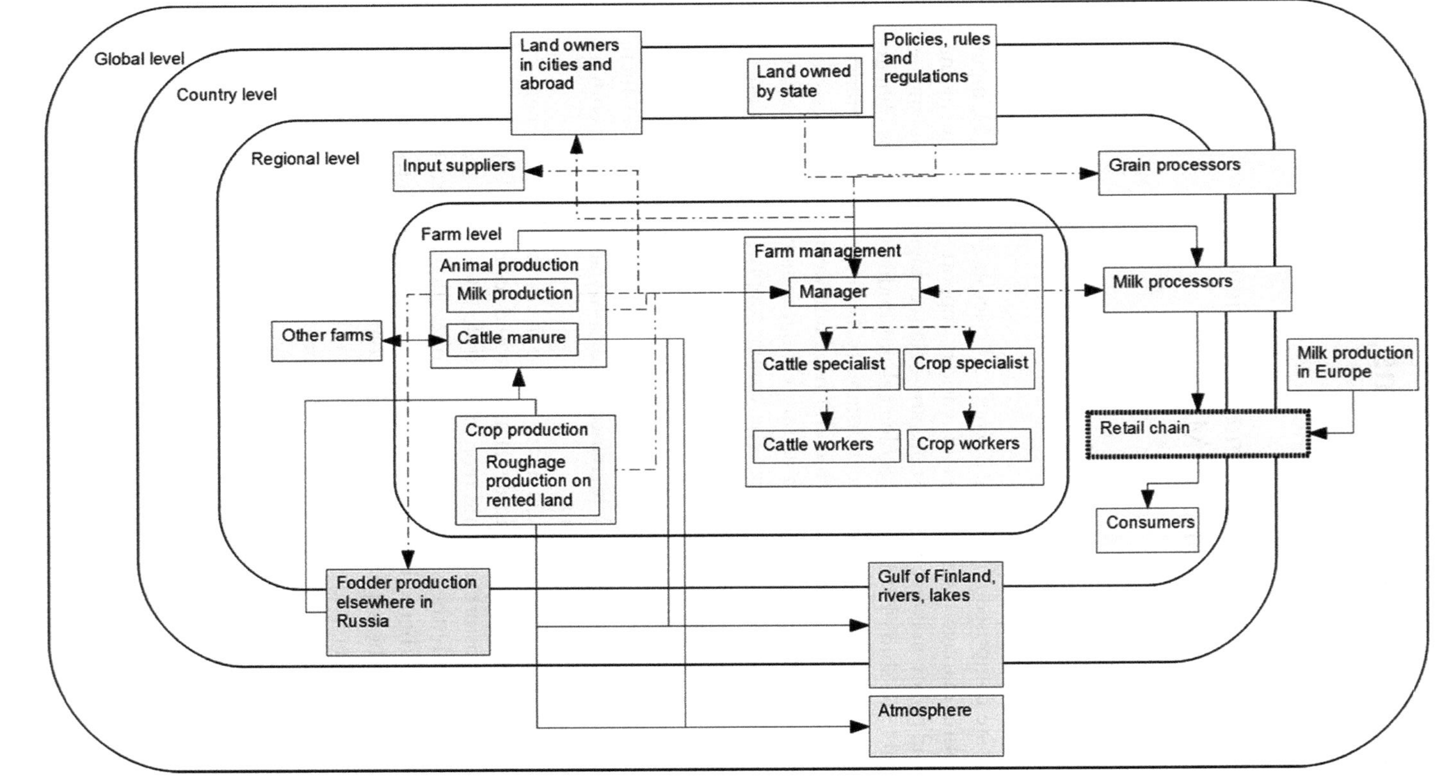

Figure 13.1 A conceptual model of social and ecological components and their relations in a food system, illustrated by the case of the dairy system of Leningrad Oblast in Russia

Note: Social interactions are marked with broken lines and material (e.g. product) flows with unbroken lines.

fodder, thus increasing vulnerability to fluctuations in global market prices and policies.

The most prominent differences between the Finnish and Russian dairy systems are in their scale: Russian dairy farms are holdings many times larger due to the fact that Finnish dairy farms are mostly family-owned. Furthermore, in Finland, milk processing is consolidated and contract-based, whereas, in Russia, there is great diversity in size and contracts of processors. Lastly, Finland and Russia have differences in access to technology. In recent years, the spike in the EU price of raw milk in 2007, followed by the instability of the financial situation and the growth in milk production in dairy farms, has resulted in producer prices as low as 0.20€ cents per litre in 2009 in many EU countries. The embargo on food supplies from European countries to Russia, increased production costs, the entry of new EU member countries with lower costs, animal diseases and changes in agricultural and environmental policies have all tested the ability of the dairy production systems of these countries to function, creating a high demand for resilience and the adaptive capacity at all levels of the various milk supply chains.

Retailers, probably the most powerful actors in the current European agrifood systems, are in a key position in food demand chains also regarding dairy products and beef. They are in a position to ensure consumer access to food, despite price volatility, but also to ensure the access of farmers and processors to the market. Farmers, on the other hand, also hold a key position in the food supply chains by maintaining milk and fodder production while facing climate change and as they directly interact with the input and the processing industries. Farmers are important actors not only at farm level, but as the main managers at the field level.

In this chapter, we synthesise the studies we have conducted in an attempt to operationalise resilience in the Northern European food systems. We explore the determinants of resilience from the viewpoint of the key actors from both the food demand and the supply chain. Our hypothesis based on our previous work was that social networks allowing: (1) the compensation of key actors; (2) the integration of material and energy flows; and (3) response diversity in various parts of a food system are among the key determinants of resilience.

Hypothetical determinants of food systems resilience

To identify the key determinants of food systems' resilience, we operationalised resilience as the capacity to maintain or quickly return good performance when facing multiple plausible futures (Kahiluoto and Himanen 2012), shocks or variability. Good performance was – at the dairy system level – indicated by access to affordable food by consumers, while at the farm level it was indicated by continuity, profitability and environmental performance, and at the field level it was indicated by forage and fodder grain yield. The major factors of change that are presumed to be critical for the performance of dairy systems were considered to be input and output price volatility and weather variability. This operationalisation was also tested and developed through the results of the empirical qualitative studies (Figure 13.2).

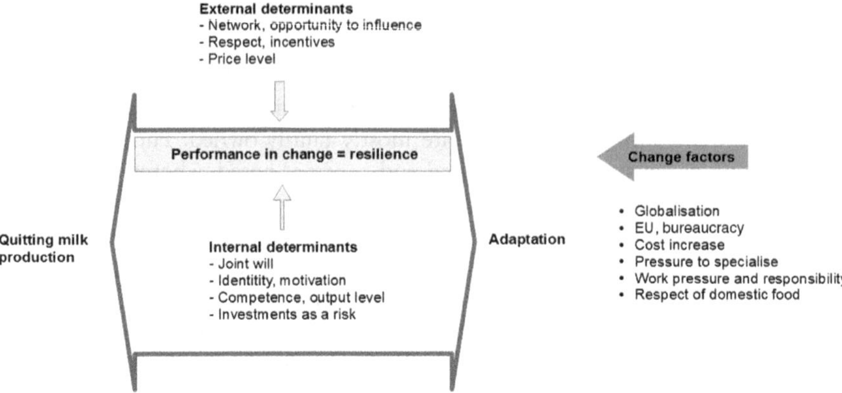

Figure 13.2 Operationalisation and critical characteristics for resilience of a dairy system to social-ecological variability and change

Social networks of milk supply chains

The way change affects a food system depends both on the characteristics of the shock and the system addressed. Minor changes disturb system operations only temporarily, whereas major ones can cause a system to collapse. Certain characteristics make a system more tolerant and improve its ability to adapt to change and recover. Managing resilience requires understanding the critical changes and how the components and functions of the system respond. The identification of the determinants of a system's ability to maintain key functions and to take advantage of any new opportunities is the starting point (Gitz and Meybeck 2012).

Scientific literature on the type of social networks that favour a system's resilience emphasise a flexible, diverse and moderately integrated system design, which has replaceable components (Janssen *et al.* 2006). The ability to compensate for a loss of critical functions increases flexibility and independence from individual actors, whose function may change (Olsson *et al.* 2004). Consequently, a broad-ranging supply network can provide leeway for a company when the prices of inputs rise or fluctuate due to global change. Hence, the capacity to adapt and transform, when changes prevent successful operations in the existing conditions, requires a diverse social network as well as economic, social and cultural capital (Folke *et al.* 2010). In addition, the ability to identify and build interactions founded on trust and feedbacks between actors can enhance the performance of systems in the long run (Walker and Salt 2006).

Integration of material and energy economy in dairy systems

In agriculture, especially in the developed world, fertiliser, fodder and energy expenses are significant, while, at the same time, market variation and extremes in the prices of these inputs have become more common. Following on from that observation, the integration of socio-ecological systems could be a key element in enhancing the resilience of food systems also (e.g. Cumming *et al.* 2005; May *et al.* 2008). Integrated, recycling farming systems may reduce dependence on external inputs, reducing vulnerability to price fluctuation. Moreover, by recycling the nutrients of organic waste and by-products as well as cascading energy, it is possible to compensate for fossil inputs (Rufino *et al.* 2009; Kahiluoto *et al.* 2011). However, currently nutrient flows in food systems are relatively open: manure is used inefficiently in fields, the organic waste produced by food systems is rarely recycled as fertiliser and the energy utilisation of organic waste is still relatively minor. The integration of farming systems has been studied, especially in the developing world, where higher resilience to climate change in terms of profitability has been reported among integrated rather than specialised farms (Niggol Seo 2010). In this study, the nutrient and energy economy of dairy farms was conceptualised by including all major nutrient and energy flows of the systems.

Response diversity in food systems

Diversity appears to play a key role in providing resilience and the metaphorical seeds for renewal, thus allowing food systems to adapt to change and disturbance. In particular, the ability to renew and reorganise after a disturbance depends on the heterogeneity of reactions within a function (Elmqvist *et al.* 2003). Therefore, it is important to distinguish the critical diversity to manage resilience and adaptive capacity in food systems. For example, at the supply chain level, if there is a weather anomaly or a strike, do all of the retailers' supply channels collapse or will some suppliers remain working despite the disturbance? And, in the field, when facing heatwaves and drought, do all species suffer or will some animal species and crops be more tolerant of the occurring stress? The consequences of a disturbance will be different depending on the extent to which the components within a system are affected and suffer.

Although an established concept in ecology (Elmqvist *et al.* 2003), there are few empirical examples of response diversity within managed ecosystems showing how grass species vary in their tolerance to grazing (Walker *et al.* 1999), how barley cultivars vary in their sensitivity to weather (Hakala *et al.* 2012) and how biomass production is enhanced during drought stress by mixing drought-resistant spruce with fast-growing aspens (Man and Greenway 2013).

A food system that contains a high degree of response diversity at various hierarchical levels is hypothesised as resilient to various stresses and disturbances and able to provide renewal. Response diversity can be assessed at various food system levels and dimensions, such as in information and knowledge systems, market channels, income opportunities, fodder crops or cultivars.

Empirical analysis

We adopted a mixed qualitative-quantitative approach to increase our in-depth understanding of the attributes that represent and determine food system resilience at various food system levels. In this section we present a series of empirical studies conducted in Finland and in Russia. First, a Delphi study on *determinants of adaptive capacity of food systems* involving a representative set of Finnish food system actors (Kahiluoto and Himanen 2012) is discussed. Second, qualitative-quantitative interviews to study the *social networks of milk supply chains* and the *material and energy economy in dairy systems* in Finland and in North-west Russia are reported. Third, the *response diversity of the food system* was studied at the retail and field levels in Finland by using various sets of quantitative data (Kahiluoto and Himanen 2012; Kahiluoto *et al.* 2014).

The Finnish Delphi study included a discussion workshop and two web questionnaire rounds with selected stakeholders representing various levels of the food chain from farms to consumers. The qualitative-quantitative interview data on the social networks of milk supply chains and on material and energy economy comprised 23 interviews conducted with current and former Finnish and Russian dairy farmers, milk processors and regional authorities. There were 11 dairy farmers and two milk processors in the Finnish interviewee set. The Russian interviewees included seven dairy farmers and two milk processors. The data was collected through semi-structured interviews which were tape-recorded and transcribed. To get a broad range of variation for the hypothesised determinants of resilience, dairy farms were selected that differed in terms of the following characteristics:

1. *rate of social networking*: the farms had no or a low rate of cooperation or they had a high rate of cooperation through joint ownership, contracting and knowledge sharing;
2. *nutrient and energy economy*: the farms used primary or secondary nutrient sources, and fossil or renewable energy sources;
3. *diversity of functions*: the farms were specialised dairy farms or they also practised crop production, meat production, the direct selling of raw milk or the contracting of agricultural machinery.

For the purpose of quantifying the impact of response diversity in the food system, we used the following data sets: (1) for the *supplier diversity* on sales and the price set by retailers, we used the retailers' sales data set of prices and purchases for around 30 retail stores; (2) official statistics from TIKE and Statistics Finland, and (3) FAOSTAT price indices (Kahiluoto and Himanen 2012). The response diversity at the field level was quantified (Kahiluoto *et al.* 2014) by using the MTT Official Variety Trial data for barley and forage crops, the weather data of the Finnish Meteorological Institute and farm data for validation. Barley and forage grasses were chosen for the case study because they play a key role in dairy farming in Northern Europe.

Initial findings

The actors from the various levels of the Finnish food system suggested transparency, dialogue and collective learning across the food system as being among the main determinants of the capacity to adapt to an uncertain future. The ability to take advantage of new opportunities was also considered very important and this is understood to work best when a food system is benefitting from collective learning. Energy and nutrient sovereignty were also highlighted as major determinants of food system resilience, reflecting the perceived vulnerability of the current streamlined provision of these critical inputs of the food supply chain – in which farms and farmers are seen as the most vulnerable actors, especially when facing climate change. The above views of the experts in the Delphi study set the framework for the search for specific factors of resilience, which were identified in the social networks, the integration of waste-based nutrient and energy flows and in the need for increased diversity within the food system.

Looking for stability in times of turbulence: contrasting strategies in Finland and Russia

According to the interviewees, shifts in policies, access to land as well as market competition and demand were considered to be the most important change factors in the operational environment of the dairy system (Figure 13.2). These factors, especially unpredictable shifts in public environmental regulations, were in fact perceived as more critical than weather and market variability. The determinants of resilience were considered partly internal, partly external to the farms, and thus some were considered beyond the control of the farming community. Among the determinants there were social, economic and ecological factors. However, social attributes played the most important role, especially relationships within a farm family, but networking with other actors in the dairy system, such as with other farmers, processors and input producers, was also critical.

Human relations on a farm were found to be crucial for farm performance and continuity according to the interviewees. In Finland, this usually means the relationship between the farming couple and their children, with the frequency of divorce being a major threat to the continuity of dairy farms. In Russia, the most important human relationships on the farms are between the farm manager, the experts in charge of various parts of the farm activities and the farm workers. Trust among these actors is essential to manage the whole farming system in optimal ways and to avoid conflict, for example, by preserving the balance between the volume targets of cropping and the health and production targets of animal nutrition, which are often run by different experts in Russian large-scale farming.

The interviewees perceived the interaction on and between farms as important, especially with regard to knowledge sharing and peer-support, but also for collaboration and animals sales, etc. Connections between farms and the authorities were emphasised in relation to the introduction and control of regulations and the incentivising of sustainable production, such as manure exploitation during cropping or the minimising of emissions in Russia. In both countries, the setting of regulations and policies was primarily perceived as an important uncertainty factor and considered a source of frustration rather than an enabling factor.

The most important determinants for resilience varied according to the actor's perspective. From the perspective of a farmer or landowner, both in Russia and in Finland, the option to rent land and thus maintain or expand farming activity, would seem to be important but, for reasons of ownership, it is not a guaranteed asset to ensure continuity, and increasing the extent of fields is costly. For farms, especially in Russia around St Petersburg, but also in Finland, an increasing number of landowners who provide land for rent are investors in cities far away, or even abroad. Thus, farmers have to have contacts with both a local, but usually a declining, rural community and ever more remote landowners in order to secure access to land. Nonetheless, if a farm owner came from within a farming community, this was considered a guarantee of farm continuity, in both countries, despite the changing environment.

The option to buy inputs, such as concentrated feed from various sources, appears to be essential for resilience. The corresponding option to sell milk to several buyers, preferably to major global enterprises as well as to local dairies producing high-quality products, and thus offering a higher price, was perceived to be an important way to ensure stability of income and continuity in Russia. Due to the higher quality requirements of the local cheese manufacturing dairies, the chance to provide milk to large-scale global food processing companies helped secure demand when milk quality fluctuated due to, for example, the quality of the fodder. While many determinants of resilience were found to be the same in the socio-economically contrasting regions, diversification strategies were much less applied in Finland. For instance, in the sales channels, in Finland diversity was replaced by the security created by the cooperative ownership of the major processor of the milk produced on the farms. The farmers identify themselves with the cooperative and were proud of its successes in adding value to its dairy products and thus its ability to keep the prices stable and satisfactory.

Integration of material and energy economy: paradigm changes on farms

The approach of intentionally striving for independent action regarding the critical energy and nutrient inputs – by efficiently recycling nutrients and cascading the energy of the farm or food system waste – was only applied by some pioneering farmer groups. This was in Finland mainly due to economic obstacles, and in Russia, there were also technological obstacles to such strategies.

In Finland, the creation of strong buffers against increasing and varying input prices was found to result from the satisfactory, stable producer price for raw milk provided by the dairy cooperative with its successful strategies, such as advanced product development; second, the continuous increase in the productivity of dairy cattle; and third, the agricultural subsidies which reduce dependence on input prices. Nevertheless, the same factors which protect the Finnish dairy system from input price increase, on the other hand, counteract the transformation of the aforementioned nutrient strategies, which would be required to adapt to the long-term shifts in price levels and the demand for public goods.

Further barriers to the transformation of the current system and the creation of an independent and more efficient and sustainable nutrient and energy economy in dairy farming include the farmers' identity as a producer, which affects them by making the possible decline of milk productivity a risk they are not willing to take. Linked with the notion of identity are other barriers such as the requirements for new knowledge and skills in order to implement changes in farming strategies.

The perceived changes in the nutrient economy have been policy-led. In Finland, the changes were characterised by applying simply 'less of the old' (less phosphorus fertilisers) rather than by a transformation to a new strategy of efficient recycling of secondary nutrients. In Russia, the awareness of the problems has led to expressions of shame regarding the current strategy of piling manure as if it were waste. Changes in the energy economy of farming have been even smaller than in the nutrient economy, but, until now, have been mainly price-led, while effective incentives by energy policies have not been offered to farming in these regions.

Response diversity: a novel perspective adds value

Response diversity seems to open new perspectives on the management of resilience in dairy systems. The novel approach of managing response diversity appears useful in enhancing resilience in the face of volatile global markets and climate change, for example, in terms of food price stability or yield (Kahiluoto and Himanen 2012; Kahiluoto *et al.* 2014). The supplier diversity of retail stores appears to protect sales and retail price stability. The retail stores purchasing their products from a more diverse set of suppliers (including smaller slaughterhouses, in addition to national actors), for example, were able to maintain their sales stability during and after strikes within the domestic food industry. A similar phenomenon was shown to form a buffer against global market price volatility; for instance, in the years with a high global market price for food oil, the retail stores with a higher share of domestic oil suppliers showed higher sales at a lower price, while in years with a low global price level, the opposite was the case. Consequently, an even distribution of purchases by the retail sector from among their different suppliers would seem to secure retail sales and consumer access to affordable food.

Managing resilience of fodder production through response diversity was shown by the practically significant differences among the reactions of the forage crops and cultivars to extreme weather, e.g. one cultivar notably suffers from heat stress and another from high precipitation. Since a single barley cultivar or forage crop species does not successfully respond to all stressful weather events, using targeted combinations of species and cultivars could enhance the performance of fodder production to cope with variability in the weather.

The approach is being further developed by producing practical tools for enhancing communication between breeders, farmers and other relevant stakeholders (see also Chapter 4).

Conclusion

We conclude that strategies to cope with shocks and change are important ways to complement the short-term efficiency in a rapidly changing world. Resilience in food systems is determined by social, economic and ecological factors, but social attributes, such as human relationships on a farm and networking with other actors in food systems, play a key role. The barriers to recycling nutrients and cascading energy deserve further attention to unlock the rigidity created by paradigms and policies. Generally, connectivity but also the flexibility and diversity of actor networks within the food system seem to facilitate coping with critical changes. Response diversity allows the use of diversity to enhance resilience in an efficient, targeted way on the various levels of food systems.

References

Cumming, G.S., Barnes, G., Perz, S., Schmink, M., Sieving, K.E., Southworth, J., Binford, M., Holt, R.D., Stickler, C. and Van Holt, T. (2005) An exploratory framework for the empirical measurement of resilience. *Ecosystems*, 8: 975–987.

Elmqvist, T., Folke, C., Nyström, M., Peterson, G., Bengtsson, J., Walker, B. and Norberg, J. (2003) Response diversity and ecosystem resilience. *Frontiers in Ecology and the Environment*, 1: 488–494.

Folke, C., Carpenter, S.R., Walker, B., Scheffer, M., Chapin, T. and Rockström, J. (2010) Resilience thinking: integrating resilience, adaptability and transformability. *Ecology and Society*, 15(4): 20.

Gitz, V. and Meybeck, A. (2012) Risks, vulnerabilities and resilience in a context of climate change. In A. Meybeck, J. Lankoski, S. Redfern, N. Azzu and V. Gitz (eds) *Building Resilience for Adaptation to Climate Change in the Agriculture Sector: Proceedings of a Joint FAO/OECD Workshop*. Rome: FAO.

Hakala, K., Jauhiainen, L., Himanen, S.J., Rötter, R., Salo, T. and Kahiluoto, H. (2012) Sensitivity of barley varieties to weather in Finland. *The Journal of Agricultural Science*, 150: 145–160.

Janssen, M.A., Bodin, Ö., Anderies, J.M., Elmqvist, T., Ernstson, H., McAllister, R.R.J., Olsson, P. and Ryan, P. (2006) A network perspective on the resilience of social-ecological systems. *Ecology and Society*, 11(1): 15.

Kahiluoto, H. and Himanen, S. (2012) Diversification for adaptive capacity, *MTT Raportti*, 43 [In Finnish, Abstract in English].

Kahiluoto, H., Kaseva, J., Hakala, K., Himanen, S.J., Jauhiainen, L., Rötter, R.P., Salo, T. and Trnka, M. (2014) Cultivating resilience by empirically revealing response diversity. *Global Environmental Change*, 25: 186–193. DOI 10.1016/j.gloenvcha.2014.02.002.

Kahiluoto, H., Kuisma, M., Havukainen, J., Luoranen, M., Karttunen, P., Lehtonen, E. and Horttanainen, M. (2011) Potential of agrifood wastes in mitigation of climate change and eutrophication: two case regions. *Biomass Bioenergy*, 35: 1983–1994.

Man, R. and Greenway, K. (2013) Effects of soil moisture and species composition on growth and productivity of trembling aspen and white spruce in planted mixtures: 5-year results. *New Forests*, 44: 23–38.

May, R.M., Levin, S.A. and Sugihara, G. (2008) Ecology for bankers. *Nature*, 451: 893–895.

Niggol Seo, S. (2010) Is an integrated farm more resilient against climate change? A micro-econometric analysis of portfolio diversification in African agriculture. *Food Policy*, 35: 32–40.

Olsson, P., Folke, C. and Berkes, F. (2004) Adaptive co-management for building resilience in social-ecological systems. *Environmental Management*, 34: 75–90.

Rufino, M.C., Tittonell, P., Reidsma, P., López-Ridaura, S., Hengsdijk, H., Giller, K.E. and Verhagen, A. (2009) Network analysis of N flows and food self-sufficiency: a comparative study of crop-livestock systems of the highlands of East and Southern Africa. *Nutrient Cycling in Agroecosystems*, 85(2): 169–186.

Walker, B., Holling, C.S., Carpenter, S.R. and Kinzig, A. (2004) Resilience, adaptability and transformability in social-ecological systems *Ecology and Society*, 9(2): 5.

Walker, B., Kinzig, A. and Langridge, J. (1999) Plant attribute diversity, resilience, and ecosystem function: the nature and significance of dominant and minor species. *Ecosystems*, 2: 95–113.

Walker, B.H. and Salt, D. (2006) *Resilience Thinking: Sustaining Ecosystems and People in a Changing World*. Washington, DC: Island Press.

14 Citizens and sustainable culinary cultures

Johanna Mäkelä and Mari Niva

Introduction

People's everyday patterns of eating are deeply embedded in the cultural, social and economic contexts and conditions of societies. The environmental impacts of food production and consumption are demarcated by both institutional structures and individual choices regarding how and to what extent sustainability becomes part of global food systems. At the same time, practices of food consumption are an important part of climate change mitigation and adaptation, and changes in the food system that they challenge necessarily need to be extended to what and how people eat in their everyday lives. At present, both popular and political debates and scientific discourses on sustainable food consumption focus on how the effects of climate change should be mitigated rather than on how to adapt to them. From both perspectives, the need to consider the meanings and consequences of sustainable transitions in the sphere of consumption is becoming increasingly evident (Spaargaren *et al.* 2012; Hinrichs 2014).

In this chapter, we suggest that in the face of changing climatic conditions the discourses of sustainable food consumption, climate change adaptation and supply chain resilience would benefit from developing shared conceptualisations and models of action. In developing this argument, we will rely on our scientific background in research on food consumption, culinary cultures and sustainability. This means that instead of applying a supply chain approach to climate change adaptation and resilience, we take a *practice-theoretical, everyday-life perspective* on the sustainability of food consumption. By adopting this deliberately one-sided view of the problematics of sustainability, we hope to reveal the role of lay people as stakeholders in sustainability and climate change adaptation, and to suggest new conceptualisations that may act as bridges between the spheres of production, manufacturing and consumption.

Below we first briefly outline our theoretical perspective on practices, followed by an analysis of what people actually do – or report doing – in their everyday life in order to reduce the environmental impacts of their eating patterns and what kinds of changes they are ready for. We review findings from both our own earlier studies on environmentally sustainable food consumption and those produced in other research. After that, we discuss the role of consumers and citizens as stakeholders in a sustainable food system. In the final section, we address the need for new resilient practices of food consumption that people can adopt in their everyday lives, and suggest *sustainable culinary culture* as a conceptualisation that may help thinking about sustainability from more inclusive perspectives, and in particular to understand people's efforts towards sustainable eating as embedded in the practices of everyday life. In order to facilitate consumers' resilient adaptation to climate change, both the social, cultural and economic aspects of sustainability as well as the ecological dimension need to be addressed.

Daily practices of food consumption

The Brundtland Commission's (WCED 1987) well-known definition of sustainability with its ecological, economic, cultural and social dimensions of sustainability calls for a recognition of the sociocultural aspects of food and eating. In this chapter we make use of research on consumption which has in the past few decades witnessed an increasing interest in everyday life as the actual context of consumption (Gronow and Warde 2001) and as a site of multiple factors affecting choices related to food (Halkier 2010). These perspectives emphasise that underlying the very mundane act of consuming food there are a multitude of cultural meanings of food, such as food as a source of pleasure and well-being, an arena of sociability and commensality, but also as a sphere of everyday compromises between various aspirations and meanings. Understanding these meanings and their relation to societal transitions enables us to situate the acts related to eating – which on the surface may seem very simple – into a wider and more complex social and cultural context. In addition, we argue that, in order to link the sphere of private consumption to the political agendas of climate change mitigation and adaptation, the theoretical perspectives of practices and political consumption can be useful.

By cooking meals, people transform the potential nourishment provided by nature into a product of culture, i.e. food. There is no culture without language and the art of cooking (Lévi-Strauss 1966). Because food and cooking are inseparable from culture, societal efforts to affect sustainable changes in eating patterns need to acknowledge that the potential barriers to bringing about a change are not only in human personal or psychological characteristics but also embedded in the culture and society where we live. From this perspective, individualised approaches, such as the "deficit model" (Wynne 1993) of consumer ignorance of environmental facts or the influential theory of planned behaviour (Ajzen 1991), can be criticised for assuming that the obstacles to changes are cognitive and attitudinal and reduce the question of behavioural change to a simple lack of information.

An alternative to these individualised approaches is provided by practice theory, which embraces the tripartite construction of social practices consisting of understandings, procedures and engagements (Warde 2005; Halkier 2010). In practice theory, what people do and say is seen to be shared and social instead of isolated and individual, thereby addressing people as carriers of practices rather than as decision-makers in the market. More and more, as underlined in practice-oriented perspectives to sustainability, in changing people's behaviour, the question is not simply what they should do or how they should behave. Instead, the starting point must be understanding what people actually do in their everyday lives, how their actions are constituted in social practices and intersections of a variety of practices, how people understand their actions and those of others in terms of what they think is desirable for themselves and for society, and how they are engaged in their actions through emotional and practical commitments.

Everyday life and sustainable food consumption

According to studies in advanced societies, there is no doubt that citizens are concerned about environmental problems. Europeans worry particularly about air and water pollution, chemicals, waste and depletion of natural resources, and think that environmental issues also have an impact on their everyday life (European Commission 2014a). Currently as many as 90 per cent of Europeans think that climate change is a very or fairly serious problem (European Commission 2014b). However, studies also show that people are less concerned about the environmental effects of food production compared to other sources, such as industry, transport and energy use (e.g. Vanhonacker *et al.* 2013). While the increasing public discussion on climate change has advanced the view that not only food production but also consumption contributes to environmental degradation, it is still difficult for people to assess the environmental significance of their own food consumption patterns (Hartikainen *et al.* 2014). For instance, it has been found in several studies that people believe that decreasing the use of food packaging is more important than eating less meat (Lea and Worsley 2008; Tobler *et al.* 2011), which is contrary to expert evaluations (Hartikainen *et al.* 2014). Considering the complexities relating to the scientific assessment of environmental impacts of food, it can, however, be asked to what extent consumers can be expected to perform such evaluations.

Research focusing on everyday life practices of sustainable food consumption has shown that people are variously willing to adopt food consumption practices that are promoted as sustainable, and that sustainable consumption is in fact in many cases driven by other than ecological factors (e.g. Lynn and Longhi 2011). For some practices, taste and convenience play a large role (such as willingness to eat seasonal products), whereas for others, health and ethical motives are significant (such as reducing meat eating) (Tobler *et al.* 2011). In addition, environmental and food policies, the historical and present roles of agriculture in society, public debates on food as well as market situations all affect ongoing discourses and practices of ecological food consumption. A Nordic comparative study demonstrates this by showing that the experienced importance of various food practices promoted as sustainable differ considerably even in countries with relatively similar societal structures and cultural heritages, such as Denmark, Finland, Norway and Sweden (Niva *et al.* 2014). The study investigated to what extent people in the Nordic countries were already active or willing to be active in buying local food, avoiding products with excessive packaging, buying organic food, eating only seasonal fruit and vegetables, eating meat twice a week at most or little at a time, and avoiding products that have been imported by air transport (cf. Tobler *et al.* 2011). Whereas engaging in buying local food was well accepted in all four countries (39 per cent were already doing this and 42 per cent were not yet but would like to), relatively large differences existed in engaging in or being willing to carry out the other activities listed. For instance, in Norway, 17 per cent of the respondents said they were already buying organic food, whereas, in Denmark, the respective share was 34 per cent. In contrast, in Norway, 29 per cent of the respondents were already limiting their meat consumption, whereas, in Denmark, 15 per cent were doing the same. In Finland, 45 per cent of the respondents avoided products with excessive packing, compared to 25 per cent in Denmark.

Social scientists have also been interested in how socio-economic differences influence sustainable food consumption. Many studies have suggested that women are more willing to make environmentally benign choices than men (Onyango *et al.* 2007; Tobler *et al.* 2011; Niva *et al.* 2014). Some studies suggest that elderly people may be more prone to make sustainable food consumption decisions than young people (Wier *et al.* 2008; Tobler *et al.* 2011; Niva *et al.* 2014), but there is also evidence to the contrary, or to no age effect (Onyango *et al.* 2007; Verain *et al.* 2012). As for the role of social status, studies point to heterogeneous directions, some suggesting that high education or high occupational positions predict making ecological food choices (Wier *et al.* 2008; Verain *et al.* 2012; Zhu *et al.* 2013), while others have concluded that they play only a minor role (Lea and Worsley 2008; Tobler *et al.* 2012). In the Nordic study referred to above, there was some indication that higher education and higher occupational positions were associated with sustainable practices, but the differences between the groups were rather small. This suggests that in the Nordic countries, engagement in activities that figure prominently in debates on sustainable food consumption is not a strongly socially stratified phenomenon. However, sustainable activities were linked to healthy eating patterns, interest in food and supporting environmental policies, such as environmental taxes, consumer information and price regulation. This kind of interlocking of various practices may be part of "a graduation effect", a term adopted from Dowler *et al.* (2010), who found that people who started procuring food from alternative food networks soon began a wider reflection on the environmental and health effects of their food practices. Nordic results also suggest that food-related interests may indeed activate reflections on food and eating in a "graduation" process, hence generating a cluster of health-related, sustainable and culinary practices.

It is also noteworthy that even though surveys on attitudes and practices may indicate that a higher social position is linked to more sustainable food consumption, studies based on consumption statistics suggest the opposite. An extensive

Finnish study based on a household budget survey showed that groups in a high socio-economic position (i.e. high income and high education) had larger per capita greenhouse gas emissions from food consumption than other groups (Irz and Kurppa 2013). Similarly, a British study suggested that though well-educated people had healthier eating patterns, their diets were not more sustainable (Harland *et al.* 2012). These varying results indicate that willingness to adopt certain kinds of ecologically-oriented practices (e.g. Niva *et al.* 2014) or discursive repertoires of ethical eating (Johnston *et al.* 2011) is not easily transformed into a lower ecological footprint of the diet. However, it is to be noted that modelling environmental impacts of eating habits is difficult and liable to measurement errors, and more research in the area is needed (e.g. Irz and Kurppa 2013).

Citizen-consumers as stakeholders in the food system

Since the early 2000s, discourses of political consumption have argued that people are taking part in sustainable development in the role of consumers rather than as citizens. In their buying decisions, consumers are expected to pay attention not only to "private virtues" of commodities, such as price, taste or healthiness, but also to "public virtues", such as environmental effects, social justice or animal welfare (Micheletti 2003). Similarly, Sassatelli (2004: 189) has described ethical consumerism as "public, other-related and therefore moral action, rather than a self-interested, private and therefore amoral affair".

However, proponents of political consumption have been criticised for adopting an exclusively market-based perspective to advancing sustainability and throwing aside the institutional and structural conditions demarcating individual choices, or the potential of more systemic approaches and policies (Jacobsen and Dulsrud 2007). In these critiques, many have concluded that consumers cannot be expected to act as forerunners of change. Even though people may well be capable of problematising the ethical and environmental aspects of consumption, their hurried everyday lives with "torn loyalities and multiple commitments and scarce resources" do not make living sustainably easy (Barnett *et al.* 2008: 23). Demands to make responsible consumption choices are interpreted through "lay normativities", and practical resources set the frames for action. Furthermore, as Johnston and Szabo (2011) have noted, despite the increasing importance of citizenship values in discourses of food, even people engaged in ethical consumption tend to emphasise consumer pleasures, and are not always very reflexive in thinking about sustainable choices or the social inequalities related to them.

In mainstream discourses of sustainable consumption, the role that people are afforded still seems to be limited to that of individualised market actors who are expected to make choices based on information and rational deliberation. As Seyfang (2007) has noted, current policy regimes and social institutions favour individualistic (competitive, hedonistic society with green growth) cultures instead of other options, such as egalitarian (participation, social justice with reduced consumption) or hierarchical (traditional, stratified society with managed growth) paradigms (cf. Evans *et al.* 2012).

The concepts of "food citizen" (Wilkins 2005) or "citizen consumer" (Lockie 2009; Spaargaren and Oosterveer 2010) have been offered as alternatives that may incorporate both market and civic roles. The former has been defined as "the practice of engaging in food-related behaviors ... that support, rather than threaten, the development of a democratic, socially and economically just, and environmentally sustainable food system" (Wilkins 2005: 271). The latter, in turn, has been offered as a concept that honours the multiplicity of factors underlying consumer choices and enables an analysis and problematisation of the relationship between action on the market and in civil society. This perspective recognises that in everyday life sustainability takes shape in practices that pertain to consumption activities but also to citizenship values and positions on sustainability as well as to the policies and politics advancing it. Spaargaren and Oosterveer (2010) develop the idea that the notion of citizen-consumer bears within it three ideal types of commitments in various human roles: environmental citizens, political consumers and moral agents. According to them, the distinction between citizens and consumers has irreversibly been dissolved, and the globalisation of consumption is the result of the interrelated political, market-related and lifestyle changes that have taken place in recent decades. These transformations make it necessary to develop new models of agency such as those proposed in theories of practice, crossing the borders between individualistic and structural perspectives on the functioning of societies.

Indeed, recent developments in food systems in many Western countries suggest that people no longer content themselves with a limited role as buyers and as the end of the product chains. Food provision systems and networks defined as "alternative", such as community-supported agriculture, urban gardening, suburban allotments, box schemes, farm shops and farmers' markets, *inter alia*, have been interpreted as a sign of reviving social and biological reconnections between producers and their markets, consumers and food, and people and "nature" (Dowler *et al.* 2010). This, in turn, suggests that people may indeed be adopting new identities that draw on ideas concerning ecological citizenship (Seyfang 2006) or food citizenship (Wilkins 2005). Such identities may prove crucial in constructing and establishing sustainable practices of food consumption also outside "alternative" food networks by circulating the meanings and know-how relating to social, cultural and ecological concerns in society.

Sustainable culinary culture

In advancing sustainability and climate change adaptation, new kinds of societal policies are needed that govern the actions of stakeholders in the food system together with a shared sense of responsibility and possibilities for action. In recent debates about corporate social responsibility in the food chain, the entire chain is held responsible for its impacts on society, the environment and economy (Forsman-Hugg *et al.* 2013). Similarly, it is recognised that citizens expect environmental policies that go beyond deficit model policies that focus on offering more information to the public. Heiskanen *et al.* (2014) point out that informing consumers, citizens or decision-makers does not suffice to generate new ways of thinking or acting. Current consumption policies do not lead to a change from "consumptogenic" to sustainable societies (Mont *et al.* 2013: 10). Instead, a wider vision and new societal norms of well-being, as well as a systemic change in society, are needed in order to release people from unsustainable practices and infrastructures (ibid.). Similarly, Jackson (2009) calls for the development of sustainable macro-economies and resilient social communities. From this perspective, the practice-theoretical approach suggesting that unsustainable patterns of consumption are "embedded in the social ordering of practices" (Evans *et al.* 2012: 114) is useful: it alters the focus from individuals to practices and envisions interventions towards sustainability that focus on practices instead of attitude and behaviour formation.

In contrast to the policy and food system level conceptualisations described above, we suggest an alternative that relates more closely to the practices of everyday life without reducing sustainability efforts to individualised perspectives. The concept of *sustainable culinary culture* addresses sustainability in food and eating as a joint effort that requires collective action and mobilisation. We understand sustainable culinary culture to involve production and distribution as well as everyday patterns of acquiring, storing, cooking, eating and disposing of food. In sustainable culinary cultures, *sustainable* embraces all dimensions of sustainability (ecological, economic, social and cultural), *culinary* refers both to the place (*kitchen*) and the action (*cookery*, *cooking*) relating to eating and *culture* relates sustainability and culinary practices to the cultures of which they form a part. Here, culture refers to the system of producing and co-ordinating meanings and knowledge, characterised by more or less shared practices, identities and values (McCracken 1988).

Inherent in the concept of sustainable culinary culture is the acknowledgement that sustainable activities in everyday life carry with them a multiplicity of meanings that do not necessarily have much to do with sustainability (cf. Seyfang 2007). People support local food networks, buy organic food or limit their consumption of animal products – or choose not to do any of these – for a variety of reasons, sustainability playing a more or less decisive role. Furthermore, as Johnston and Szabo (2011: 316) have noted, it is very laborious for people to redefine "culinary pleasure to more significantly incorporate citizenship objectives, like food system sustainability", and this kind of a redefinition often requires a simultaneous and supportive restructuring of other spheres of life both at home and at work. At this grass-roots level, there seems to be an increasing quest for engagement and what we could call "collaborative do-it-yourself involvement" in systems of food provision. In the long term, this may promote further interest in various aspects of food, including ecological considerations.

A sustainable culinary culture must be rooted in societal decision-making, cultural values and social practices. In the pursuit of climate change mitigation and adaptation, the potential resilience of already existing practices needs to be addressed, too, since the transition to sustainable culinary cultures does not imply that all current practices are inherently unsustainable. A sustainable culinary culture is about making sustainable practices normal and not something that need to be actively chosen (cf. Mont *et al.* 2013), but they can become the default option only as a result of changes in social practices involving both societal structures and individual action. Unlocking people from unsustainable practices requires transition at several levels: in legislation, in normalising and habitualising practices and in new rules and norms of conduct. The success of these transitions and changes in generating sustainability will depend on how they become embedded in everyday life.

However, some examples suggest that new resilient practices related to sustainable food consumption may be in the process of rooting in everyday life (cf. Spaargaren *et al.* 2012). Changes in meat consumption, in particular, may be interpreted as a tenable sign of resilience in eating patterns. In Finland, beef consumption has gradually been declining since the 1970s, and recent statistics also suggest that total meat consumption may be stabilising (Agricultural Statistics Finland 2013), though it is uncertain whether this is the beginning of a new trend or a reflection of the unstable economic situation. Historically meat has been a prestigious food that is self-evidently served at festive occasions, and it is today a normalised part of the diet of a large majority of Westerners (Latvala *et al.* 2012). Yet, there are signs that, in the Western world, meat may be on the verge of losing its position as the centre of the dining table and the plate. The increase of veganism, vegetarianism and flexitarianism can be seen in, for instance, the more prominent role of vegetarian options in cafés, restaurants and canteens. Indeed, food services can play a vital role as advocates for change by, for instance, offering 'climate lunches' (Grönholm 2014) and facilitating resilience by helping to embed sustainable eating into structures of everyday life. Food services at schools and workplaces are a good example of intermediaries that can enhance climate change adaptation in a mundane context (Risku-Norja *et al.* 2012; Wahlen *et al.* 2012). Similarly, nutritional recommendations that are applied in public food services are now – at least in some countries – beginning to serve as guidelines not only to advance nutrition but also environmental sustainability (Nordic Council of Ministers 2014). The increasing attention paid to the avoidance of food waste is yet another sign of efforts to bring sustainability – and to perhaps also revive the virtue of frugalism – into the food system.

In thinking of and advancing sustainable culinary cultures, the everyday life perspective implies that attention must be paid to those aspects of eating that the systemic perspectives tend to ignore. One of these is commensality as one of the central features of eating. Traditionally, and even today, eating shared meals has strongly been attached to family life and cohesion. However, new forms of sociability have lately emerged, suggesting that the commensality of eating is perhaps not only based on kinship but also on other kinds of networks, such as housing communes or friends cooking and eating together. Such networks may be interpreted to be resilient communities, which may also act as carriers of sustainable transitions.

Conclusion

In conclusion, we suggest that sustainable culinary cultures imply that food consumption must become more explicitly and overtly political than it is today. This calls for a more comprehensive understanding of the workings of global food systems. To this end, ethical, environmental, food security and social justice considerations need to attain an increasingly prominent position in public discourses and policies on food. In addition, practical means and possibilities for people to act as political consumers in their everyday lives are needed.

All this speaks for sustainable culinary cultures encompassing both the contexts and transitions of practices related to food production, manufacturing, distribution and consumption. It is difficult to break away from unsustainable practices without an understanding of the complexities relating to food consumption and eating in everyday life. Practice-based policies, societal structures and redefined norms for good life are all needed to advance and facilitate resilient sustainable culinary cultures that are embedded in everyday practices and in the ways that they demarcate food consumption.

References

Agricultural Statistics Finland (2013) Consumption of food commodities per capita, 1990–2013 (table). Available at: www.maataloustilastot.fi/en/balance%20sheet%20for%20food%20commodities (accessed 29 September 2014).

Ajzen, I. (1991) The theory of planned behaviour. *Organizational Behavior and Human Decision Processes*, 50: 179–211.

Barnett, C., Clarke, N., Cloke, P. and Malpass, A. (2008) The elusive subjects of neo-liberalism. *Cultural Studies*, 22: 624–653.

Dowler, E., Kneafsey, M., Cox, R. and Holloway, L. (2010) "Doing food differently": reconnecting: biological and social relationships through care for food. *The Sociological Review*, 57: 200–221.

European Commission (2014a) Attitudes of European citizens towards the environment. *Special Eurobarometer 416/Wave EB81.3 – TNS Opinion & Social.* Available at: http://ec.europa.eu/public_opinion/archives/ebs/ebs_416_en.pdf (accessed 10 September 2014).

European Commission (2014b) Climate change. *Special Eurobarometer 409/Wave EB80.2 – TNS Opinion & Social.* Available at: http://ec.europa.eu/public_opinion/archives/ebs/ebs_409_en.pdf (accessed 11 September 2014).

Evans, D., McMeekin, A. and Southerton, D. (2012) Sustainable consumption, behaviour change policies and theories of practice. In A. Warde and D. Southerton (eds) *The Habits of Consumption.* Studies across Disciplines in the Humanities and Social Sciences 12, Helsinki Collegium for Advanced Studies, Helsinki, pp. 113–129.

Forsman-Hugg, S., Katajajuuri, J-M., Riipi, I., Mäkelä, J., Järvelä, K. and Timonen, P. (2013) Key CSR dimensions for the food chain. *British Food Journal*, 115: 30–47.

Grönholm, P. (2014) Ilmastolounas syntyy kauden kasviksista [Climate lunch is created from the season's vegetables]. *Helsingin Sanomat*, September 25, 2014; A10.

Gronow, J. and Warde, A. (eds) (2001) *Ordinary Consumption.* London: Routledge.

Halkier, B. (2010) *Consumption Challenged: Food in Medialised Everyday Lives*, Farnham: Ashgate.

Harland, J.I., Buttriss, J. and Gibson, S. (2012) Achieving eatwell plate recommendations: is this a route to improving both sustainability and healthy eating? *Nutrition Bulletin*, 37: 324–343.

Hartikainen, H., Roininen, T., Katajajuuri, J-M. and Pulkkinen, H. (2014) Finnish consumer perceptions of carbon footprints and carbon labelling of products. *Journal of Cleaner Production*, 73: 285–293.

Heiskanen, E., Mont, O. and Power, K. (2014) A map is not a territory – making research more helpful for sustainable consumption policy. *Journal of Consumer Policy*, 37: 27–44.

Hinrichs, C.C. (2014) Transitions to sustainability: a change in thinking about food systems change? *Agriculture and Human Values*, 31: 143–155.

Irz, X. and Kurppa, S. (2013) Inter-household variations in environmental impact of food consumption in Finland MTT Discussion Papers 1/2013. Available at: http://jukuri.mtt.fi/handle/10024/481553 (accessed 18 August 2014).

Jackson T. (2009) *Prosperity Without Growth? The Transition to a Sustainable Economy*. London: Sustainable Development Commission. Available at: www.sd-commission.org.uk/data/files/publications/prosperity_without_growth_report.pdf (accessed 25 September 2014).

Jacobsen, E. and Dulsrud, A. (2007) Will consumers save the world? The framing of political consumerism. *Journal of Agricultural and Environmental Ethics*, 20: 469–482.

Johnston, J. and Szabo, M. (2011) Reflexivity and the whole food market consumer: the lived experience of shopping for change. *Agriculture and Human Values*, 28: 303–319.

Johnston, J., Szabo, M. and Rodney, A. (2011) Good food, good people: understanding the cultural repertoire of ethical eating. *Journal of Consumer Culture*, 11: 293–318.

Latvala, T., Niva, M., Mäkelä, J., Pouta, E., Heikkilä, J., Kotro, J. and Forsman-Hugg, S. (2012) Diversifying meat consumption patterns: consumers' self-reported past behaviour and intentions for change. *Meat Science*, 92: 71–77.

Lea, E. and Worsley, A. (2008) Australian consumers' food-related environmental beliefs and behaviours. *Appetite*, 50: 207–214.

Lévi-Strauss, C. (1966) The culinary triangle. *New Society*, 22: 937–940.

Lockie, S. (2009) Responsibility and agency within alternative food networks: assembling the "citizen consumer". *Agriculture and Human Values*, 26: 193–201.

Lynn, P. and Longhi, S. (2011) Environmental attitudes and behaviour: who cares about climate change? University of Essex, Institute for Social and Economic Research. Available at: www.understandingsociety.ac.uk/system/uploads/assets/000/000/023/original/Understanding-Society-Early-Findings.pdf?1355226993#page=109 (accessed 10 September 2014).

McCracken, G. (1988) *Culture & Consumption: New Approaches to the Symbolic Character of Consumer Goods and Activities*. Bloomington, IN: Indiana University Press.

Micheletti, M. (2003) *Political Virtue and Shopping: Individuals, Consumerism, and Collective Action*. Basingstoke: Palgrave Macmillan.

Mont, O., Heiskanen, E., Power, K. and Kuusi, H. (2013) *Improving Nordic Policymaking by Dispelling Myths on Sustainable Consumption*. TemaNord 2013: 533. Copenhagen: Nordic Council of Ministers.

Niva, M., Mäkelä, J., Kahma, N. and Kjærnes, U. (2014) Eating sustainably? Practices and background factors of ecological food consumption in four Nordic countries. *Journal of Consumer Policy*, DOI: 10.1007/s10603-014-9270-4.

Nordic Council of Ministers (2014) *Nordic Nutrition Recommendations 2012. Integrating Nutrition and Physical Activity*, 5th edn. Nord 2014:002. Copenhagen: Nordic Council of Ministers.

Onyango, B.M., Hallman, W.K. and Bellows, A. C. (2007) Purchasing organic food in US food system: a study of attitudes and practice. *British Food Journal*, 109: 399–411.

Risku-Norja, H., Jeronen, E., Kurppa, S., Mikkola, M. and Uitto, A. (eds) (2012) *Ruoka: oppimisen edellytys ja opetuksen voimavara* [Food: condition for learning and resource for teaching] Ruralia Institute Publications 25. Helsinki: University of Helsinki. [In Finnish].

Sassatelli, R. (2004) The political morality of food: discourses, contestation and alternative consumption. In M. Harvey, A. McMeekin and A. Warde (eds) *Qualities of Food*. Manchester: Manchester University Press, pp. 176–191.

Seyfang, G. (2006) Ecological citizenship and sustainable consumption: examining local organic food networks, *Journal of Rural Studies*, 22: 383–395.

Seyfang, G. (2007) Cultivating carrots and community: local organic and sustainable consumption. *Environmental Values*, 16: 105–123.

Spaargaren, G. and Oosterveer, P. (2010) Citizen-consumers as agents of change in globalizing modernity: the case of sustainable consumption. *Sustainability*, 2: 1887–1908.

Spaargaren, G., Oosterveer, P. and Loeber, A. (eds) (2012) *Food Practices in Transition. Changing Food Consumption, Retail and Production in the Age of Reflexive Modernity*. London: Routledge.

Tobler, C., Visschers, V.H.M. and Siegrist, M. (2011) Eating green: consumers' willingness to adopt ecological food consumption behaviors. *Appetite*, 57: 674–682.

Tobler, C., Visschers, V.H.M. and Siegrist, M. (2012) Addressing climate change: determinants of consumers' willingness to act and to support policy measures. *Journal of Environmental Psychology*, 32: 197–207.

Vanhonacker, F., Van Loo, E.J., Gellynck, X. and Verbeke, W. (2013) Flemish consumer attitudes towards more sustainable food choices. *Appetite*, 62: 7–16.

Verain, M.C.D., Bartels, J., Dagevos, H., Sijtsema, S., Onwezen, M. C. and Antonides, G. (2012) Segments of sustainable food consumers: a literature review. *International Journal of Consumer Studies*, 36: 123–132.

Wahlen, S., Heiskanen, E. and Aalto, K. (2012) Endorsing sustainable food consumption: prospects from public catering. *Journal of Consumer Policy*, 35: 7–21.

Warde, A. (2005) Consumption and theories of practice. *Journal of Consumer Culture*, 5: 131–153.

WCED (1987) *Our Common Future* (the Brundtland Report). Oxford: Oxford University Press.

Wier, M., O'Doherty Jensen, K., Mørch Andersen, L. and Millock, K. (2008) The character of demand in mature organic food markets: Great Britain and Denmark compared. *Food Policy*, 33: 406–421.

Wilkins, J. L. (2005) Eating right here: moving from consumer to food citizen. *Agriculture and Human Values*, 22: 269–273.

Wynne, B. (1993) Public uptake of science: a case for institutional reflexivity. *Public Understanding of Science*, 2: 321–337.

Zhu, Q., Li, Y., Geng, Y. and Qi, Y. (2013) Green food consumption intention, behaviors and influencing factors among Chinese consumers *Food Quality & Preference*, 28: 279–286.

15 Food waste and related climate impacts in Finland

Kirsi Silvennoinen, Juha-Matti Katajajuuri, Hanna Hartikainen, Lotta Heikkilä and Anu Reinikainen

Introduction

Roughly one-third of the world's global food production is lost or wasted, which amounts to about 1.3 billion tons per year (Gustavsson *et al.* 2011). Food waste is both ecologically and economically unsustainable because the environmental impacts of producing food as a raw material and processing it into food for consumption are rendered pointless if it goes to waste. Improving efficiency in food production and consumption as well as changing the general diet in Western countries is vital to ensure the future food supply of the world for up to nine billion people (Foley *et al.* 2011). The United Nations reported that the food the world wastes in a year accounts for more greenhouse gas emissions than any country creates in a year (including other activities that cause greenhouse gases, for example, emissions from housing and travelling), except for China and the United States. The report estimated that the carbon footprint of the food produced but not eaten is equivalent to 3.3 billion tonnes of greenhouse gas (GHG) emissions per year (FAO 2013), which is approximately 500 kg/capita/year.

When considering the climate impacts of food waste, the important issues are the volumes and the types of food wasted. The contribution is dependent on the diets and food cultures of each geographical region. The distribution of emissions varies between regions and according to a United Nations study (ibid.), the emissions are highest in Asia, Europe and North America. Asia has high amounts of GHG emissions due to losses during rice production. Very low emissions have been reported from Sub-Saharan Africa where food waste consists of roots and tubers that have a low carbon footprint. Europe and North America have high emissions due to food waste which consists of relatively high amounts of cereals and meat, as well as vegetables grown in greenhouses.

The European Commission (2010) concluded that the total climate impact of the food waste created by the entire food chain of the EU27 was approximately 170 million tons of GHG emissions per year, which corresponds to about 3 per cent of the total EU27 climate impact. A recent food waste study from the UK found that that the GHG emissions resulting from avoidable food and drink waste arising from UK households accounted for approximately 17 million tonnes of GHG emissions, which corresponds to 1.7 per cent of the UK's domestic GHG emissions (WRAP 2012). The GHG savings that would result from preventing all avoidable food waste in the UK would be equivalent to taking every fourth UK car off the road.

In Finland, food amounts to over one-third of the environmental impact resulting from private consumption, including food production, processing, wholesale and retail, restaurants and households (Seppälä *et al.* 2009). When examining the impact of food on the climate, it amounts to approximately one-quarter of the climate impact of private consumption, whereas the impact on water systems is even more significant due to eutrophication.

In this chapter, we will show how we have conducted our food waste measurements for different parts of the food supply chain and arrived at the results of the volume of food waste. Regarding climate change adaptation and especially the mitigation perspective, one of our research interests was to analyse the magnitude of the climate impact of unnecessary food waste in the food chain, especially with regard to Finland. We will also present the results of the climate impact of food waste. In addition, we will discuss the economic value of household food waste.

Materials and methods: food waste studies in Finland

The empirical findings in this chapter are based on a series of studies conducted in Finland between 2010 and 2014. The studies were performed by the MTT Agrifood Research Finland (Natural Resources Institute Finland from the beginning of 2015) and its research partners. The aim of these studies was to identify the volume and type of Finnish food waste, and how much food waste occurs during the different stages of the food chain. The household sector was predicted to be the largest generator of food waste from earlier studies, which is why our empirical research specifically considered households.

Food waste definition

In our series of studies we concentrated mainly on avoidable food waste. Food waste was defined as "food and raw material that was produced for food but removed from the food chain, although it could have been consumed if it had been handled, stored or prepared differently". Regarding liquids, only milk was included in the study because measuring all liquids was seen as too difficult, however, liquid milk products have a very significant share of Finnish food consumption.

The definition of food waste in primary production was slightly different to that for food waste in other parts of the food chain. First of all, the study on food waste in primary production included the whole of the food flow that was originally produced for human consumption. The part of the food flow that did not end up being produced for human consumption (or food processing) was termed "side flow". Furthermore, food termed "edible side flow" – the term given to food produced for human consumption, which was still suitable for human consumption when it was removed from the food supply chain to be recovered or disposed of – was defined as "food waste". Therefore the main difference between food waste in primary production and the other stages of the food chain is that only edible side flow was considered food waste in primary production, while, in other stages of the food chain, spoiled or otherwise contaminated food is considered waste (Hartikainen *et al.* 2014). Furthermore, another big difference was that in primary production food and, respectively, food waste consisted of raw material, and thus the food waste in primary production also included inedible parts, such as peels and husk.

Household data collection: diary study and mixed waste sorting

We collected the research data in 2010 and 2012 by carrying out a kitchen diary study and a waste compositional analysis study, respectively, concentrating on the volume and the composition of food waste in households.

Prior to the diary study, the participants filled in an online background questionnaire and they were equipped with electronic kitchen scales, as well as a booklet about the diary and detailed instructions on how to weigh and record their waste and the reasons for the waste. A total of 420 households participated in the study, of which 380 households (1054 people) finished the study acceptably. The households weighed their food waste every time they disposed of food on a daily basis. The study period lasted two weeks and the results were recorded in a diary (Koivupuro *et al.* 2012; Silvennoinen *et al.* 2014).

The focus of the waste compositional analysis study was to produce detailed information on the amounts and types of avoidable solid food waste in households in the Helsinki metropolitan area. Different types of households were distinguished in the sample according to the number of apartments in a building: 1, 2–9, 10–20 and more than 20 apartments. We also sorted and weighed food according to type such as vegetables, bread, fruits, potatoes and meat. Lastly, the food was classified into unopened packages, open packaging and food without packaging (Silvennoinen *et al.* 2013; Silvennoinen and Korhonen 2013).

Food industry, retail and food services

In 2010, we carried out a study concentrating on mapping the volume and composition of food waste in 72 outlets in food services and restaurants. The waste was divided into three categories: (1) kitchen waste, for example, cooking, spoiled products and raw materials; (2) serving waste, such as overproduction; and (3) plate leftovers (Silvennoinen *et al.* 2012; Silvennoinen *et al.* 2012b). The retail sector study was carried out by interviewing various parties in retail chains, waste management and other associated actors (Stenmark *et al.* 2011). The study did not include the weighing of food waste to determine the actual amount of waste. Hence, there was no statistical data available regarding the amount of food waste in the retail sector. The generation of food waste in the

Finnish food industry was studied by collecting information, via questionnaires and interviews, on the amount of food waste of the Finnish food industry. Further information was gathered from the corporate responsibility reports of food companies and other relevant literature.

Primary production

In 2013, we conducted a study by estimating the amount of food wasted in primary production (Hartikainen *et al.* 2014). A number of products (iceberg lettuce, strawberries, wheat, potatoes, beef, pork and milk) were chosen to study food waste in primary production. The data was collected directly from the participants using questionnaires and interviews as well as from publicly available statistics to estimate side flows and food waste for each product. Since the food waste amounts were not weighed, the figures are only estimates. The system boundaries for the study were when the crop was ready to be harvested, when the animal was born and when the milk was drawn from the cows. To estimate the total amount of food waste in primary production and processing, the data from the selected products was complemented by data from statistics and literature.

Climate and economic impact of food waste

We estimated the climate impact of household food waste, according to the food categories, by using numerous data sources (e.g. Williams *et al.* 2006; Katajajuuri 2008, 2009; Prime Minister's Office 2009; Usva *et al.* 2009; Kauppinen *et al.* 2010; Pulkkinen *et al.* 2011; Silvenius *et al.* 2011; Virtanen *et al.* 2011; Saarinen *et al.* 2012), when aiming to identify acceptable, eligible and relevant GHG emission estimates for different food product categories in Finnish conditions. A few generalisations were required regarding the available data. For instance, while pork and beef waste were measured and reported together, the GHG emission estimate for this category produced separate averages for beef and for pork. The average was based on the annual relative consumption of beef and pork.

Additionally, in parallel with the product category approach – at the household level, we made some rough approximations for the average GHG emissions per tonne of food wasted for the whole food chain: for households, for the sectors of primary production, retail and restaurants, as well as a partial analysis of industrial food waste. The approximations were made using a slightly modified version of the method used in the European Commission food waste report (2010).

For the economic impacts, we made our estimates by using publicly available statistical data from Statistics Finland, TIKE Agricultural Statistic and the National Consumer Research Centre. The study on economic impacts is restricted to the food chain stages beyond the farm gate. In future, the scope of the economic analysis needs to be extended to include agricultural production.

Food waste volume and content in Finland

Households

During the two-week diary study period, the households produced 882 kg of avoidable food waste and the amounts for each household varied from 0 to 23.4 kg. When extrapolated to describe food waste over a period of one year, the average annual avoidable food waste varied from 0 to 160 kg per person, this is equivalent to an average of about 23 kg of food waste per capita/year. The waste compositional analysis resulted in similar figures: avoidable food waste in mixed waste and separately collected biowaste amounted to 22 kg per capita/year in the Helsinki metropolitan region. The amount of food waste differed between these two studies and the waste analysis did not include home-cooked food or liquids. The food groups responsible for the most waste were home-cooked food, prepared food, vegetables, bread and milk products. More than 40 per cent of all food was still unspoiled when discarded. About 15 per cent of all food was in unopened packages when found in the sorting analysis process.

We found that the size of the household directly correlated with the amount of waste produced – the more people there were in a household, the more waste was produced. When examining waste per person, we found that single households in general produced more waste than others. Single women, in particular, produced the most food waste (Silvennoinen *et al.* 2014). When analysing the correlation between the waste amounts and the gender responsible for food purchases, we found that food waste was considerably higher in those households where a woman did the shopping than in households where a man did the shopping or where a couple shopped together or took turns shopping. Furthermore, in the households where a woman bought groceries alone, the household wasted more fruit and vegetables (Koivupuro *et al.* 2012).

Food services and the retail sector

The amount of food waste generated by the food service sector varied from 7 per cent to 28 per cent of cooked food, depending on restaurant type, and was estimated to amount to 75–85 million kilogrammes per year. This covers about one-fifth of all food handled and prepared in restaurants and the catering industry. Most food is wasted in children's day care, about 27 per cent, which is equal to 1–2 million kilogrammes. However, the amount wasted in kilogrammes is not large compared to other food service sector actors like schools and restaurants, where discarded food amounts to about 18–20 million kilos per year. In fast food restaurants, the food waste amount is the smallest. The findings also suggest that the main cause of food waste results from providing buffets for customers. Furthermore, it was found that legislation, the business concept, product development and procurement, management systems, managers, professional skills, communication and diners all affect the creation and reduction of food waste in service sector companies. The results reveal how diverse the management of food waste is throughout the service sector and how a holistic approach is required to prevent and manage waste. In order to control food waste in restaurants and the catering business, an acknowledgement and recognition of the food waste issue are required.

We estimated the total food waste of the Finnish wholesale and retail business to be 65–75 million kilogrammes or 12–14 kilogrammes for every Finnish citizen. The main product groups resulting in food waste in stores are fruit and vegetables and bread. Other products resulting in waste are dairy products, fresh meat and fish, and convenience food. The least food waste came from tinned goods, dried or frozen food, and other food products with a long expiry date.

The food industry

Based on the calculations, 75–105 million kilogrammes of edible food is wasted annually in the Finnish food industry. This corresponds to roughly 3 per cent of the total production volume of the industry sectors included in the study. Not all of the edible food that is possibly wasted in the sectors included in the study is included in the estimate as a share of the edible material in a side-stream. That is due to the fact that it could not be evaluated based on the data obtained for the study. The type of side-streams excluded from the calculations occurred in the sorting and peeling of vegetable and fruit, the milling of cereals and the loss of hull and bran material, and side-streams from the slaughter of animals, such as blood, intestinal organs, skin, etc.

Primary production

It was estimated that the amount of edible side flow, thus food waste, is around 2 per cent of the total food production. This food waste corresponds to around 90–110 million kilos of food a year. The food waste volume in primary production and in other sectors is shown in Table 15.1.

The food chain

When comparing the result of this study – around 15 per cent of all food is being wasted – to other studies, our results seems rather low. Some international studies

Table 15.1 Avoidable food waste and the climate impact (CO_2 equivalent) of food waste in the Finnish food supply chain

Sector	*Households*	*Food services*	*Retail sector*	*Food industry*	*Primary production*	*Total*
Food waste						
Total mill. kg/year	120–160	75–85	65–75	75–105	90–110	425–535
Per person kg/year	22–30	14–16	12–14	14–20	17–21	79–101
Climate impact						
Mill. kg CO_2 eqv.	350	210	170	220	200	1150

Note: The climate impact is calculated for food waste from households (125 mill. kg/year), food services (80), retail (70), food industry (100), primary production (100) and total (475).

(EU 2010; Gustavsson 2011) have shown rather large food waste percentages, even up to 30 per cent. The reasons for this high variation between waste studies may be due to the different definitions, methods and scopes of the different food waste studies. Our studies and the presentation of the results have mainly considered avoidable edible food waste and have not included other food-based organic waste. This is a significant exclusion as the volume of the organic waste can be about two-thirds of the total volume of food waste.

Climate and economic impact of food waste in Finland

Climate impact of food waste

The climate impact of household food waste was approximately 350 million kg of GHG emissions (CO_2 equivalent) per year, which is equal to the annual carbon dioxide emissions of 100,000 passenger cars. This calculation was based on the climate impact estimates for different product categories. The climate impact was difficult to estimate for many product categories, especially for convenience food, which included products such as ready-made casseroles and other meals, hamburgers and pizzas, all of which include many different types of raw material (Katajajuuri *et al.* 2014).

In general, animal products, such as meat, dairy and cheese, carry a relatively large carbon footprint in comparison to other products. For instance, the amount of vegetable waste was much greater when compared to the amount of cheese wasted in households, but the carbon footprint of cheese waste was higher than the carbon footprint of the waste vegetables. The meat products disposed of as waste amount to 4–11 per cent of the total carbon footprint of food waste, which is one of the highest carbon footprints alongside convenience food and snacks. These issues are important when planning and directing waste prevention initiatives.

With regard to the entire Finnish food system, and when using a more streamlined approach adopted from the European Commission (2010), the total climate impact of food waste, including households, retailers, restaurants, the food industry and primary production, was approximately 1150 million kg of GHG emissions per year, which is around 2 per cent of the total of Finland's annual GHG emissions. The share that resulted from households was 30 per cent of the total climate impact. The contributions of each sector to the total climate impact are presented in Table 15.1.

Economic impact of food waste in households

The value of avoidable food waste in the households was estimated to be around 80–125€ per capita/year and the combined economic value was roughly 550 million euros (Hartikainen *et al.* 2013; Silvennoinen *et al.* 2013). These values cover only the price of the food wasted in households, not the costs arising from other sectors, such as working hours and waste management. Finnish households consumed about 600 kg of food (TIKE 2012) and spent around 2175 euros on food per capita per year 2012 (OSF 2014). Avoidable food waste was thus 4–5 per cent of the food bought, according to its mass and 4–6 per cent according to its economic value.

According to the sorting study in Helsinki area in 2013, the biggest economic value categories were prepared food and snacks, and meat products like pork, beef and fish (Silvennoinen *et al.* 2013). Those two groups covered two-thirds of the total value. Bread covered 15 per cent of the total value and vegetables only 6 per cent, although they contributed 16 per cent of the total mass of the food waste.

Mitigating and adapting to climate change with food waste reduction targets

A quarter of the climate impacts of domestic consumption results from food. Therefore, if a significant amount of food is going to waste, it follows that we should seek to reduce food waste. Moreover, food demand is increasing rapidly and climate change has been confirmed by strong scientific evidence. Therefore, action to reduce food waste can be clearly linked to the measures required to adapt to climate change. In other words, we need to use all the available measures to adapt to climate change. Therefore, reducing food waste would play a significant role because it is one of the most significant contributors to GHG emissions.

Many initiatives to mitigate food waste have already taken place in Finland in recent years. These initiatives multiplied after the results of food waste studies, such as the studies presented in this chapter, were revealed. Collecting reliable information, comparative statistics and developing a more reliable methodology regarding food waste are necessary in order to reduce and monitor food waste. While the start has been good, many improvements are still required in the different stages of the food chain in order to mitigate food waste.

Discussion and cooperation between the entire food chain in Finland and other countries is also required: waste measurement harmonisation and clearer statistics, new campaigns, food banks, surplus canteens and other initiatives would also help to prevent and minimise food wastage. The applicable new rules and guidelines from, for example, the Finnish Food Safety Authority, Evira (2013), are significantly helping charity organisations and companies that donate food. However, though the contributions of public authorities are essential for solving food waste problems, the public sector alone cannot solve the food waste issue. Social innovations that connect different parties in society can also create new customs and trends for food and eating habits are required. A change in attitudes to achieve a permanent decrease in waste and its related climate impacts is the long-term aim.

From the point of view of climate change adaptation and especially mitigation, the prevention of food waste offers new options for the reduction of GHG emissions. Food waste represents unnecessary GHG emissions, which are generated throughout the food supply chain. There would seem to be great potential for decreasing unnecessary climate impacts by preventing and minimising food waste, especially in households, retail and catering. Nevertheless, the reduction potential is theoretical since it is also probable that if people produced less food waste at the household level, they would save money, and use that to buy other products, such as clothes and electronic equipment, all of which have a climate impact too. This is one type of "rebound effect", and other corresponding potential rebound effects can also be found in the production and manufacturing sector as well. All in all, one should keep in mind that while food waste reductions play a significant role, there is need for improvements in all sectors to decrease overall climate impact.

Conclusion

The production of food that is lost in the food supply chain causes a significant and unnecessary impact, resulting in an increase in GHG emissions. A huge amount of resources are used to cultivate, produce, store and distribute food that is not consumed, thus, by decreasing food waste, these resources could be saved or used elsewhere. The potential for diminishing the amount of food waste throughout the food chain is significant. Even if consumers and households are responsible for the majority of food waste – and therefore its climate impact – action should be taken by the wholesale and retail, restaurant and catering, and business sectors as well as the food industry and agriculture.

References

European Commission (2010) Preparatory study of food waste across EU 27. Technical Report. Available at: http://ec.europa.eu/environment/eussd/pdf/bio_foodwaste_report.pdf (accessed 2 January 2015).

Evira (2013) Foodstuffs donated to food aid. Available at: www.evira.fi/files/attachments/en/food/manufacture_and_sales/ruoka-apuohje_16035_2013_en_final.pdf (accessed 2 January 2015).

FAO (2013) *The Food Wastage Footprint*. Available at: www.fao.org/docrep/018/i3347e/i3347e.pdf (accessed 2 January 2015).

Foley, J.A., Ramankutty, N., Brauman, K.A. *et al.* (2011) Solutions for a cultivated planet. *Nature*, 478: 337–342.

Gustavsson, J., Cederberg, C., Sonesson, U., Otterdijk, R. and Meybeck, A. (2011) *Global Food Losses and Food Waste*. Rome: FAO.

Hartikainen, H., Timonen, K., Jokinen, S., Korhonen, V., Katajajuuri, J-M. and Silvennoinen, K. (2013) Ruokahävikki ja pakkausvalinnat kotitalouksissa – Kuluttajan matkassa kaupasta kotiin, *MTT*, Jokioinen.

Hartikainen, H., Kuisma, M., Pinolehto, M., Räikkönen, R. and Kahiluoto, H. (2014) Food waste in primary production and food processing. MTT series. Available at: http://jukuri.mtt.fi/bitstream/handle/10024/485067/mttraportti170.pdf?sequence=1 (accessed 2 January 2015). (In Finnish.)

Kauppinen, T., Pesonen, I., Katajajuuri, J-M. and Kurppa, S. (2010) Carbon footprint of food-related activities in Finnish households. *Progress in Industrial Ecology: An International Journal*, 7(3): 257–267.

Katajajuuri, J,-M. (2008) Ruoan ympäristövaikutukset [Environmental impacts of food]. *Futura*, 3(2008): 38–46. (In Finnish.)

Katajajuuri, J,-M. (2009) Climate impacts of food products and meals, paper presented at a Climate Smart Conference Lund, Sweden, 23–34 November 2009.

Katajajuuri, J,-M., Silvennoinen, K, Hartikainen, H., Heikkilä, L. and Reinikainen, A. (2014) Food waste in the Finnish food chain, *Journal of Cleaner Production*, 73: 322–329.

Kauppinen, T., Pesonen, I., Katajajuuri, J.-M. and Kurppa, S. (2010) Carbon footprint of food-related activities in Finnish households. *Progress Industrial Ecology*, 7(3): 257–267.

Koivupuro, H.-K., Jalkanen, L., Katajajuuri, J.-M., Reinikainen, A. and Silvennoinen, K. (2010) Elintarvikeketjussa syntyvä ruokahävikki [Food waste in the supply chain]. *MTT Report*, 12.

Koivupuro, H., Hartikainen, H., Katajajuuri, J-M., Silvennoinen, K., Heikintalo, N., Reinikainen, A. and Jalkanen, L. (2012) Influence of socio-demographical, behavioural and attitudinal factors on the amount of avoidable food waste generated in Finnish households. *International Journal of Consumer Studies*, 36(2): 183–191.

Official Statistics of Finland (OSF) (2011) *Annual National Accounts*. Available at: www.stat.fi/til/vtp/index_en.html (accessed 27 November 2011).

Official Statistics of Finland (OSF) (2014) *Households' Consumption*. Available at: http://tilastokeskus.fi/til/ktutk/2012/ktutk_2012_2014-02-28_tie_001_en.html (accessed 17 December 2014).

Prime Minister's Office (2009) *Government Foresight Report on Long-term Climate and Energy Policy: Towards a Low-carbon Finland*. Publications 30/2009. Available at: www.vnk.fi/julkaisukansio/2009/j28-ilmasto-selonteko-j29-klimat-framtidsredogoerelse-j30-climate_/pdf/en.pdf (accessed 2 January 2015).

Pulkkinen, H., Hartikainen, H. and Katajajuuri, J.-M. (2011) Elintarvikkeiden hiilijalanjälkien laskenta ja viestintä. *MTT Report* 22. Jokionen.

Saarinen, M., Kurppa, S., Virtanen, Y., Usva, K., Mäkelä, J. and Nissinen, A. (2012) Life cycle assessment approach to the impact of home-made, ready-to-eat and school lunches on climate and eutrophication. *Journal of Cleaner Production* 28: 177–186.

Seppälä, J., Mäenpää, I., Koskela, S., Mattila, T., Nissinen, A., Katajajuuri, J.-M., Härmä, T., Korhonen, M.-R., Saarinen, M. and Virtanen, Y. (2009) Environmental impacts of material flows caused by the Finnish economy. *Suomen ympäristö 20/2009* Suomen ympäristökeskus (SYKE), Helsinki.

Silvenius, F., Katajajuuri, J.-M., Grönman, K., Soukka, R., Koivupuro, H.-K. and Virtanen, Y. (2011) Role of packaging in LCA of food products. In M. Finkbeiner (ed.) *Towards Life Cycle Sustainability Management*. Dordrecht: Springer, pp. 359–370.

Silvennoinen, K., Katajajuuri, J.-M., Hartikainen, H., Jalkanen, L., Koivupuro, H.-K. and Reinikainen, A. (2012) Food waste volume and composition in the Finnish supply chain: special focus on food service sector. Paper presented at fourth international symposium on energy from biomass and waste, Venice, Italy, 12–15 November 2012.

Silvennoinen, K., Katajajuuri, J., Hartikainen, H., Jalkanen, L., Koivupuro, H. and Reinikainen, A. (2014) Food waste volume and composition in Finnish households. *British Food Journal*, 116(6): 1058–1068.

Silvennoinen, K., Koivupuro, H.-K., Katajajuuri, J.-M., Jalkanen, L. and Reinikainen, A. (2012b) Ruokahävikki suomalaisessa ruokaketjussa [Food waste volume and composition in the Finnish food chain]. Summary in English. *MTT Report*, 41, Jokioinen.

Silvennoinen, K. and Korhonen, O. (2013) Food waste volume and composition in Helsinki region households. In *Perspectives on Managing Life Cycles Proceedings of the 6th international conference on life cycle management in Gothenburg 2013*. Chalmers University of Technology, The Swedish Life Cycle Center.

Silvennoinen, K., Pinolehto, M., Korhonen, O., Riipi, I. and Katajajuuri, J.-M. (2013) Kauppakassista kaatopaikalle, ruokahävikki kotitalouksissa: Kuru 2011–2013 -hankkeen loppuraportti. *MTT Report*, 104, Jokioinen.

Stenmark, Å., Hanssen, O., Silvennoinen, K., Katajajuuri, J.-M. and Werge, M. (2011) *Initiatives on Prevention of Food Waste in the Retail and Wholesale Trades*. Stockholm: Swedish Environmental Research Institute.

TIKE (2013) Agricultural statistics: balance sheet for commodities 2012. Available at: www.maataloustilastot.fi/en/balance-sheet-food-commodities-2012-preliminary-and-2011-final-figures_en (accessed 2 January 2015).

Usva, K., Saarinen, M., Katajajuuri, J-M. and Kurppa, S. (2009) Supply chain integrated LCA approach to assess environmental impacts of food production in Finland. *Agricultural and Food Science*, 18(3–4): 460–476.

Viinisalo, M., Nikkilä, M. and Varjonen, J. (2008) *Elintarvikkeiden kulutusmuutokset kotitalouksissa vuosina 1966–2006* [Changes in the consumption of foods in households during the years 1966–2006]. Helsinki: National Consumer Research Centre.

Williams, A.G., Audsley, E. and Sandars, D.L. (2006) *Determining the Environmental Burdens and Resource Use in the Production of Agricultural and Horticultural Commodities*. Main Report Defra Research Project IS0205. Bedford; Cranfield University and Defra.

Virtanen, Y., Kurppa, S., Saarinen, M., Katajajuuri, J-M., Usva, K., Mäenpää, I., Mäkelä, J., Grönroos, J. and Nissinen, A. (2011) Carbon footprint of food: approaches from national input–output statistics and a LCA of a food portion. *Journal of Cleaner Production*, 19(16): 1849–1856.

WRAP (2012) *Household Food and Drink Waste in the United Kingdom 2012*. Final report. Available at: www.wrap.org.uk/sites/files/wrap/hhfdw-2012-main.pdf.pdf (accessed 2 January 2015).

16 Food processing companies, retailers and climate-resilient supply chain management

Ari Paloviita

Introduction

While most firms and supply chains have become familiar with the CO_2 mitigation, less clear is their acquaintance with climate change adaptation and supply chain disruptions. Although the risks associated with climate change are recognised by many businesses, few firms are actively responding to those threats and deploying specific adaptation measures. West (2014) defines risk management as "the culture, processes and structures that are directed towards realising potential opportunities, while managing adverse effects". Here, two sides of climate change risk are acknowledged: potential opportunities and undesired impacts. Hence, building anticipatory adaptation and supply chain resilience to climate change deserves explicit attention in supply chain management.

Supply chain design should incorporate resilience (Leat and Revoredo-Giha 2013) as well as vulnerability assessment (Beermann 2011). Food supply chains are increasingly vulnerable to both extreme weather events and long-term climate change. Furthermore, economic, environmental and social impacts from gradual changes in mean climate conditions, greater climate variability and intense weather extremes are likely to increase in the future. Agriculture, the food processing industry, the retail sector and consumers are all affected by these impacts, directly or indirectly. Reducing greenhouse gas (GHG) emissions in the food supply chain is a necessary action, but building resilience to the already unavoidable climate-related impacts, which threaten food supply chains, is another task. For this chapter, supply chain adaptation is defined as longer-term, anticipatory adjustments to the observed or expected impacts of climate change, while supply chain resilience is defined as the adaptive capacity of the supply chain to absorb the impacts and to learn and to recover from external impacts.

Climate change adaptation and food supply chain management are examined from the perspective of food processing companies and retailers. From the food supply chain perspective, adaptation strategies and measures to climate change are heavily directed towards agriculture, with little emphasis on other phases of the food supply chain. The food processing industry and supermarkets have become the dominant players in the European food supply chains over the past 30 years (Bourlakis and Bourlakis 2004: 222). On the other hand, their success has been greatly dependent on their upstream supply chain relationships with their suppliers and downstream supply chain relationships with their customers and consumers. We begin with an overview of the key characteristics of the food supply chains in the European context and then discuss supply chain risks, vulnerability to climate change, adaptation activities and food supply chain resilience. The chapter conclude with a discussion of the value chain approach to climate change adaptation and the importance of partnerships with producers and consumers.

Key characteristics of food supply chain

Global food industry and retail

According to Ramsey (2000), the internationalisation of the food supply chains took place between 1945 and 1980, which was followed by the globalisation phase. The globalisation of retailing is a relatively recent phenomenon, whereas food processing and manufacturing have had global characteristics for a long time. However, supply chain control has shifted from manufacturers to retailers in Europe and in the United States, where supermarket retailers are taking the lead (Marion 1998; Bourlakis and Bourlakis 2004: 222). The emergence of food retailers (supermarkets) as the dominant force in the food supply chain and the expansion of retailers across European borders are one of the key characteristics of structural change in the contemporary European food system (Fearne *et al.* 2001: 57). Hence, food sector enterprises have taken a global perspective on food supply chains when aiming for growth, speed and profitability. Increasingly large multinational food companies dominate the global food system, which can potentially lead to the "McDonaldization" of the food society (Ritzer 1993). International expansion – as an important growth strategy for food enterprises – forces companies to seek new markets in Latin America and Asia, as North America, Japan and Western Europe approach market saturation and population stagnation (Pullman and Wu 2012: 185). As a consequence of global growth strategies, the global food system relies increasingly on industrialised production and centralised distribution networks. On the other hand, globalised food supply chains have enabled consumers to have year-round access to almost any food product.

Concentration and consolidation of food industries and retailers

National grocery markets, especially in Northern Europe, are characterised by a high level of concentration as the balance of power has shifted to favour food retailers (Fearne *et al.* 2001: 63). In fact, concentration and consolidation in the food industry are increasing all over the world. However, the EU agricultural policy seems to favour small-scale farming, though other segments of the food system are shifting to large-scale production and delivery. In contrast, US agricultural policy favours large-scale farming and food processing (Pullman and Wu

2011: 253). According to Pullman and Wu (ibid.: 253–254), there are five major negative effects of food system consolidation: (1) power concentration affects the terms of supplier contracts, e.g. low supplier pricing; (2) consolidated food companies have an influence on food policies, e.g. GMO policy; (3) concentrated production facilities have negative impacts on health, animal well-being and the quality of life in communities e.g. by eliminating local small competitors; (4) consolidation requires more organised suppliers to meet the minimum volumes, e.g. full truck shipments; and (5) the low consumer pricing of consolidated companies may not last, e.g. price fixing. In Europe, the market share of the top three food retailers ranges typically from 30 per cent to 50 per cent (FoodDrinkEurope 2013). However, in Ireland, Sweden and Denmark, it is above 70 per cent. The most concentrated retail sector is in Finland, where two retailers, S-Group and K-Group, dominate nearly 80 per cent of the national grocery market. According to FoodDrinkEurope (2013), countries with a higher food retail concentration tend to experience a high level of private label penetration. Hence, private label selling arrangements between large retailer groups and food processing companies/manufacturers are becoming more common in Europe. In Finland, the market share of private label food products is nearly 25 per cent in S-Group and 80 per cent in Lidl (Talouselämä 2014).

Food cooperatives

Food cooperatives play a significant role in Europe, both in mainstream and alternative food supply chains. The continued existence of food cooperatives affects the supply chain dynamics in terms of upstream and downstream supply chain relationships. In food supply chains the cooperatives are typically producer-owned or consumer-owned cooperatives. In many European countries there are very large producer-owned cooperatives, especially in dairy, meat and input supplier industries. In many countries the majority of the meat and milk produced by farmers is collected by cooperatives. The turnover of the largest producer-owned cooperatives ranges from 1–10 billion euros. There are also large-scale cooperatives in the wine, fruit and vegetable sectors. For example, according to the German Cooperative and Raiffeisen Confederation, almost all German farmers, gardeners and winegrowers, as well as 90 per cent of all bakers and butchers, are members of a cooperative. Europe's largest producer-owned cooperatives can be found in the Netherlands, Denmark and Germany. The highest cooperative membership intensity (more than 80 per cent) can be found in the Netherlands, Greece, France, Germany, Ireland and Finland. Very high membership intensity (50–80 per cent) also exists in Denmark, the UK, Belgium and Austria (Cogeca 2010; Corneros Reguero 2013; Preusse 2013; DGRV 2014).

In addition, consumer cooperatives retain a significant market share in food retail in many European countries, especially in Finland, Scandinavia, the UK, Ireland, Italy and France. The largest food wholesaler/retailer in Finland, S-Group, is a cooperative with a market share of 46 per cent in the Finnish food retail markets. The regional cooperatives of the S-Group are owned by co-op members and supported by the Finnish Cooperative Wholesale Society (SOK). In addition, there is a broad variety of alternative cooperatives for farmers as well as consumer-owned food co-ops, which have specialised, for example, in locally produced food and organic food.

Small and medium-sized food companies

Although the global food industry is increasingly centralised, 99 per cent of the food enterprises are small and medium-sized companies (SMEs) (FoodDrink-Europe 2013). In addition, micro-companies (less than 10 employees) typically represent more than half of the all food enterprises. In France, the distribution of micro-companies to total companies is 90 per cent. Both the US and European food systems have developed a bimodal distribution concentration, which means that larger firms are increasingly larger, while the number of smaller firms has increased (Rogers 2001). SMEs operate mainly locally and regionally. Hence, SMEs are the key actors in local and regional food systems, which can include different types of alternative food supply chains. While the largest companies seek economies of scale through vertical integration in food distribution and an increase in the amount of diverse customer segments with a mass market orientation, the food supply chains of SMEs are typically shorter, more transparent and focused on niche marketing strategies based on local, regional, traditional and seasonal food products (Rogers 2001; Hughes 2004: 109–112). According to Pullman and Wu (2012: 256), the diversity of the food system, i.e. diverse agricultural production, small-scale processing and small-scale distribution, creates resilience, allowing it to adapt to climate change, policy change and resource issues.

Climate change adaptation in food supply chains

Risks and supply chain vulnerability

Food supply chain risks resulting from climate change can be assessed locally, regionally, nationally or globally. Most of the food processing companies operate locally or regionally using mainly local or regional suppliers and by selling their products to local or regional customers. Hence, within their relatively short supply chains, assessing local or regional vulnerability to climate change is their primary concern. The largest food processing companies have national supply networks, which are often complemented by global sourcing networks. Their main concern is supply chain vulnerability at the national level, but they are also affected by the risks occurring in global supply chains. Large retailers are actively involved in long, interdependent networks of global supply chains, which can be undermined by different types of threats and can be very vulnerable regarding climate change (Beermann 2011). Hence, overcoming vulnerabilities in the global supply chain is critical for them.

There are both physical and regulatory risks associated with climate change for food processing companies and retailers. In addition, there are financial risks, litigation risks, reputational risks and competitive risks involved (Nitkin *et al.* 2009: 18). Physical risks in the food supply chain are mostly faced by primary production and agriculture because their activities are directly affected by the weather and climate conditions. Extreme weather events may have catastrophic effects on local farms, communities and infrastructure. In addition, disruptions in the supply of agricultural raw materials may have serious consequences along the whole food supply chain. Long-term gradual changes in the climate are more difficult to observe and the risks from these gradual changes can grow over time without immediate warning signals. In addition to agriculture, the energy sector is a critical factor in the food supply chain, but its position in terms of climate change adaptation is complex. However, disruptions in energy supply in agricultural production, food processing and manufacturing as well as in transportation and retailing pose a serious risk to all supply chain operations. Furthermore, water supply is necessary for most of the food supply chain operations and any permanent shifts in water supply should be addressed by the companies.

Adapting to climate change and building resilience

Climate change adaptation in the food supply chain can be thought of as part of the continual process of risk or resilience management by food processing and retailing firms. However, adapting their behaviour so that it becomes economical and sustainable is a slow process, especially as the benefits of climate change adaptation may take decades to take effect. As the majority of the food processing companies and manufacturers are small firms, their overall awareness of the extent of the required adaptation may be vague. The general assumption is that SMEs are more vulnerable to climate shocks, but are not prepared for the impacts of climate change (West 2014: 240). SMEs simply do not have the resources to conduct vulnerability assessments or other relevant measures. On the other hand, large retailers in the food supply chain may consider climate change adaptation a marginal activity as the direct risks of climate change occur elsewhere in the supply chain.

Sheffi (2005) suggests that companies can develop resilient supply chains by increasing redundancy, building flexibility or changing corporate culture. It is easy to agree with Sheffi that building flexibility and changing corporate culture are essential, whereas redundancy has a limited utility. In the food supply chain, redundancies can be built, for example, by holding an extra food inventory and by having many food suppliers. Redundancy, however, can be counterproductive to efficiency (ibid.).

Aligning procurement strategy with supplier relationships is one of the key actions in developing built-in flexibility (Sheffi 2005). A company can either rely on a small group of key suppliers with deep relationships, or it can have an extensive supplier network of arm's-length suppliers with shallow relationships. The majority of food processing companies, i.e. small companies, naturally have a relatively small group of suppliers, whom they know intimately and who can be monitored rather easily. Large food processing companies rely either on a limited group of contract suppliers or more extensive supplier networks. Retailers have a tradition of using extensive supplier networks with arm's-length relationships. Companies with a small group of local suppliers or a limited group of contract suppliers are more knowledgeable about their partners as well as the risks and vulnerabilities involved in the relationships compared to companies with an extensive supplier network. Thus, achieving full knowledge of supply chain disruptions and other risks related to climate change is very much dependent on supply chain relationships.

Along the downstream supply chain, building resilience requires cultural change, including continuous communication among employees, empowerment, cultural values and flexibility (Sheffi 2005). Hence, the ability to manage cultural change will distinguish resilient companies from other companies. According to Pullman and Wu (2012: 256), regional food supply chains typically emphasise the importance of communities, fair wages, trustworthy relationships and equitable power structures, which can be seen as the cornerstones of cultural resilience. Problems arise when supply chains become longer and information flows are interrupted by intermediate actors. The European horse meat scandal in 2013 demonstrated information interruption in a food supply chain and the weaknesses of an increasingly globalised food supply chain: food processing companies and manufacturers were not able to monitor their suppliers accurately and horsemeat was used in products sold as beef. As a result, global food supply chains are now expected to strengthen the capability of their control systems to assess the potential vulnerabilities of the different parts of the supply chain (DG Health and Consumers 2014).

Value-chain approach to climate change adaptation

Partnerships with producers

The vulnerability of small farms to climate change can put entire food supply chains at risk. For example, climate change will alter the relative productivity of various regions and affect input costs (Porter and Reinhardt 2007). Hence, the geographical location of a farm is crucial with respect to its exposure and sensitivity to climate change. There is a growing global network of international suppliers from various locations with higher exposure and sensitivity to climate change. A strategic approach to climate change requires comprehensive vulnerability assessments, which should be conducted either by food processing companies or by large sourcing and logistics companies supporting retailers.

Buyers in the food supply chain, i.e. food processing companies and manufacturers as well as wholesalers and retailers, are better positioned relative to primary suppliers, i.e. farms, to meet climate change risks. First, buyers and intermediaries can easily replace their suppliers. For example, outsourcing raw material production makes a food supply chain more flexible especially if the productivity of various regions declines (Porter and Reinhardt 2007).

Food manufacturers or retailers may even relocate the hub of a supply chain away from an area that is overly exposed to extreme weather events (West 2014). Second, regarding rigid supply structures, such as those based on contract relationships, the food industry and retailers can use their negotiating power with small farms. On the other hand, alternative food supply chains can emerge if the most powerful supply chain players misuse their institutionalised power. In many ways, the considerable adaptive capacity of retailers makes them the most resilient actor in the food supply chain. However, the extent to which food processing companies and retailers are dependent on farmers to supply food inputs for downstream value-adding processes is the key determinant of their vulnerability to climate change (Benedikter *et al.* 2011). Therefore, implementing climate resilience action in partnership with farmers may be framed in win–win terms because they emphasise long-term benefits for both supply chain partners. These partnerships can include both vertical and horizontal collaboration (Leat and Revoredo-Giha 2013).

Farmers clearly need to change to increase their adaptive capacity and decrease their vulnerability to climate change. Besides climate change risks, farmers are facing various economic and regulative risks, which have consequences for their welfare and livelihood. Food processing companies and retailers do not need to change as urgently as farmers. However, they are the food supply chain actors who could facilitate change in terms of adaptation to climate change along whole supply chains. By building food value chains based on long-term strategic partnerships with producers, the food industry and retailers, climate change adaptation could be tailored to specific situations and the needs of populations. This obviously needs to be supported by the provision of incentives and assistance from relevant institutions, governments and third-party organisations (Leat and Revoredo-Giha 2013).

Exploiting the vulnerabilities of others decreases trust and mutual confidence in the supply chain. As farmers can easily become victims of the policies of more powerful supply chain actors (see e.g. Benedikter *et al.* 2011), it is crucial that rights and responsibilities – with respect to climate change adaptation – are balanced in the food value chains by sharing information on climate change risks and its potential effects as well as by implementing risk-sharing protocol, shared governance structures and shared decision-making (see e.g. Stevenson and Pirog 2008).

Local communities and regions hold *local and regional data and information* that is critical for helping food processing companies and retailers undertake vulnerability assessments (Amado and Adams 2012). On the other hand, food processing companies and retailers have more comprehensive data on supply chain performance and the full lifecycle impacts. The hotspots for risks in a supply chain can be identified by sharing information with other supply chain members. Also, information on adaptation costs should be shared along with other economic information and data, e.g. the true cost structures of production and transaction costs. According to Liverman and Ingram (2010: 204), regions make sense in terms of environmental change, e.g. climate and weather-related perturbations, because the physical coherence of regions enables environmental and food system data collection at the regional level.

Climate change risks are not evenly distributed in the food supply chain, as farmers face the most direct risks that can disrupt a supply chain. As the farm-level and the community-level risks are also supply-chain risks, *risk-sharing protocol* should be a part of the collaborative partnership. At the regional level, improved intraregional trade, strategic food reserves and transport facilities can enhance food security (Liverman and Ingram 2010: 205).

Proactive governance refers to assistance, which is provided to value chain participants in meeting legislative ethical, environmental and social standards for supply chains (Kaplinsky 2000). In a food supply chain, large processing companies, manufacturers and retailers could decrease the vulnerability of supply chains by providing assistance to their supplier farms and communities in the form of increasing their adaptive capacity at local and regional level. According to Liverman and Ingram (2010: 205), food security and environmental interaction should be considered at the regional level due to the emergence of regional governance. Hence, shared governance structures might be more suitable for regional food supply chains than for global supply chains.

Shared decision-making in the food value chain should be based on fairness and justice, including adequate profit margins above production costs and the predictability of agreements among partners (Stevenson and Pirog 2008). Climate change adaptation is a slow process and requires commitments to long-term investment for adaptive capacity and resilience.

Partnerships with consumers

Changes in demand and in societal and cultural preferences were identified as a potential *indirect* climate change risk in a German study on the corporate climate adaptation strategies of the food industry (Beermann 2011). For example, changes in eating habits and demand for certified products were identified as the potential indirect impacts of climate change. Adaptation to climate change in the food supply chain ultimately depends on what consumers want and how their behaviour and practices change. However, the complexity of the food supply chain and a lack of supply chain transparency may increase the vulnerability of consumers and hinder adaptive behaviour and practices. The behaviour and practices of consumers regarding their consumption and post-consumption behaviour, e.g. waste management, will be a key feature of their adaptive capacity. Promoting climate-resilient diets and food choices as well as minimising the adverse impacts of food waste can enhance the resilience of whole supply chains. Food processing companies and retailers could find opportunities related to climate-resilient food products and climate-resilient food markets. Moreover, reverse logistics management could enhance closed-loop food supply chains through the better utilisation of food waste.

Consumer vulnerability is a concept, which reflects a state of powerlessness arising from an imbalance in marketplace interactions or from the marketing messages and products (Baker *et al.* 2005). Modern, concentrated food supply chains may indeed increase the dependency of consumers on external factors, such as the food industry and large super- and hypermarkets. Urban consumers have very little control over the food supply chain, which may increase their feelings of vulnerability. A consumer response to this experienced vulnerability is adaptation, which includes positive behavioural and emotional coping strategies (Baker *et al.* 2005). However, unlike farmers in food production, the majority of the consumers in Western Europe are not used to coping with vulnerabilities in food consumption. For example, the last real vulnerability test for Finnish consumers was experienced during World War II, when national food rationing came into force. After the 1950s, Finnish consumers, like most Western European consumers, have become less self-reliant and more dependent on industrialised and globalised food systems. In practice, contemporary consumers live from hand to mouth because only a few consumers have the capacity to grow food themselves or have storage capacity, such as a chest freezer or root cellar that can help them survive winter.

Some consumers have adopted a coping strategy for alternative food supply chains. Community-supported agriculture (CSA) is the latest alternative trend in Europe. In CSA, consumers make an economic commitment by buying a share in a farm, which produces food for them. Consumers also share the risks related to farming, for example, losses caused by weather events. There are 10,000 CSA farms in the US, 1600 CSA farms in France, but only 13 CSA farms in Finland, where this business model is still in its infancy (Helsingin Sanomat 2014). In addition, consumers have opportunites to join the food cooperatives and food circles of the cities, which distribute locally produced food directly from farms to consumers.

Alternative food supply chains represent a very marginal supply chain model compared to retail-driven and food industry-driven conventional supply chains. Hence, in the current food system, food processing companies, manufacturers and retailers are the key players for partnering consumers in the building of resilient food supply chains. A food processing company or manufacturer is responsible for value chain governance in the upstream supply chain. For example, they need to be informed about potential environmental, social or ethical risks in food production. From a consumer vulnerability point of view, sharing information about supply chain risks with consumers is critical. Food packaging information is an important element in communication but insufficient for informing consumers about supply chain vulnerabilities or resilience. Partnerships between the food industry and consumers may be built in collaboration with consumer associations or community groups. The goals of these partnerships can include, for example, increasing the extent of consumer knowledge about agriculture and the rural environment, demonstrating the complexity of the food supply chain and distributing the results of supply chain vulnerability assessments. In other words, the main aim is to increase trust and mutual confidence in the food supply chain.

Vertical collaboration between retailers and food processing companies/manufacturers is crucial not only in terms of business transaction, but also for enhancing resilient relationships between procesessors and retailers. Hence, from the relationship management point of view, social psychology can provide useful approaches for healthy and resilient relationships. From the perspective of information management, information on vulnerabilties in the upstream supply chain should flow smoothly from industrial actors to retailers. In some product groups, upstream supply chain governance regarding vulnerabilities and resilience should be managed by retailers. Supply chains for fresh fruits and vegetables, for example, do not include a separate processing or manufacturing phase. The vulnerability of the banana or pineapple supply chain should be monitored and assessed by retailers or their sourcing and logistics companies.

On the other hand, retailers are increasingly investing in local and regional food supply chains with local and regional farmers and processors. Direct relationships with producers will help retailers to learn about local and regional conditions for production, including climate-related issues. In addition, retailers are increasingly aware of the need to develop value-added and knowledge-added lines to support the consumers' perception of quality (Marsden *et al.* 2000). As part of climate change adaptation, partnerships between retailers and consumers should promote knowledge-sharing and learning about risks and opportunites in the supply chain in order to decrease the experience of vulnerability that consumers may feel.

Conclusion

Climate change risk is only one of a wide range of risks the food supply chain is exposed to. Hence, climate change risk and climate change adaptation should be seen as part of a much broader risk management framework that takes into account various vulnerabilities in the food supply chain. A value chain approach could provide win-win benefits for supplier farms, food processing companies, retailers and consumers. This requires information-sharing, risk-sharing, shared governance and shared decision-making via partnerships. In Europe, food processing companies and retailers should be able to identify vulnerabilities at the local, regional, national and global supply chain levels in order to define the goals and scope for climate change adaptation. Iterative processes of transformational adaptations or long-term adjustments towards resilience require different types of changes in organisations. To achieve that, structural change in organisational logic, cultural change and most of all change in adaptive behaviour are required to facilitate continual organisational learning processes regarding risks and vulnerabilities. Furthermore, changes in social practices, institutions, cultural values and knowledge systems may promote social and technological innovations for climate change adaptation. One of the key outcomes of a climate-resilient food supply chain management should be the building of trust between suppliers, buyers and consumers as well as the resilience of supply chain relationships. Hence, food processing companies, manufacturers, wholesalers and retailers need to redefine their relationships with farmers and consumers to enable food supply chain empowerment that can proactively respond to climate change.

Acknowledgements

This research was funded by the Academy of Finland through the project A-LA-CARTE (decision no. 140870) and by Kone Foundation through the research project "Future Food Security in Finland".

References

Amado, J.-C. and Adams, P. (2012) Value chain climate resilience: a guide to managing climate impacts in companies and communities. Available at: www.oxfamamerica.org/static/oa4/valuechainclimateresilience.pdf (accessed 18 June 2014).

Baker, S.M., Gentry, J.W. and Rittenburg, T.L. (2005) Building understanding of the domain of consumer vulnerability. *Journal of Macromarketing*, 25(2): 128–139.

Beermann, M. (2011) Linking corporate climate adaptation strategies with resilience thinking. *Journal of Cleaner Production*, 19: 836–842.

Benedikter, A., Läderach, P., Eitzinger, A., Bunn, C. and Cook, C. (2011) Adaptation framework: adaptation of food supply chains to the impacts of progressively changing climate. Available at: http://dapa.ciat.cgiar.org/wp-content/uploads/2011/07/Adaptation-Framework-Report.pdf (accessed 18 June 2014).

Bourlakis, C. and Bourlakis, M. (2004) The future of food supply chain management. In M.A. Bourlakis and P.W.H. Weightman (eds) *Food Supply Chain Management*. Oxford: Blackwell Publishing.

Cogeca (2010) Agricultural cooperatives in Europe: main issues and trends. Available at: www.agro-alimentarias.coop/ficheros/doc/03020.pdf (accessed 31 October 2014).

Corneros Reguero, E.M. (2013) The case of Hojiblanca. *Options Méditerranéennes*, 106: 111–116.

DG Health and Consumers (2014) Horse meat: one year after: actions announced and delivered. Available at: http://ec.europa.eu/food/food/horsemeat/ (accessed 4 November 2014).

DGRV (2014) The German cooperatives in Europe. Available at: www.dgrv.de/webde.nsf/272e312c8017e736c1256e31005cedff/2e65c54b0c6567d6c12577cb0046b705/$FILE/Cooperatives_EU.pdf (accessed 31 October 2014).

Fearne, A., Hughes, D. and Duffy, R. (2001) Concepts of collaboration: supply chain management in a global food industry. In J.F. Eastham, L. Sharples, and S.D. Ball (eds) *Food Supply Chain Management: Issues for the Hospitality and Retail Sectors*. Oxford: Elsevier.

FoodDrinkEurope (2013) Data & trends of the European food and drink industry 2012. Available at: www.fooddrinkeurope.eu/publication/data-trends-of-the-european-food-and-drink-industry/ (accessed 31 October 2014).

Helsingin Sanomat (2014) Mikä ihmeen CSA? Available at: www.hs.fi/kotimaa/Mik%C3%A4+ihmeen+CSA/a1401424695200 (accessed 19 June 2014).

Hingley, M., Mikkola, M., Canavari, M. and Asioli, D. (2011) Local and sustainable food supply: the role of European retail consumer co-operatives. *International Journal of Food System Dynamics*, 2(4): 340–356.

Hughes, D. (2004) Food manufacturing. In M.A. Bourlakis and P.W.H. Weightman (eds) *Food Supply Chain Management*. Oxford: Blackwell Publishing.

Kaplinsky, R. (2000) Spreading the gains from globalisation: what can be learnt from value chain analysis? Brighton, IDS Working Paper 110, Institute of Development Studies, Sussex.

Leat, P. and Revoredo-Giha, C. (2013) Risk and resilience in agri-food supply chains: the case of the ASDA PorkLink supply chain in Scotland. *Supply Chain Management*, 18(2): 219–231.

Liverman, D. and Ingram, J. (2010) Why regions? In J. Ingram, P. Ericksen and D. Liverman (eds) *Food Security and Global Environmental Change*. London: Earthscan.

Marion, B.W. (1998) Changing power relationships in US food industry: brokerage arrangements for private label products. *Agribusiness*, 14: 85–93.

Marsden, T., Banks, J. and Bristow, G. (2000) Food supply chain approaches: exploring their role in rural development. *Sociologia Ruralis*, 40: 424–438.

Nitkin, D., Foster, R. and Medalye, J. (2009) Business adaptation to climate change: a systematic review of the literature. *Network of Business Sustainability*. Available at: http://nbs.net/wp-content/uploads/NBS_Systematic-Review_Climate-Change.pdf (accessed 18 June 2014).

Porter, M.E. and Reinhardt, F.L. (2007) A strategic approach to climate. *Harward Business Review*, October 2007: 22–26.

Preusse, T. (2013) In the spotlight: cooperatives. *Agrifuture Autumn*, 13: 18–19.

Pullman, M. and Wu, Z. (2012) *Food Supply Chain Management: Economic, Social and Environmental Perspectives*. New York: Routledge.

Ramsey, B. (ed.) (2000) *The Global Food Industry: Strategic Directions*. London: Financial Times Retail and Consumer Publishing.

Ritzer, G. (1993) *The McDonaldization of Society*. Newbury Park, CA: Pine Forge Press.

Rogers, R.T. (2001) Structural change in US food manufacturing, 1958–1997. *Agribusiness*, 17: 3–32.

Sheffi, Y. (2005) Building a resilient supply chain. *Harvard Business Review*, 1(8): 1–4.

Stevenson, G.W. and Pirog, R. (2008) Values-based food supply chains: strategies for agri-food enterprises-of-the-middle. In T.A. Lyson, G.W. Stevenson and R. Welsh (eds) *Food and the Mid-Level Farm: Renewing an Agriculture of the Middle*. Cambridge, MA: MIT Press, pp. 119–143.

Talouselämä (2014) Kotimaisuus tuli kaupan merkkeihin. Available at: www.talouselama.fi/uutiset/kotimaisuus+tuli+kaupan+merkkeihin/a2241285 (accesssed 18 June 2014).

West, J. (2014) *The Long Hedge: Preserving Organizational Value Through Climate Change Adaptation*. Sheffield: Greenleaf Publishing.

Index

Page numbers in **bold** indicate tables and in *italics* indicate figures.